CORPORATE BOARDS

CORPORATE BOARDS

Strategies for Adding Value at the Top

Jay A. Conger

Edward E. Lawler III

David L. Finegold

JOSSEY-BASS
A Wiley Imprint
www.josseybass.com

Published by Jossey-Bass
A Wiley Imprint
989 Market Street, San Francisco, CA 94103-1741   www.josseybass.com

Jossey-Bass books and products are available through most bookstores. To contact Jossey-Bass directly call
our Customer Care Department within the U.S. at (800) 956-7739, outside the U.S. at (317) 572-3986 or
fax (317) 572-4002.

Jossey-Bass also publishes its books in a variety of electronic formats. Some content that appears in print may
not be available in electronic books.

Library of Congress Cataloging-in-Publication Data

Conger, Jay Alden.
    Corporate boards: strategies for adding value at the top/Jay A. Conger, Edward E. Lawler, III,
    David L. Finegold.
        p. cm.—(The Jossey-Bass business & management series)
    Includes bibliographical references and index.
    ISBN 0-7879-5620-1 (alk. paper)
    1. Boards of directors. 2. Corporate governance. 3. Strategic planning. I. Lawler, Edward E.
II. Finegold, David L., 1963- III.Title. IV. Series.

    HD2745.C564 2001
    658.4'22—dc21   00-054592

Printed in the United States of America
FIRST EDITION
HB Printing   10 9 8 7 6 5 4 3 2

THE JOSSEY-BASS BUSINESS & MANAGEMENT SERIES

CONTENTS

PART THREE: BOARDS IN THE FUTURE   121

INTRODUCTION

Corporate boards are in the spotlight. Investors, governments, communities, and employees are scrutinizing their performance and challenging their decisions. As a result of this attention, boards themselves have become more proactive. Rare today are boardroom meetings that look like Soviet May Day parades, with a string of well-orchestrated, "good news" presentations. Instead, there is a great deal of experimentation with initiatives to empower boards. It is unlikely that this tide of change will reverse itself. A number of powerful drivers are likely to maintain the interest in corporate governance for years to come.

One principle driver is the increased focus on the role that senior leaders play in corporations. The management literature is awash with books which argue that leadership at the top of corporations is critical to providing vision, implementing strategy, creating successful corporate transformations, and so on. Given the importance attributed to executives, it is only natural that attention should be directed toward the very people who oversee, advise, and select a company's most senior managers.

A second principle driver is pressure from the investment community. In the last decade, we have witnessed a dramatic rise in shareholder activism. This rise has been directly coupled with the growing power of institutional investors, especially pension funds. Such funds have enormous assets and future obligations that they must cover. For example, the California Public Employees' Retirement System (CalPERS) alone must be capable of paying to its beneficiaries some $20 billion *a year* by 2020. The stock portfolios of these funds are so large and diversified that they generally take long-term positions across a wide spectrum of sectors and different forms of investment. Because they use this diversified, long-term investment strategy, pension funds have incentives to work to improve organizational effectiveness. This approach stands in sharp contrast to that of day traders or many managers of mutual funds who generally make shorter-term bets on stocks that can outperform the market. When performance problems arise, pension fund managers have an incentive to exercise what Alfred Hirschman describes as a *voice strategy* of striving to influence change, rather than an *exit strategy* of selling off their investments.[1] Because the largest of pension funds, such as CalPERS and TIAA/CREF, invest in a wide array of firms, however, they do not have the time or resources to become closely involved in overseeing each firm. Instead, these funds have taken the blanket approach of becoming lead advocates for national improvements in corporate governance procedures that they believe will in turn lift the performance of the entire market.

Among many fund managers, there is a belief that a strong board is a vital element in ensuring such returns. They believe that boards can directly enhance shareholder value because directors can intervene in crises, provide strategic guidance, and find, advise, and reward high performing CEOs. As a result of these beliefs, numerous large, private money managers are willing to pay premium equity prices for companies with strong, independent board governance. For example, in a recent survey of fifty money managers representing $850 billion in assets, McKinsey & Company and the Institutional Investor found that on average these individuals were willing to pay an equity premium of 11 percent.[2]

Moreover, the regulatory environment since the early 1990s has become increasingly favorable toward shareholder activism. For example, in 1992 the Securities and Exchange Commission relaxed rules that limited investors' ability to coordinate among themselves to advance governance initiatives. This is in contrast to periods in the twentieth century when political forces were generally against shareholder activism. For instance, in 1933 the Glass-Steagall Act made it difficult for banks to be investors in public corporations, preventing them from playing the active role that banks in Germany have played in the governance of firms. The Investment Company Act of 1940 discouraged mutual funds from getting involved in corporate governance.[3] The current U.S. environment, however, is one that is more favorable toward shareholder power. As a result, we see today a greater number of institutional investors who are active interventionists. It is not surprising that the majority of their initiatives are focused on influencing boards.

The final principle driver responsible for generating interest in boards is the news media. Today, all the major business magazines regularly feature articles on boards as well as publish special issues devoted to the assessing of governance practices. For example, *Business Week* has a regular ranking of the top twenty-five and bottom twenty-five boards in America. The issue's cover typically exclaims in bold type, "The Best & the Worst Boards: Our Report Card on Corporate Governance." Besides drawing attention to the names of well-known companies on its list worst of boards, the magazine lists the details of their "sins": "Small, cozy board dominated by CEO"; "Board loaded with insiders and friends of founder CEO"; "Unwieldy board of twenty-seven members rife with potential conflicts."[4]

Media coverage of boards is likely to continue to increase. In part this is because boards are generating more news. As they respond to shareholder concerns by becoming more active in governance, there have been more high-profile firings of chief executives who fail to perform. Boards are also being called on to make key decisions involving record numbers of mergers and acquisitions, often choosing between competing bids for their firms. The increased press coverage is also being driven by the emergence of corporate leaders as major celebrities. Forty years ago, few Americans knew who ran most large corporations. Now, CEOs like Bill Gates, Michael Eisner, and Jack Welch are among the figures most frequently written about and quoted in the media. Along with their celebrity status has come a dramatic increase in scrutiny from the press of their companies' earnings and overall performance.

The huge stock awards to U.S. CEOs have also drawn often unwanted media attention to boards. These reward packages stand in sharp contrast to the pay of CEOs in other countries and to that of many U.S. workers, who experienced record levels of downsizing and saw only small increases in their real earnings during the sustained economic growth of the 1990s. Corporate boards of directors have come under the journalist's magnifying glass because board members approve CEO pay packages and so are ultimately the individuals most accountable for the astronomic increase in the wealth of U.S. CEOs.

Beyond these three principle drivers, the new challenges boards will be facing are likely to be even greater than those they faced during the 1980s and 1990s. The continued globalization of the economy and of corporations and rapid advances in information technology will present especially potent challenges. Globalization raises a number of issues about how multinational corporations should be governed, particularly when they have no major country of residence. At the present time, there are several companies that have dual citizenship in a sense. Shell and Unilever, for example, have corporate headquarters in both the United Kingdom and the Netherlands. In the future, we may well see many corporations that have either no real citizenship or else a citizenship of convenience, as currently exists with some shipping lines that are incorporated in friendly offshore islands. Even corporations with major national homes face the problems of creating boards that can deal with their global businesses operating in very diverse government and cultural situations.

Boards must also face the challenge of adapting to modern information technology. As the Internet becomes a major tool of business, the appropriate time frames for decisions are becoming shorter and shorter. As a result, speed of action is going to be critical to the future effectiveness of boards. Today's boards often do not meet frequently enough, nor are they sufficiently up-to-date on technology issues. Therefore, they may not be in a position to respond quickly to a rapidly changing business environment. The Web is also likely to change the kind of information boards can and do receive. Finally, technology will change the audit function of boards, as much of this work will be done by computer-based systems.

Today's Governance Initiatives: Are They Working?

Over the last two decades, an enormous amount of effort has been spent exploring and devising new governance initiatives. Most of these initiatives aim to create boards that are more responsive to shareholders. They do so by attempting to balance the tremendous power in the CEO's hands by increasing the power of boards to act as genuine custodians of the organization.

A number of the more promising ideas for empowering boards have now become widespread practices among the largest U.S. firms, including the following: conducting formal board appraisals of the CEO, having a greater proportion of outside directors, selecting a broader profile of directors so that the board is more representative of society, holding meetings with only outside directors, requiring directors to own stock, and working with written board governance guidelines. Table I.1 shows the frequency with which some of these ideas are used by large U.S. corporations. The table is based on survey data collected by the Korn/Ferry organization and analyzed by the authors. Data from the Korn/Ferry survey is cited throughout this book to establish what practices are used by firms and to determine the effectiveness of the different practices. The data collection and analysis procedures that were used in this survey are described in the Appendix at the end of this book.

In addition, as we noted earlier, institutional investors (such as pension funds), the media, and a growing number of watchdog organizations have become powerful activists for boardroom reform, keeping the topic in the public spotlight. Overall, significant changes in board composition and operation have been made over the last twenty years. Some might even say that we are in the golden age of corporate governance, given that more new initiatives have been launched and changes made than in any other time period.

At the same time, it is not clear whether these initiatives have made boards more effective in the governance process and as a result enhanced the effectiveness of their organizations. In other words, it is not clear whether today's initia-

Table I.1. Usage of Governance Practices.

Governance Practice	Percentage Reporting This Practice in 1999
Outside directors meet in executive sessions without CEO present	68.5
Directors are required to own shares in the company	63.9
There is a formal process for evaluating CEO performance	66.2
There are written guidelines on corporate governance	65.3
Board holds annual retreat or special session to review corporate strategy	53.8

Source: Data from Korn/Ferry survey, 1999.

tives have indeed improved the board as both a watchdog and a source of counsel. In addition, some of the most promising initiatives—for example, board and individual director evaluations, nonexecutive chairs, lead directors, limits on the number of board memberships a director can hold, and having foreign nationals as board members—still remain largely ideas and have yet to become commonplace practices, as shown in Table I.2.

Another difficulty is that there has been limited research on whether the most popular of the governance "best practices" do indeed enhance board effectiveness. Moreover, some of the assumptions behind certain practices may be faulty. For instance, it is widely assumed that paying directors principally in stock is a sound practice. The thinking goes that directors will be more motivated to ensure high shareholder returns if they personally share in both the ups and downs of a company's market performance. The reality is that most directors are already financially well off. For many of them, money may not be a primary motivator. To believe that a single pay practice can ensure high performance fails to understand the fuller range of drivers that motivate the behavior of directors.

It is also widely assumed that the adoption of certain best practices by a board ensures not only a highly effective board but one that can deliver outstanding business results over the long term. Popular business magazines and institutional investors such as CalPERS have reinforced this mind-set by developing checklists of best practices, assuming "the more the better." Yet this line of thinking may itself be faulty. Take, for instance, the cases of Campbell Soup Company and Compaq Computer.

In 1996 and 1997, Campbell Soup was ranked by *Business Week* as number one in its survey of "best boards" among public companies. In 1997 the magazine commented, "Over the past year, what was already one of Corporate America's most highly acclaimed boards got even better. Outside directors took full

Table I.2. Usage of Board Membership Practices.

Membership Practice	Percentage Reporting This Practice in 1999
There are no term limits for directors	91.8
A member of the board is a foreign national who lives and works overseas	25.3
There is a nonexecutive chair who is not a present or former employee	2.9
There are no limits on the number of boards on which the CEO and outside directors can serve	78.0
The entire board's performance is formally evaluated on a regular basis	37.4
Individual directors' performance is evaluated on a regular basis	20.4

Source: Data from Korn/Ferry survey, 1999.

control of the search for a new CEO, rewriting the book on a board's role in management succession. And to ensure that each director makes a strong contribution to the boardroom, Campbell has initiated performance evaluations for all. 'This board is obsessed with self-improvement,' says John M. Coleman, Campbell's general counsel."[5] In 2000, Campbell Soup appeared once again on *Business Week's* list of "The Best Boards of Directors" with a ranking of number three.

By 1999, however, the company's core soup division began to experience earnings problems—to the point that its president, Mark Leckie, resigned. Leckie himself had been brought in only a year-and-a-half earlier and was one of several division presidents to leave over the last few years. The company's stock, which stood in the upper end of the fifty-dollar range in late 1998, slipped to $42 a share within the first few months of 1999. On the day in January when the company announced lower earnings, the stock dropped a chilling 13 percent.[6] The earnings problem was attributed to a dip in soup purchases by grocery stores, caused in part by a decision made by Campbell's management to discontinue its traditional end-of-quarter promotional discounts.[7]

Whatever the actual circumstances, the question naturally arises whether a top-ranked board in the United States should have been able to prevent such an outcome from happening. In years prior to 1999, could the directors have encouraged the company's senior management to place a far greater emphasis on new avenues for growth outside the core product line? At the very least, should they have advised CEO Dale Morrison to better manage Wall Street's expectations? After all,

Morrison had publicly set long-term sales growth goals at between 8 and 10 percent and earnings-per-share growth in the low to mid-teens range.[8] In hindsight, such goals were setting up Wall Street to be disappointed. With soup consumption nationwide up only 1 to 2 percent and Campbell's market share at already three-quarters of the market, such growth goals appear to have been unrealistic.

Similarly, Compaq Computer was ranked number four among the nation's best-governed boards by *Business Week* in 1996 and number three in 1997. Throughout the 1990s, the company had a remarkable growth record to match its board's reputation. Then in 1999, after a series of earnings shortfalls, the board suddenly fired chief executive Eckhard Pfeiffer—the man who had transformed Compaq from a personal computer manufacturer to a hardware juggernaut supplying everything from mainframe servers to high-speed networking equipment to laptops.

In hindsight one can see that several of the company's strategies initiated in the early to mid-1990s began to run into trouble by the end of the decade. For example, its acquisitions of Tandem Computer and especially of Digital Equipment proved to be difficult to integrate. Compaq was also slow to enter the fast-growing Internet distribution channels that Dell Computer was powerfully exploiting. In addition, there was a talent exodus. Five of the company's top eleven executives left over a two-year period, either due to retirement or to clashes with Pfeiffer and CFO Earl Mason. Again, the natural questions one might ask are, Why did the board not respond sooner to the growing problems? How could its strong governance not have anticipated the problems with Digital and the growth of Internet distribution channels?

The point we wish to make with the examples of Compaq and Campbell is that simply being a "best practice" board is in itself no guarantee of a firm's future performance. It may enhance the probability of better performance, but it alone is not enough. One reason is that boards have limits on their ability to act in a speedy manner to solve major problems. A second reason is that they have imperfect information. They are removed from the day-to-day operating issues of the organization.

Most directors hold demanding full-time positions elsewhere, making it difficult for them to possess real-time, deep information about the companies they oversee. In addition, a fundamental part of business involves taking risks. Boards must choose strategic and tactical initiatives to address emerging opportunities and challenges under circumstances where the ultimate outcomes of decisions are largely unpredictable. Even the wisest of boards can make strategic mistakes or find themselves in marketplace or economic crises that no governance practice can avert.

Finally, there are important issues related to the best practices themselves. In some cases, they may be adopted simply as window dressing. In some cases, they may be adopted without a firm understanding of how to implement them. Other times, boards may be reliant on too few practices. The presence of multiple and complementary practices is necessary to have an impact. For example, certain practices may be effective at meeting the interests of one set of stakeholders but not another. In addition, each board is unique, and the choice of specific practices needs to reflect this reality. Finally, organizations change over time, so practices themselves need to be continually updated. In sum, the adoption of best practices is a complex process—one that this book directly addresses. Thus it is critical that we become more realistic about the actual impact of governance practices. They are by no means a magic bullet.

At the same time, we believe that boards can and often do add value. As will be reviewed in Chapter Two, our studies of boards and governance practices show that good governance practices can indeed help company performance. Our research also shows that the performance of a board is significantly related to the financial performance of its firm. The right practices can enhance the watchdog function of a board and enable it to act more rapidly and effectively when opportunities and problems arise. Boards can provide constructive feedback and guidance to the CEO and to his or her senior management team. They can bring a network of contacts and sources of knowledge that can be of great value to the company. In other words, we are optimistic about the value of board governance practices. At the same time, we must view their impact in a realistic light—not expecting miracles.

The right board practices are a necessary but not a sufficient condition for having an effective board. For example, as we just mentioned, they can be adopted for the wrong reason. One CEO told us that he adopted them because investors were impressed by them, and he believed that by adopting them his company's stock price would be improved. We suspect that a number of CEOs share his viewpoint. We also feel that it is possible for a board to be effective without adopting all of the practices. The adoption of practices only increases the probability that the right behavior will occur, but effective governance can happen for other reasons.

What Is an Effective Board?

For us, some of the most interesting and fundamental questions concerning today's best practices in corporate governance center around what we mean by an *effective board* and what behaviors make a board effective as a group. These questions can be answered only by first determining what roles an effective board should play. The vast majority of U.S. governance practices are concerned with enhancing board effectiveness with respect to *shareholder value*. Most boards equate the owners of the firm with those who control its equity. This perspective may be too narrow a mandate, considering the changes that have been unfolding in the business world over the last half-century. Employees, suppliers, and communities are each increasingly "investors" in firm-specific assets.[9] The definition of board effectiveness may therefore need to change from a narrow emphasis on the *shareholder* to a broader emphasis on *stakeholders*. The adoption of a stakeholder perspective is consistent with important trends that are unfolding in the global business environment, especially those concerned with knowledge workers and supplier relationships. Moreover, in the United States we find ourselves in a legal environment that largely supports this view. For example, since 1985, at least twenty-seven states have enacted laws that allow directors to consider stakeholders beyond the company's shareholders in making a major business decision. Stakeholders, in this case, are defined as groups whose interests are tied to the company, such as creditors, suppliers, employees, and the community.

Let's start with one of the most critical stakeholders—employees. Thanks to the rise of the knowledge worker, a growing percentage of a company's value no longer resides in physical assets, such as buildings or pipelines or equipment or inventory. Increasingly, the skills that reside in the employees' minds are a company's greatest asset. Some firms, such as advertising agencies, software providers, and management consultancies, depend almost entirely on intangible knowledge assets. In some of the world's more valuable companies, such as Microsoft and Cisco, most of the value is in the intangible assets that are created by employees. Human capital can oftentimes be scarcer than traditional investment capital. Similar to the capital that arrives in the form of equity investments, knowledge capital can and will go to where it receives the highest personal return.

The core dilemma, as Peter Drucker has commented, is that "knowledge workers own the means of production. It is the knowledge between their ears. And it is a totally portable and enormous capital asset. Because knowledge workers own their means of production, they are mobile."[10] The most glaring example of the mobility of knowledge capital can be found in Silicon Valley, where talented people are constantly moving between firms. Knowledge workers are simply another form of investor. Employees make firm-specific investments when they spend a portion of their career at a particular employer. On top of the career investment, more and more employees today receive shares of their employer's company as a portion of their compensation.[11] In essence, they choose to invest themselves in certain organizations. Presumably, those firms that are seen as the most attractive in terms of career, work, and rewards draw in greater pools of knowledge capital—not unlike a highly attractive stock that draws in a greater number of investment dollars. We therefore need to think of today's knowledge workers as part *owners* of the corporation; like external shareholders, they share in the risk.

The problem for boards seeking to represent the interests of this more broadly defined set of owners is that measurements have not caught up with the rising importance of the knowledge worker. In other words, what a company measures internally are its tangible assets, not its human assets. Few companies, even those highly dependent on human capital, have any measurements for their human assets beyond employee climate surveys. For example, Bill Gates explained in *Business Strategy Review,* "Our primary assets, which are our software and our software-development skills, do not show up on the balance sheet at all."[12] Felix Barber notes the irony: "If a company were as ill-informed about its capital performance as most companies are about their employee performance, it would be in serious trouble with the investor community."[13] This is a core problem for any board that oversees companies increasingly dependent on knowledge workers.

Similarly, supplier relationships have been changing over the last two decades. Driven in large part by the need for faster product introductions, just-in-time production, lower inventory carrying costs, outsourcing of low-margin activities, and consistent quality, companies have been increasing their reliance on outsourcing at the same time that they have sought to reduce the number of their suppliers. This shift has entailed a move toward building longer-term relationships with a few suppliers who then become strategic partners. This move is especially common in the manufacturing and high-technology sectors. As a result of these changes, suppliers are now making larger and larger investments on behalf of their clients. They may build warehouses and on-site production facilities specifically for their clients. They may have their own staff in permanent residence at the client's site. They may do research and development to meet the client's product needs. Suppliers are therefore making firm-specific investments. They are in essence becoming *investors* in companies to whom they supply. In this light, they are not unlike shareholders and employees.

In contrast to many equity investors who hold diversified portfolios, employees and suppliers are often making investments in a single firm. Employees have a portfolio of one, suppliers a portfolio of several. It could therefore be argued that both groups are taking a higher risk than are equity shareholders. In the case of suppliers, their switching costs are higher. Given these trends, a convincing case can be made that directors should define the effectiveness of their companies' performance around serving a broader stakeholder-based model. The traditional shareholder model too narrowly defines the actual investors in a company. Boards must far more seriously consider all the various parties that have specialized, at-risk investments in the organization—recognizing that certain stakeholders may be of greater importance than others.[14] As we explore the board governance practices in the chapters that follow, we will purposively employ a stakeholder frame in discussing how boards can enhance their effectiveness.

Because it is behavior that counts with respect to boards, not the practices per se, we will look at boards through the lens of group and organizational effectiveness. Specifically we will look at the conditions and behaviors that lead groups to be effective. Group effectiveness is the product not of simply one element but rather a combination of behaviors and practices converging to create an effective unit. The research on organizational effectiveness clearly shows that in order for groups to be effective decision makers, they need *information, knowledge, power, rewards* that motivate, and *opportunities* to perform their duties as a board. In the chapters that follow, we will use this framework of five dimensions in analyzing boards to determine what is necessary in order for boards to engage in effective governance behavior. In order to translate our analysis and findings into concrete steps that boards can use to improve their effectiveness, we also will provide key principles and exemplary practices at the end of Chapters Three, Four, Five, Six, and Seven.

CORPORATE BOARDS

PART ONE

WHAT SHOULD BOARDS DO?

CHAPTER ONE

CRITICAL BOARD ACTIVITIES

What are the critical activities of the board? Although there is no definitive answer to this question, there is general consensus as to which are the most important activities. This consensus is shaped by the multiple responsibilities of boards, as well as by practical issues concerning what boards are actually capable of doing. For example, as mentioned in the Introduction, boards have legal responsibilities; they have responsibilities to shareholders, to communities, and of course to members of the organization. The difficulty is that all these groups put pressure on boards to engage in somewhat different activities.

Given the divergent demands of stakeholders, boards face a fundamental problem with regard to their focus. According to a survey conducted by the National Association of Corporate Directors (NACD), CEOs believe that their directors should focus on company performance.[1] But to what extent can boards actually influence performance? The issue is confounded by serious constraints on board members' time and influence. Most boards meet less than once a month, and often for a single day or less when they do convene. Outside the boardroom, directors typically hold full-time jobs and are therefore unable to spend more than a few hours a month on board activities beyond directors' meetings. Most directors of large corporations do not hold management positions within the company, so the knowledge, information, and power they need in order to understand and intervene at the operating level of the company are simply not at their disposal. The result is that boards face serious limits in their ability to meet all the potential demands placed on them. They can realistically and effectively deal with only a small number of issues that face the corporation. Boards must focus their energies where they have the greatest leverage and on those responsibilities for which they will be held most accountable. This leads to an obvious question: Given the practical constraints on boards and their legal mandate, what should their principal responsibilities include?

The Debate: What Are the Board's Key Responsibilities?

When one surveys academics, board directors, and CEOs on what a board's primary roles should encompass, the variety of responses reminds us of an old parable. It is the tale of several men who are asked to identify a very large object completely hidden by a canvas. Each man has only a small slit cut into the canvas through which to feel the object with their hands. They are also stationed at completely different points along the object. Not a single individual is able to guess what it is—an elephant. One man had guessed it to be a cord (the tail), another described it as a piece of leather (the ear), and another thought it was an old tree trunk (the leg). Similarly, perspectives on the primary roles of the board are about as divergent, depending on whether you are an academic, a CEO, an inside director, an outside director, a shareholder, or a governance activist.

In the academic literature, for example, there are widely diverse perspectives. Agency theorists emphasize the board's primary role as monitoring the behavior and performance of executives.[2] Resource dependence theorists argue that boards, through their members' networks with other organizations, exist to help companies obtain key resources, such as capital and business partnerships.[3] Legal scholars focus on the roles that boards must satisfy to fulfill their legal responsibilities as overseers of the corporation,[4] including representing the interests of shareholders, selecting and replacing the CEO, and guarding against any infringement of the law. Management experts, in contrast, stress the crucial service role that board directors play in providing strategic advice to top management and in promoting the reputation of the company externally.[5]

Directors themselves have differing and sometimes ill-defined views of their proper roles on boards. For example, when board members responded to the 1999 Korn/Ferry survey, outside directors were more than twice as likely as chairpersons and three times as likely as inside directors to attach maximum importance to "reviewing CEO performance." Surprisingly, inside directors placed more emphasis on "responsibility to shareholders" than did outsiders; outside directors placed more importance on "duty to employees" than did insiders.

According to one survey, CEOs believe that, in addition to corporate performance, the two most important issues that boards should address are strategic planning and CEO succession.[6] In our interviews, CEOs had clear but varied perspectives as to the primary roles of directors. For example, we found that most focused on only two or three key responsibilities that they felt were important—surprisingly not many more than that. For some, boards were foremost a resource for thinking through strategic moves. For other CEOs, the director's role as coach was most important. For still others, succession planning was the primary role. One CEO even drew the analogy that directors were like salmon whose task was simply to create the next generation of leadership:

> I come from the school of thought that the board is like a Pacific salmon with basically one function, which is to swim upstream until you get to the top. There you drop your egg and die. In this case, the egg is the new CEO. The board's task is to keep fighting and trying to hold their position in the stream's current until they get up to a place or time in the company's life when they need a new CEO either because of [the CEO's] age or the person is no good or whatever, and then directors have to select a new CEO. That is their dominant responsibility in my view. That's the dominant role for being on the board.

The one theme that was consistent in our CEO interviews was the value placed on the directors' role as a sounding board or, as one CEO told us, "an incorruptible coach." A good board essentially serves as the CEO's confidant. Nicely summarizing the point, one CEO explained,

> When you get to be the CEO, you don't have very many people you can talk with. You can't sit around and speculate with your direct reports, particularly about things that impact them. So it is incredibly useful if you have directors you can trust and think are competent, with whom you can share ideas and with whom you can dialogue about important issues. So first and very importantly, I need directors I can talk with about the strategic direction of the company or about personnel moves. The second thing is to have directors who are sufficiently knowledgeable about the company to raise red flags. I think this is very, very useful.

Beyond the viewpoints of academics, directors, and CEOs, we know from research on organizations that other factors can have an impact on directors' roles. For example, the stage of a company's development dictates which roles and responsibilities should receive the most attention. A growing high-tech start-up is far more likely to require the resource and service functions of the board than is a large public corporation owned predominantly by institutional shareholders, for which the legal and agency roles take precedence.

One measure of the relative importance of various responsibilities is simply the amount of time invested on each, as revealed by the survey results presented in Table 1.1, which shows how directors report spending their time in board meetings.

The most frequently discussed topics have to do with the issue of corporate strategy. The number one issue in major strategy decisions involves mergers and acquisitions, followed closely by decisions concerned with forming strategy, monitoring strategy implementation, and identifying threats and opportunities. These data clearly suggest that the major focus of board discussion is on the strategic direction of the corporation and particular major decisions involving acquisitions and mergers.

What is often neglected by the differing perspectives on what boards should do is a consideration of the potential for conflict among the various roles. For instance, a board composed of individuals with strong connections to the corporation (for example, the firm's banker, its lawyer, key customers, and the like) may be well designed to bring in resources, but it can lack the independence needed to exercise effective supervision of the CEO. Earlier we mentioned the critical role of board members in counseling and advising the CEO on strategic management issues. Research indicates that this is often best facilitated by the board members' having a personal relationship with the CEO. Not so surprisingly, when board directors know and see the CEO socially or as friends, the CEO is more comfortable in asking them for advice and listening to their opinions. These days, however, boards are increasingly called on to make tough decisions about the appointment of new CEOs and the removal from office of existing ones. Just as it is difficult for

Table 1.1. Time Spent as Perceived by Board Directors.

Topic	Mean
Identifying possible threats or opportunities to the future of the company	3.4
Shaping long-term strategy	3.5
Monitoring and evaluating strategy implementation	3.4
Planning for management succession	2.8
Building external relationships that strengthen the company	2.8
Bolstering the company's image in the community	2.4
Evaluating and rewarding the performance of senior management	3.1
Advising during major decisions such as mergers or acquisitions	3.8

Note: 1 = Almost no time; 5 = Most time

Source: Data from Korn/Ferry survey, 1999.

any manager to be both coach and disciplinarian for their subordinates, so it can be equally difficult for boards to critically evaluate a CEO who is a good friend. Therefore, a conflict can arise between the board's role as evaluator and appointee of the CEO and its role as friendly adviser to the CEO.

Another area where conflict can arise is the advocacy roles that directors assume. A board so concerned about shareholder interests and consistent share price gains may not support investments and initiatives that only show profitable results in the long term. Or they may disapprove of investments that benefit other stakeholders at the cost of the company's shorter-term share valuation.

In conclusion, the responsibilities of boards have inherent tensions between them that can cause boards to be compromised. Moreover, there are limitations of time, knowledge, and influence that constrain the breadth of their responsibilities. Given these factors, this chapter will explore what activities boards can and should engage in. We examine this issue, first, by looking at what boards are legally required to do and, second, by exploring the activities boards need to perform to fulfill their broader responsibilities.

The Primary Responsibility of Boards: Their Legal Mandate

According to state incorporation laws in the United States, boards have legal responsibility for the management of a company. The downside, of course, is that directors today can face a wide range of liability claims based, for example, on violations of employment discrimination regulations or failure to comply with environmental protection requirements. Surveys show that companies involved in acquisitions, mergers, or divestitures are especially prone to liability claims. Even a rapid drop in a stock's price or sudden weakness in a company's financial performance can produce a flood of class action lawsuits against corporate directors. Given this environment, it is no longer permissible for directors to "be responsible" simply by monitoring the business and the company's CEO. Instead boards are now expected to take a leadership role themselves, and this role has become quite broad. In its review of court decisions to date, *Liability of Corporate Officers and Directors,* one of the preeminent legal handbooks in the field, highlights the six primary roles of present-day directors:

1. Approving major corporate actions.
2. Providing counsel to the corporation's management, particularly its CEO.
3. Overseeing the performance of management by setting objectives and measuring actual results against those objectives, as well as being responsible for selecting and, if necessary, removing the CEO.

4. Ensuring effective procedures for auditing so that the board is well informed about the corporation's financial status. This includes not only the selection but also, if necessary, the dismissal of the independent auditor and the establishment of uniformly organized audit committees.
5. Providing access for nonmanagement personnel to corporate decision making—in other words, ensuring that consumers, employees, suppliers, social groups, and other stakeholders are given recognition during boardroom discussions and decisions.
6. Monitoring the company's investments on a regular basis to ensure they comply with the law.[7]

Beyond these roles, state jurisdictions generally agree that directors must uphold and adhere to three basic duties vis-à-vis the companies they serve: the duties of diligence, obedience, and loyalty. The *duty of diligence* as defined by most state statutes requires that directors make business decisions on an informed basis, and act in good faith and with an honest belief that their actions were taken to serve the best interests of the corporation.[8] A central tenet of the diligence duty is that directors be as well informed as possible before undertaking any decision. The *duty of obedience* refers to a requirement that directors themselves must obey the law and that they must ensure that the corporation itself obeys the law. They must not commit what are called ultra vires acts—any act that is performed without the authority to commit it. In essence, directors must confine their activities within the powers conferred by the company's corporate charter and its articles of incorporation, regulations, and bylaws. The *duty of loyalty* requires directors to avoid conflicts of interest. They must refrain from personal activities that either take advantage of or injure the corporation: "A director may not deprive the corporation of profit or advantage which his skill and ability may bring to it or enable it to make in the reasonable and lawful exercise of its powers. This rule requires 'an undivided and unselfish loyalty to the corporation.'"[9]

Although these three duties set general legal parameters for directors' obligations, the courts at the same time recognize that not all actions taken by directors will benefit the corporation or in hindsight appear to have been the best course. States have therefore established what is called the *business judgment rule,* which can be invoked in liability cases as a defense when directors are presented with claims of mismanagement or breach of care. This rule focuses on the duty of diligence surrounding the actual *process* of decision making and de-emphasizes the decision outcome: "the business judgment rule provides that courts should not examine the quality of the directors' business decisions, but only the procedures followed in reaching that decision, when determining director liability."[10] This rule recognizes that the courts themselves are not well equipped to evaluate business judgments and that decisions must often be made under conditions of imperfect information and under pressures to decide quickly.

Although these are the essential legal guidelines for director duties, the legal environment is in constant evolution. On the one hand, the business judgment rule allows for considerable leeway in terms of company outcomes related to directors' judgments. On the other hand, new areas of the law concerning the environment and employment are making their presence felt at the very top of companies in liability suits against directors. What is clear, however, is that the courts themselves are most concerned about the *process and procedures* involved in making decisions: that directors undertake their responsibilities with the best interests of the corporation in mind, that they be well informed, that they act within the bounds of the law, and that they act without conflicts of interest. But those procedures and legal requirements say little about where a board can best leverage its limited time and influence. From our research and that of others, it is clear that boards need to focus on certain specific responsibilities.

Key Activity Areas for the Board

In what activities should boards engage to fulfill their responsibilities? Their activities can range from assisting the CEO with strategy formulation to advising on developmental initiatives for the executive team. Given the constraints of time and influence, however, the challenge becomes one of maximizing the board's impact on the performance of the CEO and of the company by knowing where to put the directors' focus to its greatest advantage.

Using the criterion of high leverage shaped by issues of practicality, greatest influence, and legal oversight, we can identify seven areas in which boards should be active: (1) giving strategic direction and advice, (2) overseeing strategy implementation and performance, (3) developing and evaluating the CEO, (4) developing human capital, (5) monitoring the legal and ethical performance of the corporation, (6) preventing and managing crises, and (7) procuring resources.

Giving Strategic Direction and Advice

Fundamental to the operation of any business is its strategy. Although boards are rarely in a position to develop detailed strategy, they are in an excellent position to provide input and advice to the CEO and his or her senior management team regarding the company's strategic direction. Because of their special relationship with the firm, boards can be expert advisers that can be trusted to keep information and plans confidential. They also have a strong vested interest in seeing that the plans are successful. They can contribute opinions, viewpoints, and information that are not always readily available to the company's management.

When board members come from different backgrounds and spend their time in different countries, companies, and types of organizations, they can provide a wealth of information about the potential effectiveness of aspects of a company's strategies. Their "outsider" perspective allows them potentially to challenge fundamental assumptions about company strategy. Explaining how to approach the review of a turnaround strategy proposed by a CEO, one board director illustrated this advantage to us:

> [In difficult situations] I ask for a verification of all of the assumptions that went into this thing [the turnaround plan]. You're going to take losses [initially] with the expectation of [later] big gains, but is the market going to let you make those gains? Is the market going to buy your product, or are you going to have to take market share away from your competitors? Will the market switch instead to another product? Will your shareholders stay with you during this time, and if they don't and the stock price starts to collapse, are you a candidate for a takeover? Those are the pertinent questions you have to ask, and you have to be satisfied at the end of the day that most of your concerns have been allayed.

Because directors are not involved in the day-to-day development of the strategy, they are often in a position to provide an objective and detached critique of its potential effectiveness. In the words of one CEO whom we interviewed, a good board also has little to lose careerwise by being candid—in contrast to the subordinates of the CEO: "Boards can contribute by acting as an incorruptible coach for the CEO; they have no fear of retribution from him. So they can tell him the truth—a rare commodity for a guy running a company. They can tell him how his strategies really appear to them. They can challenge him in a very aggressive way."

Boards are often particularly good at identifying events in the larger environment that may not be taken into consideration by the strategic plans of corporations. For example, directors may be familiar with issues in the investment community or the economy or the political scene that are not on the radar screen of members of management, who are working within the more limited worldview of the corporation. Thus board members can call attention to changes involving major technological, social, and regulatory events that could demand a dramatic reformulation of strategy or that call into question the existing strategic initiatives. Because they are not consumed by the day-to-day demands of the marketplace and Wall Street, boards may also be able to encourage a focus on strategy that is more long term than that of the CEO.

The board also needs to formally approve the strategic direction of the organization. This is, of course, a particularly important step when the strategic direction involves a major investment of financial and human capital. In many respects, the board is uniquely qualified to weigh the pluses and minuses of large investments, again because of its outsider's perspective.

There is little doubt that board members want to be involved in strategy. In our interviews with board members, we consistently found that board members want to understand the strategy of the business and want to have opportunities to shape and influence it. They clearly feel that they have a great deal to add to business strategy and that they should play an active role in its formulation.

There are limits to directors' involvement in strategy formulation, however. Although board members can indeed provide a broader and more eclectic perspective on strategy than company insiders can, they usually do not have in-depth knowledge of the organization itself nor of the details of the company's business. Thus the challenge is to use their knowledge of the external environment and their expertise as a sounding board to formulate strategies that match the capabilities and competencies of the organization with the realities of the external environment. Meeting this challenge is not easy, but it is clearly an area, if not the major area, in which boards can add value to a corporation.

Overseeing Strategy Implementation and Performance

Research on organizational effectiveness strongly suggests that developing a valid strategy is only the first step in creating an effective organization. Many strategies fail not because they are flawed in concept but because they are poorly executed. Thus it is critical that boards play a role in advising, evaluating, and monitoring strategy implementation. Because board members are oftentimes CEOs or former CEOs themselves, they can draw on a personal history of implementation experience. Directors are in an excellent position to evaluate implementation efforts because of their ability to take a relatively detached look at the performance of the organization.

In the case of a failing or failed strategy, boards must be in a position to challenge senior management to change strategies or, if appropriate, change the approaches that are being employed to implement the strategy. If a new strategy is needed, the board must also be capable of assessing whether the current management team is the best group to develop and implement that strategy. If that team is not the right group for the task, the board must be able to replace the CEO and perhaps other members of the senior management team.

If the board determines that responsibility for execution problems of a strategy does not rest with the senior management team, then directors must be capable of providing senior management with advice on strategy implementation and organizational change. Although clearly the board cannot manage the details of the change effort, it can and should provide counsel on the overall plan. The board should also carefully monitor the implementation of major change efforts to ensure that strategies are implemented as described and are providing promised returns. Such monitoring is especially important in the case of complex initiatives, such as the installation of enterprise resource planning systems, e-commerce systems and initiatives, new organizational structures, and major changes in financial information systems.

Boards can best monitor strategy implementation by setting benchmarks to measure progress and by drawing on objective sources of information, such as customer or employee surveys commissioned by outside organizations. Benchmarks should not be simply financial accomplishments. A board might consider other measures—for example, customer satisfaction rates, new product development rates, or the addition of salespeople.

The board must remain extremely vigilant as the implementation unfolds. One board member who is also a CEO explained,

> If there are midcourse corrections to be made, the board has to increase its oversight and demand answers along the way. . . . You should also get an independent appraisal of what is happening in the company. What is the market saying is wrong about the company? For example, is it staying with old models and styles too long? Is it spending too much or not enough on R&D? You need some third-party opinion. I'd want a third-party consultant or several consultants to give a report to the board on what they think. And if they are reluctant to do this in the presence of management, I would not have a hesitation to say we want to meet in private as a board without management being present.

Boards should also do the same for any financial and capital investment commitments that are part of the strategic plan. Boards must not only approve capital investments but also monitor their development and payback. Hand in hand with an assessment of the effectiveness of change efforts and the implementation of strategy and capital investments, the board must conduct ongoing assessments of the CEO and his or her senior executives, as we discuss in the next two sections.

Developing and Evaluating the CEO

One of the most important actions that a board can take is to evaluate the CEO and the top management team. No one else in the organization has the authority or the data to perform this activity. Because environments are changing so rapidly and the performance demands facing organizations are changing at an accelerating rate, boards need to be proactive with respect to the performance of CEOs and senior executives. Boards that wait for the formal retirement or succession process to address poorly performing CEOs are increasingly subject to criticism. In a few cases, boards have been ousted because they have failed to replace poorly performing senior executives.

The board is uniquely positioned to evaluate and facilitate the development of the CEO. They can set developmental goals for the CEO and even tie the pay of the CEO to his or her development and performance. No other part of the organization or the stakeholder community has a comparable combination of legal mandate, information about the company and its executives, and expertise needed to evaluate, develop, and select a CEO. An effective board should have an ongoing knowledge of the organization's performance and the CEO's performance that allows it to do a candid and realistic evaluation of the CEO relative to CEOs in competitor organizations. Boards should also be able to help the CEO recognize areas of needed personal improvement and to guide the CEO's continuing development. In our interviews, we found that directors were often helpful in getting CEOs to be better leaders, to more effectively orchestrate change efforts, and to spend more time on the development of their subordinates. Sometimes boards can encourage CEOs to monitor their time management or shift their allocation of time to priorities. In one case we studied, board members had the CEO cut back on his external activities to devote more of his time to leading internally.

When a new CEO is required, it is the responsibility of the board to identify and appoint someone. In many ways, this is the key test of how effective a board has been in its role of encouraging the development of executive talent in the organization. If there are no suitable candidates internally, the board needs to be capable of overseeing an external search. New CEOs are increasingly being recruited from the outside precisely because talent is not available internally. Once again, boards are in a unique position to compare the internal talent of the organization with the candidate(s) identified in an external search.

Developing Human Capital

The board's responsibility for the evaluation and development of talent in the organization should not and cannot stop with the CEO. The board needs to be positioned to look at all members of the senior management of the organization and to be involved in planning their development. Performing this activity ties directly to the board's responsibility for selecting CEOs and ensuring that an organization has a continuous internal supply of senior management talent. Again, the board should have within itself the expertise to evaluate comparatively the management talent of the corporation and to determine if the correct investments are being made in developing management talent for the future.

It is beyond the capability of most boards to get involved in development of individuals below the most senior management levels. Nonetheless, it is not beyond their capability to monitor the development systems of the organization to determine if they are adequate and are likely to produce the kind of talent it takes to sustain organizational effectiveness. In some respects, this is a nontraditional area of activity for many boards. Employee development is something that is often not reviewed by boards because it is seen as an internal organizational matter. There is, however, a strong argument for change here. As we discussed in the Introduction, human capital has become increasingly important, and its allocation is a critical determinant of organizational effectiveness. Thus, just as boards monitor the systems and processes used to move financial capital within an organization, they similarly need to look at the systems and processes that are used to move and allocate key human talent. They need to analyze the investments that are being made in human capital and determine whether these are adequate and whether they fit the strategic agenda of the business. The new reality is that the key to organizational effectiveness increasingly relates to the procurement, allocation, and retention of human capital; the board therefore needs to monitor the processes that are used to perform these critical activities and to determine how effective the organization is at managing its human capital.

Monitoring the Legal and Ethical Performance of the Corporation

As noted earlier in this chapter, monitoring the ethical and legal behavior of senior management and the corporation is a critical responsibility of the board. Directors must have access to information about the company's ethical and legal behavior, and they must act whenever problems occur. Thus they need to visibly and proactively monitor the manner in which senior management and the corporation conduct business. Carrying out this role effectively is critical to mitigating against outsiders (for example, lawyers representing shareholders and employees, or government agencies) who might otherwise become involved in identifying and correcting problems. It is far more disruptive and dysfunctional for an organization to have to respond to outside groups that challenge its behavior. Furthermore, given their insider status, boards can at times recognize early warning signals concerning unethical and illegal behavior that might precipitate a major problem for the organization.

As part of their monitoring behavior, boards need to be certain that the appropriate communication channels for detecting problems exist in the organization and are operating effectively. This means going beyond simply choosing a good audit firm and ensuring that effective financial controls are in place. The board needs to provide employees concerned about the legal and ethical performance of the organization with secure ways to bring problems to the attention of the board. For example, at Exxon there is an anonymous hotline employees can call to report ethical issues. The information goes directly to the general auditor of the company, who then takes it to the board's audit committee. The board also needs to be assured that the organization regularly conducts audits that look at safety, personnel fairness, and a host of other issues that can cause an organization to be in violation of legal and ethical standards.

Preventing and Managing Crises

In today's turbulent business times, corporations are frequently faced with unexpected crises and developments. These range from hostile takeovers to major product failures. When a major crisis strikes an organization, particularly if the crisis involves the incapacitation of a senior executive, the board must be prepared to act swiftly and effectively. Often this requires the directors to make a significant time commitment and to obtain a quick education in aspects of their company's operation.

What constitutes an adequate response to a crisis varies significantly depending on the nature of the crisis. For example, a crisis that involves the loss of senior leadership in an organization requires a different response than one precipitated by a hostile takeover. In the former case, the board needs to effectively substitute itself for the senior management. In the latter case, the board needs to be certain that senior management is taking into account not only its own best interests but also the best interests of the total organization and its shareholders.

By the very nature of crisis, it is impossible to know exactly what crises the organization will face and, therefore, what detailed plans boards need to prepare for dealing with a specific crisis. Because of their own limitations, boards often learn about an emerging crisis quite late. The comments of one director who has lived through several company crises sum up the problem: "[As a board member,] you don't see the red flags and signs of a crisis. . . . The real red flags are down in the operations and down in the trends such as pricing. So you have to know what questions to ask [to surface the red flags]. But most directors don't know what questions to ask."

What boards can and should do, however, is to brainstorm response scenarios that cover the major types of crises that might confront an organization in their industry. They should also prepare for the possibility of a key member of senior management being lost to the organization either through a voluntary departure or through incapacitation or death. Boards need the capability to meet and act on short notice and to step in and take charge of the organization. In order to do this effectively, they must have clear plans established beforehand as to how they will proceed in the case of a crisis.

Procuring Resources

Financial capital, human capital, business relationships, and technology are all key resources that organizations need to access in order to be successful. Boards potentially play an important role in helping organizations obtain the resources they need to be effective. By creating a board with the appropriate external contacts and relationships, an organization can gain valuable information about how to obtain needed resources from its environment. It can also develop working relationships with individuals or organizations that can help it develop its internal capabilities and competencies. Of course, what kinds of resources an organization needs will vary tremendously depending on the business strategy and the industry within which the organization operates. Thus the membership of the board needs to be strongly shaped by the types of resources the organization needs.

The importance of the resource procurement role of the board depends greatly on the size and developmental stage of the organization. In the case of relatively new organizations, resources—particularly financial and human resources—are a key issue. These firms need to create boards that are particularly helpful to the organization in obtaining financing and recruiting talented individuals as well as attracting initial customers. Often this means identifying individuals who would bring credibility to the company. For example, having a board member from a well-known venture capital firm can bring financial credibility. Technology firms seeking credibility often hire a board member or members who are recognized technical experts.

For larger and more established organizations, resource procurement is much less of a critical function of the board. It may still be important, but oftentimes it comes in the form of facilitating the creation of certain alliances, joint ventures, and partnerships. For example, relationships that directors have developed can contribute to the credibility of the organization and the amount of trust that exists between two organizations. In a well-established organization, directors' relationships are much less important in gaining access to financial capital, because the financial relationships are usually already well in place and depend on the historical financial performance of the company.

Board Roles and Company Performance

One of the most difficult challenges facing boards is how to allocate their limited time among these many important tasks. According to Korn/Ferry survey data, the average large company board met eight times per year in 1999, and much of this meeting time was devoted to reviewing company performance and to performing administrative tasks. Although directors spend considerably more time on board-related activities outside of the formal meetings—an average of 159 hours in 1997, with high-tech company chairs spending the most time (187 hours)—they still face hard choices about where to focus their efforts.

The Korn/Ferry survey asks directors to assess the effectiveness of their boards on different key dimensions of corporate governance. Analysis of the pattern of their responses suggests that directors divide their roles into two key areas: internally focused activities (for example, shaping strategy, engaging in succession planning) and externally focused activities (for example, building networks).

Boards that score more highly on either of these dimensions of board effectiveness show generally superior company performance (see Tables 1.2 and 1.3). These results are confirmed in our regression analysis, which demonstrates a very strong relationship between directors' ratings of their boards' effectiveness on these two roles and subsequent financial performance of the firm.

There are some more subtle lessons for corporate boards in how their efforts may affect the bottom line. For example, boards that focus much of their attention outside the company and score highest on the effectiveness of their external relationships do not show significantly higher stock market performance in the same year, but see a large payoff the following year.

Table 1.2. Board Roles and Stock Market Performance.

	Stock Market Rate of Return, 1996 (%)		Stock Market Rate of Return, 1997 (%)	
	High Effectiveness	Low Effectiveness	High Effectiveness	Low Effectiveness
Strategy formulation	27	17	31	32
External networking	19	18	33	22

Note: Data based on directors' ratings of effectiveness.

Source: Authors' analysis of data from Korn/Ferry survey and Compustat data.

Table 1.3. Board Roles and Company Performance.

	Return on Investment, 1996 (%)		Return on Investment, 1997 (%)	
	High Effectiveness	Low Effectiveness	High Effectiveness	Low Effectiveness
Strategy formulation	19	14	19	13
External networking	16	14	16	14

Note: Data based on directors' ratings of effectiveness.

Source: Authors' analysis of data from Korn/Ferry survey and Compustat data.

These findings suggest that having directors spend their time building relationships with outside constituencies, such as investors, possible potential strategic partners, the community, and government, is a potentially productive long-term strategy for the board. In the short term there is little payoff; because these relationships require time to cultivate, they entail directors' taking some of their focus away from internal company issues. Such external relationship building is leveraging directors' extensive personal networks of contacts, however, and in the future can produce a real increase in shareholder value.

In contrast, for boards that want or need a more immediate payback, it may be more useful to concentrate their efforts on governing the internal workings of the corporation and contributing to setting and monitoring strategy. These internally focused activities are related to consistently higher financial results for the company in both current and subsequent years. The stock market performance of firms whose boards were highly effective in performing internal roles was also superior in the year of the survey, but it was no higher in the following year than the stock market returns of those firms whose boards scored lower on these measures. Paying careful attention to how the firm is performing in relation to its strategic objectives appears to be vital to ensuring that the firm meets its financial targets and satisfies investor expectations. But too much board focus solely on internal and short-term issues may fail to yield sustained improvements in stock market returns.

Taken together, these results suggest it is vital for boards to achieve a proper balance between their internal and external activities, adjusting their focus to fit the strategic needs and financial pressures on the firm. In Chapter Two, we focus in greater detail on some of the specific practices that can enhance board effectiveness and shareholder value.

Conclusion

In this chapter, we have looked at what a board's key areas of responsibility should include. The importance of each responsibility will vary depending on the maturity and expertise of the CEO, the life cycle of the company and its industry, the financial health of the organization, the capabilities of individual directors, and the key external challenges such as legislation, environmental issues, talent in the marketplace, and so on.

Boards have a tendency to prefer certain activities over others, however. It is clear from our interviews that directors especially enjoy being involved in strategy discussions. A problem can arise when favored activities edge out time for the others. The challenge therefore is to find a healthy balance between the seven areas of responsibility. Although each role may have a particular "season" or timing given the current issues facing the company, they are each due the board's full attention in the long run.

Another problem is that directors can fall prey to the age-old trap of preferring to serve primarily in the role of counselor to the CEO rather than judge. It is not surprising that several of the CEOs we interviewed made candid comments such as this: "My guys [his directors] speak up, but I have the last vote. They challenge me, and they argue with me all the time. But they know deep in their heart, if I want to do something—if my instinct says to do it—they know I am going to do it."

CHAPTER TWO

ATTRIBUTES OF HIGH PERFORMANCE BOARDS

Having identified the seven key activities at which boards need to excel, we are now in a position to establish the characteristics that boards need in order to perform these activities. Research on organizational effectiveness and team performance suggests that there are four attributes that individuals and groups must have if they are to be effectively involved in managing an organization: *information, knowledge, power,* and *rewards* that motivate performance.[1] In the case of boards, the challenge is to specify what kinds of power, information, knowledge, and rewards boards require to do their job. Once this is established, we can determine how the board should be structured, trained, staffed, rewarded, and developed so that it will have the appropriate kind and amount of each of these four attributes. Later chapters will discuss in considerable detail how these attributes can be developed in boards; our focus in this chapter is on exploring the attributes themselves and on how they apply to the ability of boards to perform their key activities.

Exhibit 2.1 provides definitions of information, knowledge, power, and rewards as they apply to board effectiveness. It also includes a definition of a fifth attribute, opportunity, which is not normally considered in the literature on organizational effectiveness and involvement. Clearly opportunity is critical to the effectiveness of any group or team simply because most groups must have enough of it to operate. At the same time, it is not always a key differentiator between successful and unsuccessful activities. We include this attribute because boards meet only occasionally and are staffed by individuals whose work on them is a part-time job. Thus boards must operate in a way that effectively uses the limited time that board members have, and members must be willing to spend the time that is needed to create an effective board.

The Attributes of Effective Boards

The importance of the five attributes of effective boards varies depending on the activity in which the board is engaged, as do the specific features of each attribute that need to be present. In the sections that follow, we give attention to the

Exhibit 2.1. Key Attributes of Effective Boards.

Knowledge

Knowledge refers to the expertise and understanding that is resonant in a group or individual. In the case of boards, of course, knowledge involves expertise concerning such areas as business strategy, succession, finance, government, technology, society, and how organizations operate.

Information

Information refers to data about occurrences, events, and activities that affect the business. In the case of boards, the term refers to information about the operations and management of the organization as well as information about the business environment and the performance and activities of competitors.

Power

Power is the ability to make and influence decisions. In the case of boards, the term refers to the power to reach decisions about the key issues facing a company as well as the ability to have those decisions accepted and implemented by the members of the corporation.

Rewards

Rewards influence the willingness of individuals to commit their energy to perform a particular task. In the case of boards, rewards influence directors' motivation to attend meetings, read materials, spend time on corporate activities, and, of course, make decisions that will contribute to organizational effectiveness.

Opportunity and Time

Opportunity refers to the ability of groups to have the chance to make effective decisions and to perform effectively. It is a necessary precondition to the effective utilization of the knowledge, information, power, and motivation that exists in a team or work group. In the case of boards, relevant issues include the frequency and timeliness of meetings, whether meetings are of a duration sufficient for dealing with key issues, whether there is time to prepare for meetings, and whether there is the opportunity to discuss and vote on important decisions.

key features that are needed to support each of the seven board activities that we discussed in Chapter One. Rewards have their own distinctive quality, as they clearly need to be present for any of the seven activities to be carried out effectively. For this reason, we deal with rewards separately in Chapter Seven.

Giving Strategic Direction and Advice

Information, knowledge, and *opportunity* are the critical determinants of how effective a board can be in influencing a company's strategic direction. In order to be effective strategic partners, boards need a considerable amount of objective information and knowledge about the organization's business environment. Typically a board can add the most value by bringing an array of perspectives to discussions about strategy. Ideally, directors should have a strong comprehension of the competitive environment and can bring information about business, social, and technological trends to the discussion of strategy.

The information and knowledge that boards bring to discussions about strategy should also relate to issues that are internal to the organization's operations. Strategy cannot and should not be formulated without consideration of the condition of the organization's internal capabilities to execute the strategy. Thus a focus on the company's core competencies and its organizational capabilities is critical to the strategy formulation process. In order to understand and utilize information about an organization's strategy, the board needs expertise in organization design and effectiveness as well as in the technology and knowledge bases of the organization. In order to judge the potential for a new strategy to succeed in a particular firm, directors also need some expertise in change management. Thus board members need to understand both how organizations operate and how their particular organization stands relative to its competitors on its key organizational capabilities (in such areas as learning, speed to market, quality, adaptability, and customer focus). Without good benchmarks of an organization's internal capabilities, a board cannot make an assessment of the potential benefits and risks associated with different strategic options.

The issue of opportunity and time is particularly interesting with respect to strategy formulation. Because of the complex internal and external issues that are involved, a useful discussion of strategy often takes a considerable amount of time and preparation. The typical board meeting may last only a few hours and include quite a number of agenda items. Board meetings therefore often do not provide the right opportunity or setting for an in-depth discussion of strategy. Our recommendation is straightforward: separate, longer discussions of strategy need to be scheduled. Such sessions allow boards an opportunity to develop an in-depth understanding of strategic issues so that they can provide the kind of advice and direction that they are uniquely positioned to offer.

Overseeing Strategy Implementation and Performance

In order for boards to exercise effective oversight concerning strategy implementation and the performance of an organization, they need much of the same *information* and *knowledge* that is required for them to advise on the strategic direction of the firm. There are some important differences, however. In order to monitor strategy implementation, a board of course needs operating information that indicates whether the strategy is being executed effectively. Simply focusing on financial performance, however, may not provide the board with an adequate opportunity to act if the strategy is failing or needs to be altered. Good boards act far in advance of a financial crisis and before it is obvious to everyone that a strategy has failed. Particularly important are lead indicators that say whether the strategy is working in ways that will ultimately influence the financial performance of the organization. For example, if the strategy is to increase customer satisfaction and loyalty through certain types of customer-focused activities, the board needs to obtain measures that show whether the activities are indeed in place and whether they are actually increasing customer loyalty. In addition, the board needs to know whether increases in loyalty are affecting the financial performance of the company.

Effective monitoring of strategy implementation requires that boards have expertise in organizational change and change management. If an effective change strategy cannot be developed, then it is highly unlikely that the business strategy will be effectively implemented. A slightly different kind of change management expertise is needed in monitoring the implementation of change. Boards need to have expertise in the use of survey data, behavioral data, and other metrics that assess the effectiveness of change efforts. They also need to understand key organizational development processes and the conditions that are required for a change effort to be successful.

Unlike strategy development, the assessment of strategy implementation does not necessarily require boards to meet for long periods of time. Instead, boards need frequent updates that provide good information about how strategy implementation is going. Ideally this information can be distributed well in advance of regular board meetings, allowing directors to review it on their own. This conserves precious board meeting time for those key issues requiring attention. Too many boards devote a substantial portion of their scarce time together to reviews of routine operational information.

The decision-making *power* of directors can be a critical factor when it comes to monitoring strategy implementation. This is particularly true if the board feels that a strategy needs to be altered or abandoned. In such situations, a significant power struggle can take place with management. In extreme cases, problems in strategy implementation may require changes in the composition of the senior management group. This is what happened when Compaq Computer fired its CEO in 1999. Replacing members of senior management is a particularly critical issue from a power point of view. Often the greatest test of a board's power occurs when the board has either to change the company strategy or to change the senior management team because of implementation problems. A truly powerful board is required in such situations.

Developing and Evaluating the CEO

The 1999 Korn/Ferry survey results suggest that about 75 percent of the boards of large corporations actually do formal evaluations of the CEO. But successfully developing and evaluating a CEO is a complex activity. It requires the right mix of *power, information, knowledge,* and *opportunity.* Chapter Six will go into more detail on how boards can carry out evaluation and development activities with CEOs. However, it is important to note here that the key issue in CEO evaluation is *power.* Boards need to have power to evaluate, reward, and, if necessary, remove CEOs. They are the only ones who are in a position to deal with a CEO who is performing at an unsatisfactory level.

In order to guide the CEO's development, boards need expertise in leadership development and management development as well as data on the leadership performance of the CEO. The board must also have the opportunity to actually discuss the CEO's performance and develop an objective evaluation and development program. For example, unless outside directors have the capability to meet without the CEO and to control the committee that evaluates the CEO, boards often do not have more than a passing opportunity to conduct a performance assessment of the CEO. Instead of evaluating the CEO, they spend their time doing regular business reviews and transacting the normal day-to-day business of boards. In some cases, this situation is brought about by a CEO who controls the board's agenda and prefers not to be evaluated.

Perhaps the biggest problem directors face in evaluating the CEO's performance and his or her developmental needs arises if they must assess the CEO only on the basis of their contacts with him or her at board meetings, on the data presented there, and on the overall financial performance of the firm. Critical to the effective evaluation of anyone, particularly a CEO, is obtaining data from *multiple* sources. The board needs 360-degree data on the performance of the CEO in order to effectively evaluate and develop the CEO. In the case of CEOs, this means collecting data from individuals throughout the organization who are in a position to evaluate the CEO's leadership ability and impact on the organization. It may mean gathering data from the investment community as well as from key customers and suppliers.

Developing Human Capital

Boards need to be particularly concerned about the development of management talent. Developing a succession plan for the very senior levels of management is one way boards can have a significant impact. In order for boards to be effectively involved in this activity, they need *knowledge* about leadership and executive development as well as assessment. They also require *information* about the broader development activities of the organization.

In addition, they need specific information about the capabilities of individual executives in order to ensure that development activities of the organization are effective. Directors can get this information by having executives appear before the board and by obtaining systematic data about how executives are perceived in the organization. As in the case of the CEO, this information needs to be from subordinates, peers, customers, and others who come into contact with the executives.

In the case of knowledge work and technology firms, boards must also focus on the technical talent throughout the organization in addition to its executive talent. Because the technical talent is the foundation of the organization's core competencies, these individuals represent the major asset of the firm and can be more important to its success than executives. Recruiting, retention, and promotion data are vital to the board's understanding here. The tracking of "high potentials" lower in the organization may be a useful activity for the board.

Power may or may not be an issue in getting the kinds of information, knowledge, and opportunities the board needs in order for it to monitor and facilitate the development of human capital. If the CEO is concerned about being replaced or feels threatened by the development of a successor, power can become a critical issue. Indeed, in cases where the CEO does not develop successors, the board may need to intervene to ensure that developmental opportunities and plans for potential successors are in place. In today's environment where there is great competition for talent, boards must conduct regular reward audits to be assured that high-potential executives have highly competitive reward packages.

Finally, *opportunity* is critical to the board's involvement in human capital development. There may be situations where the CEO prefers not to have succession discussed and thus never puts the issue of executive development and succession on the agenda of the board. Boards must insist in these cases that development and succession issues become routine items on the agenda at appropriate points in the year. In the absence of agenda time designated for this purpose, there is a tendency for boards to become absorbed in operational issues.

Monitoring the Legal and Ethical Performance of the Corporation

The key determinant of how effectively a board can monitor the legal and ethical performance of a corporation is its access to *information*. Boards need mechanisms that allow them to probe deeply into the organization in order to detect potential legal and ethical issues. They need information from employees, suppliers, customers, communities, and government agencies that are knowledgeable about the performance of the organization. Certain groups will come directly to the board with their concerns; therefore some information is readily available to board members. The same may not be true, however, for employees and suppliers who fear retribution and may lack knowledge of how and when to access the board.

The board needs considerable *knowledge* for it to effectively monitor the legal and ethical performance of the company. Directors need knowledge of human resource management, accounting, and other functions where unethical behavior may occur. In addition, they should have a basic knowledge of where legal problems might arise and how courts might interpret and respond to them.

The presence of an independent audit committee helps ensure that the board has the *opportunity* to discuss and deal with legal and ethical issues when it comes to financial reporting. But the same is not always true where the issues do not involve financial reporting practices—for example, environmental problems or employee discrimination. These may not make it onto the board's agenda until a crisis emerges.

Power is an extremely important issue if a board needs to react to legal and ethical problems. Sometimes the only resolution to ethical problems is to dismiss employees, including members of the senior management. Obviously the board can take this kind of action only if it is able to meet to discuss how to correct problems and has the power to actually correct them. If the directors feel a problem warrants investigation, the board also needs the power to collect data independent of information provided by senior management. A skillful CEO who does not want the board to uncover legal and ethical problems can potentially keep the board from gathering data and discussing such issues by controlling the meeting agenda and by denying the board the resources it needs to gather data. When this situation occurs, the power to direct discussions and to control data gathering and boardroom time is a key issue. Boards need the power to act as independent auditors, data gatherers, and actors when investigating any issues of unethical and illegal behavior.

Preventing and Managing Crises

When organizations face crises, securing the *opportunity* to problem-solve rapidly can be one of the greatest challenges for a board. Because boards typically meet only a few times a year and their members are very busy, it can be difficult to assemble a board meeting on short notice. Thus boards may have trouble acting quickly in response either to a major crisis or to a significant opportunity. A crisis can also demand *knowledge, information,* and *time* that boards do not normally possess. Thus the board needs a rapid-response capability that includes both time to talk as well as means for quickly gathering information and knowledge that are pertinent to the issue facing the board. Such a means might be to hire outside experts to do research and gather data, as is often done with takeovers. In other situations, all or some of the members of the board must spend their own time gathering information, assessing the situation, and making decisions. A crisis almost always requires board members to spend considerable unscheduled time on issues with which they had not planned to deal, often with the consequence of having to cancel important outside commitments and activities.

As noted in Chapter One, a board can enhance its rapid-response capability by regularly performing future scans of the environment to anticipate possible threats to the organization and by conducting exercises to simulate how the board would respond to such situations. These exercises serve to build directors' knowledge of the issues they will face as well as to identify the information they will require. Exercises can speed the time of actual response by familiarizing individuals with the decision-making process for a particular crisis. Ideally, undertaking crisis response exercises may help prevent or at least reduce the severity of a crisis. For example, simulating the response to a lawsuit for fraud may uncover weaknesses in existing audit procedures, which in turn can lead to improved financial monitoring. Likewise, simulating the need to replace a suddenly incapacitated CEO may make directors aware that their succession planning process is providing them with inadequate knowledge of possible replacements.

Procuring Resources

The ability of a board to help an organization acquire key technical and financial resources is very much dependent on the *knowledge* and *information* that board members have about external resources. In the area of knowledge, boards must be quite insightful about the technological, human resource, and financial needs of the corporation. They must be able to match these needs to information about the availability of resources in the external environment. They need to know, for example, where and how capital can be obtained; who the right contacts are; and where technical expertise resides and where it can be bought, brokered, or somehow acquired. Overall, board effectiveness in the area of resource acquisition usually is dependent on the characteristics and background of individual board members and the network of personal contacts they bring to the board.

Boards as Teams

Most team research has not focused on either boards or senior management teams. Some researchers have even suggested that it may never be possible to get such groups to be effective teams.[2] Because of boards' special situation, it is true that they are unlikely to be as effective as many other teams. This point, however, only serves to emphasize the importance of doing everything possible to make them effective as a working group. Because of the board's crucial leadership role, even small improvements in a board's group effectiveness can potentially have significant impact on corporate performance. As we will discuss in the chapters that follow, we believe that there are conditions and practices that can lead to boards having an effective mix of information, knowledge, power, rewards, and opportunity.

In many of the areas mentioned in this chapter, the reality is that no board can provide significant value to an organization unless its members truly operate as a team. Much of the work that boards must do in order to produce effective outcomes involves cooperative decision making and joint efforts. Most decisions are complex, requiring multiple perspectives. Boards therefore need individuals who can pool their best information, knowledge, and efforts in order to produce a high-quality outcome.

The major challenge then is to get the board to operate not simply as a loose aggregation of individuals but as a team that actively collaborates. Creating effective teams does not happen by accident. It requires active team building. Boards are clearly a special case when it comes to team building: they do not meet as often as most teams; their membership is often very diverse in terms of the knowledge that individual directors bring to tasks; and individual board members often have very different vested interests in decisions. As a result of these characteristics, boards cannot operate the same way as the self-managing work teams that can be so effective in production environments. Nor should boards operate like finely tuned sports teams. Nonetheless, there are lessons from research on other kinds of teams that suggest basic activities in which a board must engage if it is to become an effective team. The next paragraphs briefly review these key activities.

Boards must establish a set of clearly stated basic operating procedures. Boards need to determine how they will spend their time together; they need also to define the role of various committees in supporting the work of the overall board. It is clear from our research that boards need to establish a clear line between decision areas for company management and decision areas for the board. This distinction should be established through a group charter determined by the board that specifies not just the roles and responsibilities of the board but also operating procedures for group meetings. Roles should also be specified for each board member. The description of roles should include the kinds of expertise individuals are supposed to bring to a board as well as their membership roles on committees and subcommittees.

Expectations need to be clear about the board's basic operating procedures. For example, effective teams define and reach agreement on how they will go about doing their work. They decide how agendas will be set, who will take the lead on specific issues, how decisions will be made on key issues, and how information will be gathered and shared at the board level. These operating procedures need to be agreed on by all members of the board and stated in such a way that it is possible to assess whether they are being adhered to.

Teams operate most effectively when they have rules and guidelines that cover their behavior. It is particularly important that members agree on certain process rules with respect to interactions in the team. These rules can relate to such matters as how people get recognized to talk and how individuals will share the air time in board meetings (for example, agreeing that individuals will be allowed to complete sentences and thoughts before someone else talks). Agreements about how teams operate and how they will judge their own performance are most useful when an assessment process is in place to determine how well the teams are working. As discussed in Chapter Seven, this is best done through a systematic assessment of the board itself.

Board Attributes and Effectiveness

By focusing on the different tasks boards are required to perform, we have been able to identify the knowledge, information, power, rewards, and opportunity that boards need to be effective. Testing whether the presence of these attributes actually leads to a more effective board and ultimately to improved company performance is very difficult. There are no recognized objective indicators of effective governance, and even if a board is clearly governing effectively, the board is only one relatively indirect factor affecting the overall performance of a firm.

To explore whether there is a relationship among these different attributes and board effectiveness, we analyzed data from the more than eleven hundred directors of the companies who responded to Korn/Ferry's 1996 corporate governance survey. This survey contains questions about board practices relating to each of the five attributes in our board effectiveness framework. We then analyzed whether boards that have adopted each of these practices are more effective than their peers who have not. We measured effectiveness in two ways: first, by using directors' ratings of how effectively their board performs key roles; second, by testing whether objective data on a company's financial and stock market performance was linked to different board attributes and practices.

Board Practices and Perceived Governance Effectiveness

If a practice is really useful in building a more effective board, then the directors on those boards that have adopted it ought to perceive their boards to be operating more effectively. To see if this is the case, for each practice we divided the boards into two groups—those that make high use of a practice and those that do not—and then compared the directors' ratings of their boards' effectiveness on a composite rating index of board effectiveness.

The results shown in Table 2.1 indicate that boards that score highly on key attributes in our framework have much higher ratings for effective governance.

Looking first at practices that affect power, those boards that formally evaluate the CEO, have written guidelines for corporate governance, and control the meeting agenda rate their effectiveness significantly higher than those that do not. Those boards who have better sources of information also appear to be more ef-

Table 2.1. Board Practices and Board Effectiveness.

Board Characteristics and Practices	Board Effectiveness	
	High Use	Low Use
Board spends time identifying potential risks to company	4.21	3.11
Board spends time on long-term strategy	4.12	3.08
Board has broad range of indicators for organizational effectiveness	4.03	3.09
Board benchmarks the firm against top performers in comparable industries	4.01	3.05
Board controls the meeting agenda	3.85	3.46
There are written guidelines on corporate governance	3.76	3.47
There is a formal process for evaluating CEO performance	3.74	3.42

Notes: Determination of high or low use is based on ratings by board members; effectiveness rated on a 5-point scale: 1 = Very ineffective, 5 = Very effective.

fective. Boards who have adopted practices such as having a broad range of indicators for organizational effectiveness and benchmarking the firm against top performers in comparable industries appear to perform their roles far more effectively than those who lack this information. With respect to opportunity, boards whose directors feel they spend the right amount of time on long-term strategy and on identifying potential risks to the company have much higher effectiveness ratings.

Limiting the number of inside directors on the board, another important board power factor, also appears to lead to more effective governance. On boards where 10 percent or fewer of their directors are insiders, directors rate their boards as more effective on both their internal strategic roles and on their success in building external relationships for their firms than do directors on boards with a higher percentage of insiders. Ensuring that outside directors are at least in control of the board is important; the small percentage of boards in large companies where insiders hold a majority of seats rate their own effectiveness lower than the rest of the boards.

Interestingly, the one area of board practice that shows little if any relationship to the perceived effectiveness of boards is how directors are paid. Shifting a higher percentage of director pay from cash to stock does not show any relationship to board members' perceptions of effective governance. Likewise, those boards that require directors to own stock rate their board's performance only slightly better than those that do not.

Board Practices and Company Performance

Although a practice that has a positive impact on how well directors perceive their boards to be governing is important, the ultimate test of whether it is truly a "best practice" is if it can be shown to have an impact on the company's performance. Our results indicate that adopting many of the identified board practices leads to a clear payoff in firm performance in both current and future years (see Tables 2.2 and 2.3).

The impact of some practices is particularly impressive. Directors who had better information because their boards "benchmarks the firm against top performers in comparable industries" had more than double the stock market return and 50 percent higher return on investment one year after reporting the practice than those that did not. Likewise, boards that spend the right amount of time on strategy, have a broad range of indicators for organizational effectiveness, and have the power to balance the CEO (for example, by controlling selection of new directors and key committees) oversaw companies that recorded much higher stock market returns than firms that scored lower on these practices.

Table 2.2. Board Practices and Stock Market Performance.

	Stock Market Rate of Return, 1996 (%)		Stock Market Rate of Return, 1997 (%)	
Board Practices	**High Use**	**Low Use**	**High Use**	**Low Use**
Board spends time on long-term strategy	31	17	34	25
Board has needed technical expertise	28	23	38	26
Board has power to balance CEO[a]	25	19	37	24
Board has broad range of indicators for organizational effectiveness	24	18	37	26
Board benchmarks firm against top performers in comparable industries	33	19	36	17
Board spends time identifying risks to the company	25	22	43	22
Board controls the meeting agenda	23	19	32	31
Board conducts a formal evaluation of the CEO[b]	25	18	31	28

Notes: Determination of high or low use is based on ratings by board members.

[a]Board power is measured by who appoints committee chairs and members, how the CEO is evaluated, and the amount of influence the board has over CEO succession.

[b]A yes-or-no question.

Other board practices that appear to have an impact on performance include conducting a formal evaluation of the CEO, spending time identifying potential risks to the company, and having the right technical expertise.

Table 2.4 shows that there is a relationship between the number of outside board members and economic performance. Those companies with a large number of outside members clearly outperform those with a small number. This finding reinforces the point that board power is a critical determinant of company performance.

Although it is useful to understand the impact of individual board practices on firm performance, just as vital is to understand whether the combined elements of an empowered board have an impact on effective governance and firm performance. To gain this understanding, we constructed a statistical model that examined the combined impact of *power, time, information,* and *motivation* on effective governance and company financial results, while controlling for such factors as firm size, industry, and capital intensity. We found that each element of our framework has a strong and independent statistical relationship with directors' perceptions of effective governance and that together they can explain nearly one-quarter

Table 2.3. Board Practices and Company Performance.

Board Practices	Return on Investment, 1996 (%)		Return on Investment, 1997 (%)	
	High Use	Low Use	High Use	Low Use
Board spends time on long-term strategy	18	15	20	13
Board has needed technical expertise	15	14	17	14
Board has power to balance CEO[a]	19	15	21	13
Board has broad range of indicators for organizational effectiveness	23	16	24	15
Board benchmarks firm against top performers in comparable industries	21	13	23	11
Board spends time identifying risks to the company	20	13	20	11
Board controls the meeting agenda	17	15	17	14
Board conducts a formal evaluation of the CEO[b]	15	16	17	13

Notes: Determination of high or low use is based on ratings by board members.

[a]Board power is measured by who appoints committee chairs and members, how the CEO is evaluated, and the amount of influence the board has over CEO succession.

[b]A yes-or-no question.

Table 2.4. Ratio of Inside to Outside Directors and Company Performance.

	Financial Performance			
	Return on Investment, 1996 (%)	Return on Investment, 1997 (%)	Stock Market Rate of Return, 1996 (%)	Stock Market Rate of Return, 1997 (%)
Small Number of Insiders[a]	18	21	35	43
Medium Number of Insiders[b]	16	16	22	30
High Number of Insiders[c]	13	15	27	30

[a]Less than 10% insiders

[b]Between 10% and 50% insiders

[c]More than 50% insiders

of the variation in board effectiveness.[3] More effective governance is in turn strongly related to the firm's financial performance. The single factor that has the largest direct impact on an organization's financial performance, even controlling for the ratings of governance effectiveness, is the power of the board relative to the CEO; we find that boards which conduct a formal, written evaluation of the CEO and in which the outside directors have clear control over the nomination of new directors and the successor to the CEO have significantly better returns on assets, sales, and investment than those that do not. This result suggests that maintaining some degree of formal independence between the board and the chief executive is an indispensable prerequisite to creating an effective board.

Conclusion

Our analysis found strong evidence suggesting that boards which adopt certain key attributes are able to govern more effectively and produce superior company financial performance. These attributes include the following:

- *Information* about a broad set of indicators of organizational effectiveness and about how these indicators compare with the performance of leading firms in the company's sector
- *Knowledge* of the key technological and market changes affecting the firm's future
- *Power* to counterbalance top management, which can be maintained by ensuring that outsiders hold a clear majority of board positions, control the meeting agenda, and conduct a formal, annual evaluation of the CEO's performance
- *Opportunity* to devote time to the company's long-term strategy and to identify the potential risks to the firm

PART TWO

PRINCIPLES AND PRACTICES FOR EFFECTIVE BOARDS

CHAPTER THREE

BOARD MEMBERSHIP

High performance boards can be created only if the right mix of talent is present on the board. This mix has an important influence on four of the five major attributes that we identified in Chapter Two as critical determinants of board effectiveness. Board membership has a strong influence on the *knowledge* that is present on the board, the *information* that exists within the board, the *power* that the board has, and finally the *opportunity* that a board has to be effective. Thus the characteristics of board directors are major determinants of board effectiveness. Selecting board members is therefore a critical task and one that is also particularly challenging and complex.[1]

In many ways, the process an organization uses for selecting directors stands in sharp contrast to the process for hiring its employees. In the case of employees, inexperienced individuals often are hired after they have been assessed to determine their potential. On-the-job experiences improve and develop their skills, knowledge, and competencies. If employees do not work out, they can be relatively easily replaced. In contrast, board members are typically highly experienced individuals who are expected to contribute immediately to the effectiveness of the board. In most cases, they are not easily nor quickly removed. Directors almost always serve their full elected terms and, in most cases, serve multiple terms until they step down or retire because of age or term limits or because their position outside the board has changed.[2] Board members thus need to be selected not only for their current ability to contribute to the effectiveness of the board but also with an eye toward a relatively long-term presence on the board, typically a minimum of six years.

In addition, boards are working groups. Most of their work is highly interdependent, so board members must be able to work well together. Thus, in many respects, the selection of new board members is not about picking a talented group of individual contributors; rather, it is about picking an appropriate mix of *team members*. This is the one way in which selecting board members is not all that different from selecting employees for situations where teamwork and contributing to a team effort are critical.

Obtaining effective board members is partly a matter of having the correct selection process in place, but it is also a matter of attracting highly talented individuals. Boards need to actively seek out individuals who possess knowledge and information that fit well with the strategic needs of the organization. Typically boards must first identify a particular profile or type of individual they want and then actively search for directors that fit this profile. Given the limited number of positions on a board and the time demands of board membership, there can be a scarcity of certain kinds of talent, so boards must be aggressive in recruiting members. One of the key factors that director recruits consider when deciding whether to join a board is the quality of existing board members. For example, in the 1999 Korn/Ferry survey, nearly 27 percent of directors said that the "quality of board members" was the "most important" criteria for them in deciding to accept a seat on a board. Another 64 percent said it was of "major importance" in their decision. Attracting a few high-profile directors who are leaders in their field can help create a virtuous circle.

Without the right membership composition, critical issues may never get raised, and important information and knowledge may not be brought to bear on issues that are discussed. To a limited extent, board operations can be improved with training and development, but such development activities are far more useful for improving group dynamics than they are for enhancing individual directors' underlying capabilities. Thus the selection process for boards entails looking carefully at the characteristics of individuals with respect not only to their substantive knowledge and skills but also to their ability to work together in a group, their time availability, and their effectiveness at influencing others.

Creating the Appropriate Membership

Given the diversity of expertise that is needed to understand and govern today's complex businesses, it is unrealistic to expect individuals to be knowledgeable about and involved in all phases of the business. The best boards are therefore composed of individuals with different skills, knowledge, information, and degrees of availability to contribute. Thus, in staffing most boards, it is best to think of individuals as contributing different pieces to the total mosaic that comprises the effective board.

To build an effective board, one must begin by identifying the *knowledge, information, power,* and *time* required by the board and from there assembling a set of individuals who together have all the talent and attributes needed to supply these. With this approach in mind, we examine how each of the four dimensions of board effectiveness should shape the decision about whom the board recruits.

Knowledge and Information

Because of the complexity of most businesses, it is impossible for any board member or even a small number of individuals to understand and to offer useful information about all the issues that are likely to come before a board. Thus it is important that boards carefully select individuals who have different areas of expertise. Ideally the board's pool of expertise should cover the knowledge and information areas that are necessary for the board to provide guidance on the key issues that the firm faces and to establish its credibility in the eyes of corporate stakeholders.

There are broad categories of knowledge and information that are common to all boards, in addition to unique competencies required by a particular business. Exhibit 3.1 provides a list of the generic knowledge that most boards will need at some point. Unique competencies can be determined only by doing a careful analysis of the organization's key stakeholders, the type of marketplace and organizational issues it faces, and the locales in which it operates. For example, a company's stage of development as well as the diversity of its activities profoundly determine the knowledge and information directors require. Describing his directorship on the board of a small start-up as a sharp contrast to his role on the board of a large corporation, one *Fortune* 500 chairman explained: "Our board meetings [at the start-up] are very much focused on specific management decisions . . . requiring very intense, hands-on attention. The flow of information to the directors and the level of detail is enormous. There is not a very wide gap [of information] between the management and the board. So it is very, very different from a large corporation's boardroom."

Among the boards we interviewed, we found that many do consider a number of the knowledge areas listed in Exhibit 3.1 in their selection of new directors. Certain critical areas are often overlooked, however, and as a result, a board can end up with major gaps in expertise. For example, frequently missing among many of the boards we interviewed was expertise in such areas as employee relations,

Exhibit 3.1. Key Knowledge Areas for Board Directors.

Strategy

The company's business model: Knowledge of how and where the organization makes its profits and its revenues in relationship to suppliers and customers.

Corporate strategy formulation: Knowledge of alternative strategies and knowledge of the strengths and weaknesses of the different strategy alternatives. Knowledge of the company's customer base and trends within differing customer segments that may offer strategic opportunities.

Competition: Knowledge of key competitors (their strategies, core competencies, leadership) as well as knowledge of potential competitors who might enter the industry due to shifts in the market or technology.

Global markets: Understanding of the various existing and potential international markets for the company. Fundamental knowledge about national economies and government relations in those markets.

Leadership

Senior executive coaching: Skills in coaching senior executives and helping them set goals for self-development and personal growth.

CEO development: Ability to transfer knowledge about the business, suggest learning experiences, and provide meaningful feedback to the CEO about his or her behavior.

Organizational Issues

Strategy implementation: Understanding of how strategic plans need to be implemented through organizational systems and the deployment of resources. Understanding of initiatives that build on the firm's core competencies.

Change management: Knowledge of basic change processes, such as communications strategies, tactics to overcome resistance, dedicated change management teams, and the use of benchmarks.

Group effectiveness: Understanding of information about how groups best do knowledge work and how the board can effectively get information to assist in key strategic decisions.

Organizational design: Understanding of alternative organizational designs, their strengths and weaknesses, and how they affect and relate to business strategy.

Relationships

Governments: Understanding of how to deal with corporate host governments in terms of regulatory approval and financial management.

Investors, financial analysts, and the media: Knowledge about communicating effectively with investor groups, analysts, and media representatives.

Communities and the environment: Knowledge of key communities in which the company has its headquarters and major operations. Understanding of legal and social issues concerning the environmental impact of the company's operations.

Functional Knowledge

Finance: Understanding of alternative sources of capital as well as acquisitions, mergers, and divestitures.

Audit: Comprehension of financial statements and auditing procedures.

Technical expertise: Knowledge of the key core competencies in the organization with respect to how they are obtained and managed.

Legal issues: Understanding of the particular legal issues that the organization faces in its business, from both a business and regulatory perspective.

Human resources: Understanding of the critical talent issues of the organization and, if relevant, understanding of labor relations.

Information technology: Particular focus on the impact of enterprise information systems and the Internet on the company from the point of view of internal management and with regard to the capability of these systems to provide effective interfaces with customers and suppliers.

Marketing: Understanding of and information about the company's markets and the ability to structure the organization to interface effectively with its markets.

Ethics

Ethical responsibilities: Ability to identify and raise key ethical issues concerning the activities of the company and of senior management as they affect the business community and society.

---

change management, strategy formulation, organizational development, and organizational design. One reason for these gaps is that many boards define these issues as outside their board's domain. They are seen as the prerogative of management rather than that of the board.

Although management is clearly responsible for strategy implementation and organizational change, the board must be sophisticated enough about these vital issues to assess whether management has chosen the correct approaches. When we interviewed board members about where they obtained expert knowledge in these areas, they typically told us that they rely on fellow board members who are CEOs of other firms. One CEO implicitly confirms this in a comment: "In my view, our strongest, more useful directors happen to be CEOs. You have a little more confidence in someone who has been there." His viewpoint was echoed by many others with whom we spoke and is confirmed by a recent survey, in which CEOs report strong preferences for fellow senior executives from either inside or outside their industry as board members.[3]

Having boards composed of senior executives may have been good enough in the past, but the "general" knowledge that these individuals might bring is often inadequate. The topics of strategy and change have become far more relevant for boardrooms as firms struggle to achieve strategic objectives in a rapidly changing marketplace where execution of strategy, not simply its design, determines success or failure. In many respects, these areas of expertise are no different than such areas as finance and law, in which experts are likely to be able to provide the kinds of knowledge and information needed by boards to deal effectively with such issues.

Another key knowledge gap on many boards is expertise on the international economy. Boards of U.S. corporations traditionally have been dominated by U.S. citizens. With the globalization of many corporations, this board composition represents a potential misfit between the issues the board must face and the knowledge and information that board members can bring. For example, in the 1999 Korn/ Ferry survey, 76 percent of respondents indicated that it was "very important" or "important" for a board to have a "global perspective," and almost all of those who disagreed sat on boards of firms that operated only in the United States. Yet only 13 percent of these *Fortune* 1000 firms had even one director who was not a U.S. citizen. There are, of course, a number of difficulties in having foreign nationals on U.S. boards. For example, having a director based in another country can create logistical problems with respect to scheduling meetings as well as cultural differences that may make the group process itself difficult. Great travel distances can create problems even within the United States, let alone overseas. One CEO we interviewed described the problem of the "Rocky Mountain barrier":

> We have a problem here on the West Coast with the Rocky Mountain barrier. It's very difficult to get good directors to come out here from the East Coast. We lost one good director from the east coast because in her case, she said that with ten board meetings a year she had to dedicate twenty days of travel. She said, "That's a whole month of working days going to our board. I can serve on two boards on the east coast in the same amount of time. Let alone all the wear and tear on the body to do all this back and forth."

Despite the logistics problems associated with having a multinational board, it is hard to argue with the view that a multinational company must have a multinational board. For example, Nobuyuki Idei, CEO and president of Sony, is on the board of General Motors, bringing vital knowledge as GM tries to adapt its strategy and build the alliances needed to succeed in Asia. There is some evidence that U.S. boards are indeed beginning to become more multinational. For example, 15 percent of boards in the Korn/Ferry survey reported plans to add a foreign director in 1999, up from just 6 percent the year before. At present, however, only 2 percent of the CEOs in the 1999 National Association of Corporate Directors (NACD) survey say that their board is truly multinational.[4]

There is a wide range of factors that determine exactly what kinds of knowledge a board needs to have. Given the long list described in Exhibit 3.1, it is rather obvious that no organization can expect to have directors with adequate expertise in all of these areas. Thus it is critical that a board examine its distinct situation and set priorities among these areas of expertise. From our research, we identified a number of factors that should influence the types of expertise needed by the board. Some of these crucial factors are as follows:

- Degree of globalization. As already mentioned, this is a key issue in determining how important it is to have international expertise represented on the board. Truly global organizations, which have lines of business and key competencies located outside the firm's home country, naturally need different kinds of expertise than companies that are only exporters or those that have only domestic markets and operations.

- Life cycle of the company and its industry. Start-up organizations have very different needs than more mature ones. For example, start-up organizations generally have a much greater need for access to capital, technology, and skilled human resources. They also have a particular need for credibility. One key task of boards in high-technology start-ups is often to recruit the top management team. Mature companies have greater needs concerning regulation, globalization, and so on.

- Size. Because of their complexity, large organizations typically need much greater variety of knowledge on the board, in areas such as change management, employee-union relations, and product innovation.

- Type of business. Consumer organizations particularly require marketing and information. E-commerce companies require expertise in operations and branding. Technology-based organizations rely heavily on being first to market and look for core competencies, so they have a particular need for technological expertise.

Power

The legal system in the United States and many other countries grants the board considerable power. They can hire and fire executives, audit the performance of their corporation, sell the company (with shareholder approval), and sponsor a host of activities. However, the power that boards have is not always exercised in ways that serve the key stakeholders in the organization. As has been stressed in this book, all too often the potential power of the board is either misused or not used at all, in which case the board does not contribute to organizational effectiveness.

The composition of the board's membership is a critical determinant of the kinds of power a board will have. It also shapes how that power is likely to be exercised. Research on power in organizations suggests that it can be derived from multiple sources. Specifically there are three kinds of power that are particularly relevant with respect to boards:

1. *Personal power* is based on the characteristics of the individual. It exists independently of an individual's formal authority and position.
2. *Expert power* is based on the knowledge and information an individual brings to a situation and that potentially can be exercised independently of the person's position in the organization.

3. *Position power* is based on the formal authority of the individual and is often explicitly spelled out in the organization's bylaws, structures, and operating procedures.

Board members should come to a board with expertise that is critical to the organization's performance and with the personal attributes that give them power. This seems to be recognized by both CEOs and outside directors. In responding to the Korn/Ferry survey, both groups rate willingness to confront management and to raise difficult issues as the most important characteristic they look for in recruiting board members. For example, in the 1999 survey, 95.4 percent of board directors rated the "willingness to challenge management" as either the "most important" or "of major importance" in selecting new directors.

With respect to board members, the issue of position power is complex. Simply being on a board brings a certain power, but a number of studies indicate that board members' power, particularly the willingness to use that power, is strongly influenced by the positions they hold beyond their board position.[5] Specifically, outside directors who have no direct business ties to the firm or its executives seem to be more willing to exercise power than inside directors, particularly where the power involves challenging the decisions and questioning the performance of senior management. This situation has led to boards increasingly being populated by outsiders who are independent of the CEO and the existing senior management.

At the same time, one study suggests that having significantly more outsiders may not increase the probability of the *ousting* of a poorly performing CEO. William Ocasio, a professor at Northwestern, discovered that among 114 companies, those with more outsiders deposed their CEOs less frequently when the firm was struggling financially. He suggests that inside directors have greater access to detailed information about problems and that they may be more aggressive in pushing for change, as they could move up in the organization as a consequence.[6]

At the heart of the matter is the ability of directors to form judgments concerning critical issues independent of the CEO's influence and personal stance. In other words, directors must retain their own objectivity. In part, this independence is a product of the directors' character, self-confidence, and knowledge. In part, it is a product of their working relationship with the firm. What constitutes independence is often difficult to specify. At the least, it usually means that board members are not employees of the organization, are not related to members of senior management, and do not receive non-board-related income from the company (for example, as a consultant). True independence also typically means that the board member is not involved in other business or social relations with the CEO or other key members of senior management.

In contrast, the Disney board has often been criticized because several of its "outside" directors have business connections with the firm or the CEO; for example, one director is the personal attorney to the chairman and CEO, Michael Eisner, and others have been in charitable groups with the CEO and the CEO's wife. These and other entanglements raise the question of whether board members can objectively and consistently think of the best interest of the shareholders when in fact there are personal and other relationships with the CEO that could affect their behavior on the board.

Another example of a board that lacked independent directors is the drug store chain Rite Aid. In the late 1990s, vendors and company insiders populated the board of the company.[7] In addition to the company founder and two Rite Aid executives, board members included Nancy Liberman, a partner at the company's legal advisers Skadden Arps, Slate, Meager, & Flom; and Leonard Stern, chairman of the Hartz Group, a supplier of pet products to Rite Aid. One outcome was that the board was slow to address problems caused by an overly aggressive expansion program undertaken by CEO Martin Grass. The company's debt jumped from $1.8 billion to $2.6 billion in its fiscal year 1999; its stock plummeted; and company earnings were twice restated for the three prior fiscal years, reducing pretax earning by some $500 million. In the midst of growing problems, the board's audit committee met only twice during twelve months. Eventually the CEO stepped down.

The insider versus outsider issue is only one of several tensions between other board practices and the goal of independence associated with effective governance. For example, paying directors in stock or options gives them a direct financial interest in the firm. Likewise, directors may be recruited to extend the firm's capabilities—for example, by facilitating strategic partnerships with other organizations. Both approaches, however, encourage *mutual dependence* rather than independence.

In summary, a board's power is maximized when the board is made up of independent directors. It is enhanced when these directors have world-class knowledge of many of the key issues facing the board. It is further strengthened when the directors have personal credibility along with the ability to inspire and gain respect from the CEO and other board members.

Time and Opportunity

Board members are extremely busy individuals. As a result, time availability is critical to board effectiveness. Many of the issues that boards face are complex and time-consuming, as they require the integration of market, business, financial, and legal knowledge. Constraints on time can become a serious problem during a crisis, such as a hostile takeover. Clearly a key issue to consider in the selection of board members is their time availability. There is no more certain way to create an ineffective board than to staff it with individuals who do not have time to attend critical board meetings and to undertake the necessary preparation.

This potential problem can be tackled in part by choosing individuals who themselves hold a very limited number of additional directorships. During most of his time as CEO of General Electric, Jack Welch refused to be on any outside board. He argued that being a CEO was more than a full-time job with no time left to be on boards. He only began to join boards as he neared retirement. It is hard to argue with Welch's stance, although it may seem somewhat extreme given what CEOs can often learn from being on outside boards. There is little question that no CEO should be on more than three outside boards, and ideally most should be on only one or two outside boards. In fact, this conclusion fits well with the thinking of many CEOs. In the 1999 NACD survey, most CEOs reported serving on *no* outside boards, and virtually none served on more than three boards.[8]

The situation with respect to the number of board memberships is different for individuals who are primarily committed to doing board work, either because they are retired or because they are a professional board member. In addition, some venture capitalists who hold significant ownership stakes in a portfolio of companies may sit on the boards of each of these firms. But with respect to directorships of major corporations, it would be extraordinary for an individual who is spending his or her full time doing board work to be an effective contributor on more than five or six large company boards. Thus our recommendation with respect to seeking board members is clear: find individuals who are not already on more than a few boards. In the ideal case, the maximum should be one or two boards.

In general, boards may want to seek out a few individuals who have some slack time, most likely those who are retired or who are professional board directors. Having a few board members with slack time is especially important during a major crisis, such as a legal investigation, a takeover bid, or other situations that demand heavy board involvement for a period of time. Board members who hold another full-time job may have trouble getting away for the days required to deal with a major crisis. In contrast, individuals who have slack in their schedules can often free up the time. It makes good sense to have a variety of individuals on the board, some of whom have full-time outside priorities and some of whom have flexible schedules.

Selecting the Right Members

Establishing the right membership on a board is clearly a complex process. The selection process must encompass a wide array of factors, including the knowledge and teamwork requirements of board membership and the operational efficiency of the board. Unfortunately there is no magic formula for creating a board with an optimum membership mix; however, the boards we have studied who have developed the best mix of directors did follow some common processes. A brief overview of these key processes and practices follows.

The Role of the Nominating Committee

It is critical that the board selection process rest in the hands of a board committee that is either completely or largely made up of independent directors. Many boards have nominating committees that do nothing but consider the issue of membership from the point of view of both initial recruitment and reappointment. Others have governance committees that have a somewhat broader agenda but spend a considerable amount of time identifying and recruiting board members.

The 1999 Korn/Ferry survey of directors shows that CEOs and committees composed largely of outside directors are seen as having about equal influence in determining who is nominated for board membership. This result is consistent with the 1999 NACD survey, which found that in only 7 percent of the cases did the CEO operate alone in nominating a new director, down from 27 percent in 1995.[9] Of course, ultimately the shareholders approve membership—although shareholder votes rarely go against the recommendations of the board.

In the absence of an independent nominating committee, the CEO inevitably dominates the process. In these situations, there is an enormous risk that the board will not have the power it needs to carry out its activities. Again, the board must find an appropriate balance in terms of involvement. It is vital that the CEO have input into the selection of new directors, as they will be working together closely. The CEO is also likely to be the best informed about the strategic knowledge requirements of the organization. However, if at the time of initial selection a director feels heavily indebted to the CEO for his or her place on the board, it can hinder the director's ability to exercise effective oversight of the chief executive. There is always a risk that the CEO will seek to populate the board with individuals who are unwilling to challenge the existing management. Thus it is vital that a strong, independent director chairs the nominating committee and that a majority of its members be company outsiders.

The Search Process Itself

Finding good board members is not an easy task. Given their multiple assignments, board members usually do not have the time themselves to perform searches, gather references, and handle the logistics of recruiting new board members. In many cases, search firms and full-time staff assistance from the firm's human resources department can aid in the recruitment process. What the full board or the nominating committee can and must do, of course, is specify what characteristics they are looking for in a board member.

Screening Interviews with the Board

Even though much of the recruiting process of new board members may be assigned to a search firm, it is critical that the members of the board committee carefully screen prospective board members. They should interview the potential board members with particular attention to the degree to which their behavior and interaction style fit the group process of the board. One helpful interview technique is to ask perspective board members about their experience in committees and groups. It is useful to focus on what roles they have played, how comfortable they felt in these roles, and any examples of situations in which they saw themselves as particularly constructive or positive in a group setting. To shed light on their ability to challenge top executives, it is also useful to seek out examples of occasions on which they have had to ask hard questions of a close colleague. Another litmus test in the interview process is the candidates' depth of interest in the company and its industry. Do they already appear to know a great deal? Are they visibly excited about learning about the firm? Several CEOs and directors identified a "passion index" as way of determining a director's long-term effectiveness on the board. One director captured the essence of the index: "The best directors we've had are sincerely interested or passionately interested in seeing the company and the CEO succeed. First of all, they really know the company in a great deal of detail. . . . The other clue is how closely they've thought of things. If you bring up an issue about the company, the directors are already aware of it. The first thing they do with the *Wall Street Journal* is look for us in the Marketplace section. They're the ones you want."

Have they maintained their passion for the firm or become complacent after sitting too long on the same board? In the case of reappointments to the board, before approval the selection committee should first to do a thorough review of the board member's performance. As will be discussed in Chapter Seven, this review is a critical part of the board evaluation process and a step that should be led by either the committee in charge of membership or the governance committee of the board.

Determining the Right Mix of Members

A key step in conducting a search for a new director is to establish guidelines for the membership composition of the board. These guidelines need to specify in considerable detail the kind of board members that will produce an optimal mix of directors for a given forum. The following are areas in which it is important for the board to specify membership guidelines that can be used to guide the efforts of executive search firms and others who are involved in identifying potential board members.

Knowledge Areas

Boards need to identify the knowledge areas that are priorities. Several boards we studied had developed matrices that identified key knowledge areas to be represented on their board, and then mapped these against the existing directors' competencies to determine the strengths and weaknesses of the current board. The matrix was then used to identify the gaps to be filled through selection of new directors. This approach seemed to work well and should be widely applicable to most boards.

It is important to recognize that the competencies an organization requires do change significantly over time. For example, several years ago, very few large companies would have identified the Internet as a critical strategic concern for the board. Today, it is rare to find a bricks-and-mortar firm that is not seeking to enhance its board and top management competencies in this area (see Chapter Eight). A directors' matrix needs to be updated frequently in consideration of changes in the company and its environment. The biggest challenge in creating such board-staffing charts is in developing the right list of knowledge and skills. As was mentioned earlier, boards all too often end up undervaluing knowledge in strategy formulation, human resource management, and organizational change.

One useful approach to developing a meaningful matrix is to ask existing board members what issues they feel the board should spend its time on during the year. Once this list has been developed, it can be compared to the actual knowledge and skills that are present on the board and the knowledge areas on which the board is spending its time. In our study, we found that boards typically wanted to spend more time on strategy and less on operational issues. This finding is hardly surprising, considering that strategy is such an important issue for boards. The companies that use this charting process often ended up realizing that they did not have a strong knowledge base in all of the key areas needed to influence strategy on their boards. Thus, although their boardroom discussions were useful, they were not as effective as they might have been.

A second major issue involves the realistic assessment of the strengths and weaknesses of existing board members. It is reasonable to expect most board members to have expertise in several areas, but there can be a tendency to assume that some individuals have broader expertise than they in fact do. As mentioned earlier, we found in our interviews that CEOs who were serving as directors of other companies were frequently seen as having the most comprehensive knowledge.

Certainly, if one is looking at a general level of knowledge, this is often true. But it is important to distinguish between the kind of knowledge that someone gets from having general management responsibility and the knowledge that comes from being a subject matter expert. As we have argued, there are some cases in which boards need more than general management knowledge. With respect to such topics as executive development, strategy formulation, and organizational change, boards need in-depth subject matter expertise. Therefore it is important for boards to compare the level of knowledge that individual board members have in specific subject areas with the depth of knowledge that the board needs.

Independent Directors

In addition to having guidelines with respect to knowledge and information, it is extremely important for boards to have guidelines regarding the number of independent directors they should have. On the average in U.S. public corporations, there are two inside directors and nine outsiders. In many cases (over a third of the organizations in the 1999 NACD survey), the CEO is now the only full-time employee of the organization on the board. Thus firms are currently creating boards that are largely independent of the existing management. This undoubtedly represents responses to the many calls by such investors as CalPERS and LENS for more independent board members. There are a number of arguments in favor of independent boards, particularly with respect to board power, but it is not clear that minimizing the number of insiders is necessarily the optimal approach. In some ways, the pendulum may have swung too far.

An insider can contribute information and knowledge about the company that outside directors and even the CEO may not possess. Inside directors are also in a position to learn a considerable amount about the board, which can be especially important if they are in line to succeed the existing CEO. Directors also have an ongoing opportunity to assess the inside board member to see whether he or she is a good candidate for the CEO's job.

In our interview with George David, the chairman and CEO of United Technologies, he stressed the importance of having his successor on the board. He pointed out that he himself had had the opportunity to be a board member several years before he had been made CEO. This experience gave him a significant head start on gaining the knowledge and experiences he needed to be a successful CEO. He was careful to appoint his successor to the board of directors in order for that individual to have the same opportunity to learn about the company from the board's perspective and to learn more about the board's operations.

In general, one test of whether it makes sense to have insiders on a board is to determine the degree to which they are able to add value beyond the CEO—

in other words, the degree to which they are able to bring to bear on discussions complementary information and knowledge that might not otherwise become part of the discussion.

One recent study provides evidence from analysis of proxy data that boards are more effective when some members have close social relationships with the CEO.[10] The reason for this is that the CEO is more likely to seek and listen to advice from the board if there are some directors with whom he or she has a comfortable, high-trust relationship.

Despite the potential advantages of having an insider or two along with a few outside directors with close personal ties to the CEO on the board, truly independent directors should still constitute a clear majority of the board members. With at least 75 percent of the board made up of independent directors, there should be sufficient independence from the CEO for the board to be able to exercise effective oversight of top management.

Stakeholder Representation

Boards need to develop guidelines with respect to which stakeholders will be represented on the board. In many cases, individuals who represent particular stakeholder groups possess knowledge in critical areas for the organization. Although there is a potential convergence between the guidelines concerning board knowledge and guidelines about stakeholders, it is worth separately identifying stakeholder groups that should be represented on the board.

It is hard to set general guidelines about which stakeholders should be on the board, because the relative importance of the different stakeholder groups varies among organizations. There are also important international differences in the degree to which the law mandates that specific stakeholders be represented on the board. In northern Europe, for example, representatives of the employees are commonly required to be on boards. In the United States, the United Kingdom, and parts of Asia, no such requirement exists. Significant industry differences also exist regarding what would be considered a critical stakeholder group. For instance, a natural resources company might have a representative of an environmental interest group on its board, whereas representation of this group would not be a high priority for an Internet company.

In the United States, the stakeholder group most frequently underrepresented relative to its importance is the workforce of the organization. This group rarely has a representative on the board unless the organization has a considerable amount of employee stock ownership through an employee stock ownership plan (ESOP). Yet in organizations where human capital is the major asset of the company, including a representative of the employee stakeholders on the board would seem to be a high priority. Despite the critical importance of human capital, most publicly traded U.S. organizations have no employee representatives on their boards. One reason for this is the low and declining percentage of union representation in U.S. firms. Without some vehicle for collective voice such as that provided by unions, it may be difficult to determine who the employee representative should be. Often the best approach for choosing an employee representative is simply to follow the same selection process used for selecting other board members, paying special attention to the knowledge candidates have of the organization's employees and working conditions.

Chrysler was required to put a union representative on its board for a number of years as a condition of its government bailout, but it did not continue the practice once the firm recovered. United Airlines has significant employee representation on its board as the result of an ESOP that made the firm's workers its largest shareholders. But even in that organization, such representation occurred only because of the concessions United's unions made in order to keep the airline solvent.

It would appear to be time for organizations to consider employee representation on their boards. Employees can bring a tremendous amount of knowledge to the board, and they represent a critical stakeholder in the corporation. The increasing use of stock ownership and stock option plans on a corporation-wide basis is a particularly compelling reason for including employee representation on boards.[11] Employees are in effect becoming double stakeholders in the organization: they not only work for the firm but also own a significant piece of it. Thus it only makes sense to have an employee representative as a board member.

Diversity

Particularly in the United States, boards are under pressure to diversify their membership with respect to gender and race. Historically boards have been made up almost exclusively of white males.[12] The reasons for this include the ease of communication that exists among members of a homogeneous group and the sometimes valid observation that these individuals are representative of the major stakeholders in the corporation, partially because of historical patterns of race and gender discrimination. Even those boards that are seeking to diversify their membership may find it difficult because of the high levels of competition to recruit qualified female and minority candidates in senior management positions.

Clearly times have changed, and for most corporations a compelling case can be made for having a board that has gender and racial diversity. There is in fact some evidence of change. Gender diversity is increasing in *Fortune* 500 firms, but few firms still have more than one female board member. The same situation exists with respect to minority representation. About one in four boards has minority members, but typically only one.[13]

In the best-case scenario, diversity would occur naturally as part of the selection process. In order to fill the knowledge areas and include stakeholder groups that the board needs to cover, the process would naturally lead to the appointment of a diverse board. It is likely to be a logical consequence of creating a board that can truly understand the environment and the marketplace within which the corporation operates. Support for this view that diversity contributes to board effectiveness and is therefore a good business practice is provided by a recent study that found that greater diversity of board membership is associated with higher returns to investors.[14]

But what if boards do not end up with diversity as a result of going through an appointment process that is based on looking for individuals that represent the critical skills, knowledge, information, and power that boards need in order to be effective? There clearly is no simple answer to this question, but our belief is that they should then search further in order to ensure that they have a diverse board that still fulfills the other key knowledge needs. One means of encouraging this extra effort is to set guidelines with respect to the minimum diversity goals of the board. In the absence of these, it is too easy to simply fill the board without giving serious consideration to diversity.

Age Limits

Most boards have age limits on membership. According to the 1999 Korn/Ferry survey, over 75 percent of large U.S. corporations have a mandatory retirement age, the most common limit being seventy years. A much smaller percentage of boards have term limits: less than 10 percent, according to the Korn/Ferry survey. It is easy to see why this pattern of policies exists. Limits on length of service are one way to force fresh thinking and new ideas onto a board, and serve as a less confrontational approach to dealing with poor performers. But term limits do have some negative consequences. For example, boards can lose valuable members because of an arbitrary guideline. The reality is that some board members should retire before seventy, others should retire at seventy, and still others are far from ready to retire at seventy, particularly as older people's health and life expectancy continue to improve. A *Fortune* 100 CEO told us, "I really like the idea of having two directors who are now retired because I can call on them without feeling that I am interfering with their real jobs. Retired directors are a plus. We had a former CEO of Exxon who was in his eighties who was immensely valuable. He was hugely wise."

In the process of gathering data for our study, we interviewed several directors who were over seventy and who had been forced to retire from major boards. It was clear to us that their retirement was a real loss for their boards. They were very sharp and active in the business community and could have continued to make a substantial contribution to their boards. In several cases, they joined boards of smaller start-up companies, which are generally less sensitive to formal corporate governance guidelines; these directors were very much appreciated and made a tremendous contribution.

Should boards have a fixed retirement age? In many respects, retirement limits are a poor substitute for a good evaluation process for directors. If a board develops an effective process for evaluating individual directors (see Chapter Seven), it should not need mandatory retirement guidelines. In contrast, if a board does not have a good evaluation process, then a mandatory retirement age is probably wise to have—even though it is in many respects an admission of poor board processes. By limiting the length of a director's tenure, a board is simply substituting an arbitrary rule—one that sometimes produces good results, sometimes bad results—in place of informed, rigorous decision making.

Board Size

We have left the discussion of board size to the last for a simple reason: the right size for a board should be driven by all the staffing decisions considered so far. There is no magical or ideal size for a board. The key question that must be faced is how many board members it takes to produce a board that has the right mix of knowledge, information, power, and opportunity. The answer to this question varies considerably depending on the organization's complexity, age, and demands on board members.

Although it is not possible to specify an ideal size for boards, there are some size limitations that need to be taken into account. Clearly boards can be too large. Large boards end up as legislative bodies rather than as working groups. When boards are too large, it is difficult for individuals to get sufficient airtime, it is hard to engage in true discussions, and members find it difficult to build consensus. Some researchers even suggest that larger boards are less likely to be involved in strategic decision making.[15] Power may end up diffused in large boards, rendering effective decision making difficult.

How large is too large when it comes to boards? The psychology literature on group size suggests that groups are often most effective when they have seven members, plus or minus two. Most CEOs report that their ideal board size is eight to twelve members.[16] The average size of boards surveyed by Korn/Ferry in 1999 was eleven. A group of nine to thirteen members is probably right for most corporate boards, though too small for large corporations. In the case of large corporations, the 1999 Korn/Ferry study found an average board size of fourteen. We would suggest that board size should be even larger than fourteen in cases where the need for diverse knowledge is high and where there are a number of critical stakeholder groups that need to be represented. This suggestion is supported by a recent study that has found a positive relationship between board size and corporate performance.[17] The most likely explanation for this finding rests in the point that boards are expected to fill many quite demanding roles and that it is easier to fill them when there is a large number of members.

Clearly if boards are going to have fourteen or fewer members, some individuals need to possess several sets of expertise and to be able to fill several roles. This puts a real premium on finding directors who are not only knowledgeable but also seriously committed to the role of being an effective board member.

Conclusion

In summary, the right talent mix is a crucial factor in building a board that can not only serve in a powerful advisory role but also be highly influential. To achieve both ends, careful attention must be paid to the selection of new directors and how these individuals will match the board's needs for knowledge, information, power, and opportunity.

There remains one other crucial dimension of board membership that deserves attention: the issue of leadership. Although boards traditionally think of the chairperson or CEO as their formal leader, such thinking contradicts research on high performance teams. These types of teams are characterized by shared leadership among members. In the ideal case, boards should follow this pattern. In the next chapter, we explore this critical dimension of board performance.

PRINCIPLES AND PRACTICES FOR EFFECTIVENESS

Principle: The selection of board members needs to consider the expertise and knowledge of members so that the board as a whole has the ability to understand the business, develop key executives, contribute to the design and management of the organization, and understand the business model and the technology of the organization.

Practice: Develop a board member expertise matrix or chart to use in assessing current strengths and gaps and in selecting future board directors. This matrix should include board members on one axis and key knowledge areas that the firm requires on the other. This format allows the board to quickly assess knowledge gaps and to take these into consideration when future appointments to the board are made. A critical issue in developing an effective matrix is the identification of the knowledge areas that should be represented on the board. Often what is missing is expertise in organization design, management development, change management, and business strategy. It is also important to consider company size and age. For example, board directors play different roles and require different skills as corporations grow and become more established.

Practice: Include a nonmanagement employee or a union representative on the board. It is common in Europe to have a representative of the workforce on corporate boards. A small number of U.S. corporations have done so as well. As employees increasingly come to own more stock in major corporations, it makes sense to have a representative of the general workforce on the board. Employees are not only an important group of stakeholders; they also provide a link between the board and the employee stockholder group and its views.

Principle: Board size should be partially determined by the skill needs of the board as well as by group dynamics.

Practice: Recognize that there is no ideal number for an effective board, from the viewpoint of either group dynamics or knowledge coverage. Obviously, the more diverse and complex the corporation, the larger the number of board members likely to be needed. However, there should be an upper limit to board size. Large groups of individuals are always difficult to manage and organize. A good rule of thumb is that major corporations should have at least ten members, but no more than twenty.

Practice: Boards need more than just the right mixture of technical and business expertise; they need to be able to effectively utilize the knowledge of their members and to operate as a team.

Practice: Have existing board members interview prospective new members to determine if there is a good "fit." Selecting individuals who can work well with the existing board members can help create an effective team.

Practice: Ensure that no director who is also fully employed as a CEO or senior executive in a firm should be on more than two outside boards. As a general rule of thumb, organizations should avoid selecting directors who are fully employed and already sit on two other boards.

Practice: Require directors to submit their resignation when their employment situation changes. As individual board members change their nonboard activities, they may no longer bring to the board the time, knowledge, and information that led to their original appointment. Thus, when a director's situation changes, it makes sense to review that individual's potential contribution to the board and determine if he or she still fits the board's needs.

Principle: Independent outside directors should control the board and key committees.

Practice: Make certain that at least 75 percent of board members are independent directors. In some cases, it may work best for the CEO to be the only full-time company employee on the board. For many boards, however, it is useful to have another insider or close associate of the CEO on the board to enhance communication with the chief executive. It is particularly beneficial to add the CEO's successor to the board if this individual is chosen some time in advance of his or her assuming the post of CEO.

Principle: Some board members need to be able to devote substantial time to their board duties.

Practice: Select some board members, perhaps retired or self-employed individuals, who have time flexibility and availability to respond to organizational crises such as might occur due to an acquisition or merger.

CHAPTER FOUR

BOARD LEADERSHIP

Leadership plays a vital role in the overall effectiveness of a board, as it does in any working group. But boards face unique challenges regarding the kind of leadership they require and how leadership is best distributed within the group. Many of today's governance practices are aimed specifically at ensuring a greater balance of leadership between the CEO and the directors. In principle, however, this balance should shift depending on the issue that is being considered.

By design, a board's oversight role implies that the board should have a strong leadership role within the firm. Reality may get in the way, however. Our research and that of others suggests that in the vast majority of boards, leadership still remains largely vested in the CEO. We often heard comments from both CEOs and directors that board members were too collegial, too polite to assert a strong leadership role. One director's comments convey the problem: "Unfortunately, the board are all his [the CEO's] friends. So some of the objectivity and candor one would hope for in a board isn't there." Under these circumstances, board meetings become Japanese tea ceremonies rather than dynamic, engaged discussions. Nonetheless, a few boards are experimenting with nonexecutive chairpersons and lead directors as a counterbalance to the CEO's power. In addition, important shifts have begun to occur especially in the growing leadership role of board committees. In this chapter, we will examine the fundamental leadership dilemmas in the boardroom and then offer examples of practices that serve to illustrate how boards should be led.

The Board's Formal Leader:
The CEO or a Nonexecutive Chair?

Officially, the chair is the leader of the boardroom. In over 90 percent of large U.S. firms, the CEO holds the chair position. This dual role inevitably reinforces the CEO's power as the board's de facto leader. The position of CEO brings with it a number of potential sources of power and influence. The CEO has greater access to current and comprehensive information about the state of the company than do other board members. In contrast, the typical outside director's knowledge about company affairs is extremely limited, often due to the part-time nature of the director's role and to the director's lack of experience in the firm's specific businesses. This information and knowledge deficit puts directors at a serious disadvantage when it comes to assuming a leadership role in boardroom discussions.

In addition, many directors are or were CEOs themselves and thus share in an etiquette that suggests restraint from aggressively challenging a fellow CEO or from probing too deeply into the details of someone else's business. All these factors encourage directors to defer to the CEO under most circumstances. As a result, the CEO normally determines the agenda for meetings and controls what information the directors receive. Chief executives often dominate the selection of who sits on the board and who is a member of the board's committees. Therefore, it is not surprising that in the 1999 Korn/Ferry survey less than 30 percent of the directors in large firms agree with the statement that they "have control over the board agenda," and that nearly two-thirds of surveyed directors say that the CEO has the most influence in determining director nominees.

The rare times when a board feels that it must take the lead usually occur during the selection of a new CEO, during a company crisis (particularly if generated internally), or when a change of company ownership is under consideration.[1] The fundamental problem with this "CEO model" of board leadership, however, is its lack of an effective system of checks and balances. Despite the significant steps many organizations have taken to increase board power, Jay Lorsch and Elizabeth MacIver's conclusion to their study of corporate governance is still an accurate representation even after more than a decade: "Directors see problems through the eyes of the CEO who, like a multidimensional filmmaker, writes the script, assigns the roles, directs the production, and has the starring role!"[2]

The natural advantage of the CEO is only further magnified by the fact that most CEOs in the United States also hold the position of board chair. Nevertheless, there are clear advantages to combining the CEO and chair roles.[3] By centralizing board leadership in a single individual, there is no ambiguity concerning who runs the firm. Accountability can be pinned on one person. This in turn eliminates any possibility of a dysfunctional conflict between the CEO and a board chair. Rivalries that might produce ineffectual compromises or result in drawn-out decisions simply do not occur. Combining the roles avoids the possibility of having two public spokespersons sending different messages when it comes to addressing the organization's stakeholders. It also generates certain efficiencies by having the most informed individual be the board chair. Otherwise, the CEO needs to expend significant time and energy communicating with the chair on key issues, especially before every meeting. The combined CEO-chair role may make it easier for CEOs to use the board as an adviser if it doesn't have a great deal of power. As has been mentioned throughout the book, there is a potential conflict between a strong board and a CEO who feels comfortable using the directors as a group of advisers. Finally, it may be far easier to recruit CEO talent given the very strong preference of most CEOs not to have a "boss."

Compaq Computer provides an interesting example of the problems that are inherent in finding a CEO when a strong board chair exists. Until 2000, Compaq had a strong, nonexecutive chair, Ben Rosen. In 1999, when the board opted for the second time in the 1990s to fire its CEO, Eckhard Pfeiffer, finding a strong replacement was complicated by the presence of Rosen. Several potentially strong CEO candidates reportedly did not want the job because they preferred a situation where they were both CEO and board chair and thus not accountable to a strong, independent chair and his board. In the end, Compaq ended up appointing an insider to take over the CEO role. The new CEO performed well, and this led Rosen to retire as board chair. Then for the first time, the chair and CEO positions were combined at Compaq.

The aforementioned advantages of a CEO's holding the chair role were confirmed in our own interviews with CEOs, who, almost without exception, deeply believe that the CEO should be the board's chair. Yet despite these advantages, there has been a growing debate over the past decade about whether this unity of command on the board best serves the company's stakeholders. One of the primary catalysts for the debate was the highly publicized decision in November 1992 by General Motors to separate the CEO's role from that of board chair. The impetus for the change was a crisis during which General Motors had losses approaching $7.5 billion. The CEO was replaced by GM veteran Jack Smith, who was given the mandate to run the company's day-to-day operations, while outside director John G. Smale (former chairman and CEO of Procter & Gamble) was chosen as board chair. At the time, there was an enthusiastic reception for the idea among shareholder activists and a great deal of favorable publicity produced by the media. Some three years later, however, CEO Smith assumed the board chair position as the crisis subsided. The model of the nonexecutive chair was discarded, although Smale remained head of the board's governance committee.

Although the idea of a separate or nonexecutive chair has been circulating for decades, few companies have adopted the idea. It is important to distinguish between the idea of a nonexecutive chair who is in fact a former CEO or executive in the company and one who is an independent director of the corporation. Clearly, the independent director who becomes chair is much more likely to possess an objective perspective as leader of the board than is a former CEO who in most cases has picked the current CEO to be his or her successor.

According to the 1999 Korn/Ferry survey, fewer than 9 percent of the largest U.S. firms have separate executive chair persons who are not former employees. The slow inroads made by this practice suggest strong resistance to the idea. The lack of enthusiasm for this idea is captured by the responses of CEOs to a question on the 1999 NACD survey of CEOs. When asked to provide the best reason for having a separate chair, only about 60 percent provided any reason at all. The most common response among those who did answer the question was that it ensures board independence.[4] The lack of CEO enthusiasm for having an independent chair, however, has not stopped governance commissions and activist pension funds from promoting the idea. In its study of board best practices, the Blue Ribbon Commission on Director Professionalism, a prestigious twenty-eight-member group created by the NACD and headed by noted governance specialist Ira Millstein, concluded, "Boards should consider formally designating a non-executive chairman or other independent board leader."[5] An equally high-profile group, the Committee on Corporate Governance in Canada, sponsored by the Toronto Stock Exchange, made a similar recommendation: "In our view, the board should be able to function independently of management. . . . Perhaps the simplest means for implementing this guideline is for the board to appoint a strong non-executive chair of the board whose principal responsibility is managing the board of directors."[6]

The principal arguments in favor of a separate or nonexecutive chair have to do with enhancing the ability of the board to monitor the CEO's performance. It is assumed that directors will feel more at ease about raising challenges to the CEO and executing their legal responsibilities for oversight if the board is led by a fellow director. In addition, fund managers seek to guard against cases where a CEO seeks first to serve himself or herself and only secondarily the shareholders. A nonexecutive chair whose mandate is to enhance shareholder value is less likely to be compromised, or so the belief goes.

Catherine Daily and Dan Dalton, two professors at Indiana University's School of Business, have reviewed the research to date on whether separate CEO and board chair roles do indeed produce better performance outcomes.[7] Their findings showed very mixed support for separate board leadership structures; some researchers found positive associations with firm performance, others found no differences at all. The difficulty with this research, of course, is that because so few firms have a separate chairperson who is not the former CEO, there are few empirical cases with which to test the merits of a truly independent chair. Where the chair is the former CEO, a number of problems can arise, starting with the fact he or she is likely to have chosen the new CEO. In one of our interviews, a current CEO whose board chair is the company's former CEO described the dilemma:

> If he [the board chair] has been involved in selecting the new guy to be CEO, as was true in my case, the chair is in a funny position of not being able to be critical of the new guy for some time. He's got to preserve the honeymoon aspect of it. If a new guy comes in and wants to change anything, there is also the unavoidable explicit criticism of the old guy insofar as how he did things. There is an awkward tension set up between the new guy and the old guy, which results in an awful lot of senatorial dancing around the issue of why these problems existed before and why the old guy didn't do anything about them. If the new guy comes in and wants to dramatically change direction, he has the old guy who is lurking there, either biting his tongue or, heaven forbid, arguing with him about it. If the new guy wants to kill some of the pet projects of the old guy, it is an awkward situation. Personally, I believe, in the simplest of terms, that the retiring CEO is "in the way" and should go out gracefully. If the new CEO wants to call on the wisdom of the retired CEO, he is certainly free to do that without the old guy being on the board.

Interestingly, the rationale for keeping a former CEO on as a board chairperson is usually not based on real concerns about leadership. The most common rationale we have heard in our interviews is that the arrangement will assist the incoming CEO in his or her transition to the new role. The thinking goes that the CEO's predecessor will be more available as a coach to share his or her wisdom and insight into company issues through the most senior board role. Given their freedom from the day-to-day demands of their prior role, former CEOs are also in a position to be more available to directors and other stakeholders outside of meetings. In addition, they are another resource for the board, bringing a deep knowledge of the firm's inner workings. As one chief executive told us: "I think they [the directors] would be very smart to have me stay on [as board chairperson] because I am the architect of the vision and the change that has occurred here, and I can be the coach of the next generation of managers. We've got a couple of guys coming up the ranks that I am very close to. I can help these people grow. I see myself in the next phase of my life as a kind of coach."

Sometimes, the role of chair is bestowed out of a desire to reward or placate the former CEO. For example, many directors see the chairperson's role as a "reward" for their years of service, especially in the case of long-tenured or highly successful CEOs or company founders. It is an honorarium for their years of contribution to the organization. Just as commonly, retiring CEOs simply do not want to let go. They orchestrate their move to the chairmanship so that they can remain involved in the company during retirement. But this very same desire sets in motion a potential problem: the inability of the chairperson to step back and not meddle. Reflecting on his own experiences, Denys Henderson, the former chairman and CEO of Imperial Chemical Industries (ICI), captured the dilemma: "In my own case [as a former CEO who becomes the board chair], it was difficult at first to give up day-to-day control because I was still very energetic, and it was clear that further change in the organization was required. I found it a considerable challenge to move from 'energy mode' to 'wisdom mode.'"[8]

When boards find themselves creating a separate chair position for a former CEO either to reward or placate him or her, they have compromised the board's leadership. We are strongly against former CEOs taking the chair role of their board, as it sacrifices the benefits of unitary leadership, without the corresponding gain in board independence.

The one potential exception to this rule may be for start-up firms as they evolve through different stages of growth. As we will discuss in Chapter Ten, the model of corporate governance for high-tech start-ups financed by venture capital differs in a number of critical respects from the typical large company board. In these firms, it is much more common to find a separate chairperson, representing the interests of the investors, and a chief executive charged with running the company. This chairperson is sometimes brought in from outside by the investors to ensure clear oversight as well as to provide expertise that may be missing from the firm's initial management team. In some cases, the original founder is better suited to the chairperson's role than to the CEO's role. These entrepreneurs typically have a strong vision of where the market is going and the drive required to turn an idea into a viable business proposition, but they lack the managerial skills required to take the firm to the next stage of growth. They may be best at identifying the next generation of opportunities and threats rather than running the business. When the entrepreneur recognizes this situation and is prepared to give up that day-to-day authority, then splitting the CEO's and chairperson's roles on the board can potentially work quite well. This is particularly true in a high-tech start-up environment, where the speed of competition requires that top leadership focus on discerning trends in the marketplace (which may be fundamentally changing the rules of competition) while simultaneously implementing strategic initiatives through day-to-day operations.

One example of a firm with an apparently successful division of responsibilities is the Internet service provider (ISP) Earthlink. Founder Sky Dayton first ran the company, then hired Gary Betty, an outside manager with significantly more operating experience, to become the president. After Betty had demonstrated his ability to lead the organization, Dayton made him CEO and became an executive chairman, focusing on long-term strategy and new business opportunities. When Earthlink merged with Mindspring, another large ISP, Dayton recognized that he had now worked himself out of a job, and turned over the reins to Mindspring's chairman and CEO. He moved on to cofound e-Companies, where he could again put his entrepreneurial talents to work.

Although it is difficult to achieve the proper leadership balance between the board chair and the CEO in both new and established companies, we believe that a separate chair is a preferable form of board leadership. This chair must, however, be an individual who is highly admired by the directors themselves and who has the self-confidence and industry knowledge to take a leadership role, especially during times of trouble. This person must also be someone who is dedicated to following both the company and the industry closely. In addition, the nonexecutive chair should hold few—if any—other board directorships elsewhere, given the potentially high demands of the role. For example, some have estimated that in large, diversified companies, a nonexecutive chairperson may need to spend as many as seventy-five to one hundred days a year keeping abreast of the company. We feel that this number is at the high end of the range when a company is performing well. In a crisis situation, however, it could easily be the minimum number of days required. For this reason, standing CEOs of other companies are not appropriate for the role of nonexecutive chair, given the demands on their time from their organizations. In contrast, a recently retired CEO familiar with the industry might make an ideal chairperson.

Because the board chair works closely with the CEO, the selection process should involve the CEO. At the heart of this model of shared board leadership is a balancing act between the chairperson and the CEO. The two individuals must have strong positive chemistry, yet the chair must not be afraid to challenge the CEO. In the selection process, the chemistry issue is best determined by the two individuals themselves; the chairperson's ability to challenge the CEO is best determined by the directors. The ideal selection model is to have the board nominating committee choose from a roster of candidates, having received input from the CEO beforehand.

Another factor critical to the success of this leadership model is clear and negotiated expectations about what tasks the CEO and chair will each focus on. Henderson of ICI outlines what must happen at the very beginning of the relationship: "It's important that the chairman and the CEO agree from the beginning what each person's role will be. The last thing you want is a fight over turf. The agreement should be put down in writing and eventually approved by the board. But the process of understanding each other's viewpoint is more important than the final text."[9]

The following list describes some of the possible roles of the nonexecutive chair:

Responsibilities of the Nonexecutive Chairperson

- Set board meeting agendas in collaboration with the CEO, board committee chairs, and the corporate secretary, and create a yearly schedule of all meetings
- Govern the board's activities and assign tasks to the appropriate committees
- Preside at the annual shareholders' meeting and at all board meetings
- Facilitate a candid and full deliberation of all key matters that come before the board
- Ensure that information flows openly between the committees, management, and the overall board
- Organize and preside at no fewer than two annual executive sessions comprising only outside directors to review the performance of the CEO, top management, and the company
- Annually review the governance practices of the board
- Annually review the committee charters
- Serve as an ex-officio member of all board committees

Despite the potential benefits of a nonexecutive chairperson, we believe that the position will continue to be a rarity in the United States. We say this simply because there are a number of important hurdles to be faced in adopting this form of shared leadership—all of which are significant. One is the potential for heightened legal liability for the nonexecutive chair. One board director and former CEO explained to us, "I would not accept the chairmanship of a company if I were not an employee and in the fight three hundred and sixty-five days a year. There is too much risk and exposure to do that. To expect a nonemployee chairman to be around ten days a year for board meetings, or something like that . . . and take all the responsibility of being a chairman of a company in a kind of operational sense is illogical. You cannot pay a person enough to take that kind of risk for ten days' exposure."

Beyond the legal risks, of course, there is the issue of time, as noted earlier. In our interviews, we heard over and over again that the time investment on the part of a nonemployee chair needs to be much higher than for the average board member. At a certain point, these investments become impractical for most directors. "You cannot be active in any other company or have any other activity because this [chair position] becomes a full-time job. It almost has to be someone who is retired or unemployed," explained one director very familiar with the nonexecutive chair model.

Directly related to the time challenge is the issue of knowledge. The chairperson who is or has been the company's CEO has a much richer database on which to draw when contemplating the firm's issues. In contrast, a nonemployee chair's knowledge is often similar to that of any outside director. A former CEO we interviewed who has served in the chair's role captured the dilemma:

> A nonemployee chairman is in a very stressful position. You have many of the responsibilities and accountabilities [of an employee chairperson]. But you are not in the network . . . not in the day-to-day things that happen. You read about them in the newspaper because you don't expect the CEO to call you every five minutes. Things happen that you didn't know about. You probably would have challenged them if they had been brought to your attention before they happened. There are times when you bite your tongue to the point where you are bleeding out of both corners of your mouth. It is not a very satisfactory position [to be in].

One way around some of the problems of a nonexecutive chairperson is to create a top leadership team on which one executive assumes the role of full-time chair while the other takes the CEO position. This experiment can take place as a result of a merger, in order to provide a distinct role for the CEO of each company. Some prominent recent examples include the Bell Atlantic and GTE merger, and Citigroup after its merger with Travelers. This arrangement has the advantage that the chairperson is a dedicated executive and hence has the time and detailed information needed to fulfill the job well. If entering the job as a result of a merger, the person will also have an in-depth knowledge of at least a substantial part of the organization. In today's increasingly complex global organizations, such a top team can also include individuals with potentially complementary skills to handle an array of different tasks.

The challenges in making such an arrangement work, however, are closely parallel to the problems associated with the former CEO's becoming the chairperson. Unless the roles are carefully defined from the outset, there is a real danger of overlapping responsibilities and infighting between each executive and his or her respective constituencies. Further, using this approach, the chair is not an independent director and might not establish a significant independent leadership presence on the board. Such an arrangement appears to work best when a merger brings together two CEOs of different generations, where the older individual is ready to step into less of an operating role as the chairman, while the younger person and natural successor becomes the CEO. They can then carefully divide responsibilities. For example, the chair might concentrate on identifying long-term threats and opportunities and building external relations, while the CEO focuses on defining the short- to medium-term strategy and its execution. It is also possible, of course, to hire an outsider to perform a board leadership role as an executive director, an arrangement with which Citigroup experimented when it added Robert Rubin to the team of Sandy Weill and John Reed, before Reed retired.

Other Leadership Roles for Directors

As we have discussed, the CEO is the main reason we are unlikely to see a significant increase in the number of nonexecutive chairs, despite their potential to enhance corporate governance. Most CEOs consider the idea of sharing leadership on the board cumbersome and inefficient. Their bias is toward a single leader—them. When boards are in a position where a nonexecutive chair seems impractical, yet they nevertheless wish to share the leadership role with the CEO, there are alternative forms of board leadership. A lead director position and strong committee leadership vested in outside directors can be reasonable substitutions. We explore these two forms of leadership in the sections that follow.

The Lead Director

A form of board leadership more palatable to some CEOs is to establish a lead director. Although this individual does not assume the role of chairperson, he or she is in essence the directors' representative to the CEO. Only in the case of a management crisis might the lead director actually take over as the board's formal chair. The lead director's role is to ensure that the board approaches its responsibilities in a manner that guarantees its independence and provides a source of leadership complementary to that of the CEO. The lead director is both an ombudsman and a facilitator of the governance process. For example, at Tyco International Ltd., a diversified industrial products company in New Hampshire, CEO Dennis Kozlowski made a string of acquisitions in 1995 and 1996—some of which raised concerns among the board members about the potential contribution of these acquisitions to the company. These concerns were voiced to the firm's lead director, Philip Hampton, who in turn informed Kozlowski. As a result, Kozlowski now brings to each board meeting detailed progress reports on the financial impact of the various acquisitions.

Firstenberg and Malkiel suggest a number of the specific functions a lead director might perform:

Setting the board's agenda in collaboration with the CEO, board committees, major shareholders, and other major stakeholders to ensure that multiple and independent perspectives are represented.

Acting as a regular communication channel between outside directors and the CEO, such that sensitive issues or concerns are raised in a manner that provides a voice for directors who might not otherwise raise an issue or who might wish not to have a subject discussed publicly.

Organizing sessions of the independent members of the board to privately review the company's performance and the effectiveness of the management.

Conducting exit interviews with executives who resign from the corporation to determine whether such resignations reflect problems within the organization or with the CEO's style and approach.

Meeting on occasion with major stakeholders to ascertain their concerns and expectations. Such smaller meetings at which company management are not present unless requested might encourage more open discussion than do public annual meetings.[10]

Ideally, lead directors are highly respected members of the board who also serve in another leadership capacity—for example, as the chair of a board committee. They should be outside directors who by strength of their personality and background can effectively question the CEO. Similar to nonexecutive chairs, they should also have significant executive experience. At the same time, they should not be chosen on the basis of seniority. For example, boards sometimes wish to honor long-standing members or "elder statesmen" with a lead director position, but this criterion determines little about the individual's actual ability to lead. Moreover, long-standing members may have lost a measure of their objectivity, given their long-term relationship with the CEO.

It is important to draw the distinction that the lead director *leads in terms of boardroom process* rather than in taking stands on various issues. In most cases, an effective lead director's role is not to be a "sparring partner." In our interviews with CEOs, we found that several had mistaken notions about the responsibilities of the lead director, which caused them to feel uncomfortable with creating such a position on their own boards. They assumed that this individual would be an adversary on important issues brought before the board or that this director alone would be the channel for directors' concerns. For example, one CEO commented to us, "I have trouble with lead directors. I just don't know what that position accomplishes. On certain boards I have taken a very powerful leadership position. On other boards, I have chosen not to. The dynamics of these things happen without formalizing them. I just feel that on certain issues some directors are more outspoken than others, and on the next issue another one may be."

Other CEOs have objected because they feel it is vital that a board operate as a group of peers. They fear that designation of a "lead" director will somehow reduce the governing responsibilities that all directors should share. Although these are reasonable concerns, they can be addressed at the outset by setting very clear expectations about the lead director's role and through careful selection of the individual who fills that role.

Perhaps because of these concerns, less than a third of the largest U.S. companies have a lead director, and only another 5 percent are even considering the possibility of adding one (according to the 1999 Korn/Ferry survey). Surveys of the Standard and Poor's public companies in the United States by the National Association of Corporate Directors and the Center for Board Leadership show the popularity of lead directors declining—at least temporarily. For instance, a 1997 survey showed that 23 percent of boards that responded had a lead director. By 1999, this figure had dropped to 14 percent. Many CEOs and directors may still see this role as one that is appropriate only in times of emergencies or as a ceremonial post. We also suspect that some CEOs see their board committees as the real sources of leadership and feel that having a lead director only complicates matters.

At the very least, boards should consider having a "lead director in reserve" for occasions when emergencies do arise. One of the boards we studied had what they called the fire warden. One director explained the role to us:

> Whenever you have a combined CEO-chairman, there needs to be someone who acts as a hunter-gatherer among the independent directors. While we have no formal or externally announced lead director, we in fact have a person whom we have designated as the fire warden. They look like every other director until you get to the point where you have a fire. Then they put their fire warden hat on, and they direct people to minimize the loss of life. When the fire is over, they put their hat back in the closet and go back to being a regular director. . . . [To be prepared for emergencies,] the fire warden needs to have a conversation with each of the independent directors once a quarter just to make sure the warden is in touch with concerns that they could not tell to the CEO.

Board Committee Leadership

Where we have seen the greatest emergence of leadership by outside directors in recent years is in the committees. In large part, the growing influence of committees is reflected in a shift in the composition of key committees; most committees now consist exclusively of outside directors or at least have outside directors filling a clear majority of slots, including the position of committee chair. One important by-product is that committees are now more likely to choose their chairs than in the past, when CEOs often hand selected the committee chairs; in 1999,

55 percent of directors in large U.S. firms stated in the Korn/Ferry survey that committees now chose their chairpersons, as the number of inside directors on boards has declined.

In some ways, this shift in power is not entirely surprising. CEOs rarely have the time to be active members of all of a board's committees, so they feel comfortable playing more of a consultative or advisory role and allowing the committees to lead themselves. Reinforcing this situation is the fact that the board governance movement has discouraged CEOs from playing a directive role in committees and has placed a strong emphasis on having outside directors assume key leadership roles. This emphasis is particularly vital to maintaining the independence of the compensation committee, given its responsibility to evaluate and make pay decisions for top executives. For example, one CEO commented on the shift:

> I used to tell the directors about the new committees' membership before the board meeting. I called the new chairman and asked if he'd accept the job. And I created the committees myself. Well, I don't think that is the way of the future. So now I have started to sit down with the nominating committee and tell them who I think should be the chairman. And I handed them at the last meeting a makeup of each committee. Well, they began changing the committees right then and there. They challenged me on one chairman. And they've made a couple of other changes.

Committees are also where board members can generally have their greatest influence. Many of our interviews reinforced this viewpoint. As Lorsch and Mac-Iver discovered a decade ago, board committees help directors cope with two of their greatest challenges: limited time and the enormous complexity of information they must digest.[11]

There are a number of steps that committees should proactively undertake to ensure that they not only retain but also enhance their leadership. For example, in order for outsiders to take advantage of their majority position in committees, they often need to develop action plans and positions of their own rather than be guided by those of the CEO. Because they only infrequently have a reason to get together independently of their board activities, it is important that their board activities provide them with the opportunity to work on these plans and positions. Meetings held without company executives, during which members can discuss sensitive issues concerning executive succession and corporate performance, need to become a norm. These meetings, which according to the 1999 Korn/Ferry survey take place in about 70 percent of large companies, may be the only opportunity outside directors have to develop strong positions that are contrary to the stated preferences of senior management. In addition, it is critical for committees to have the ability to meet without the CEO when they feel that events call for it. They must be able to call these meetings on short notice when they sense that a crisis or rapidly developing issue demands immediate action. It is also critical that they have a vehicle for placing issues on the board's agenda without significant advance notice. In addition, board committees must be in a position to seek outside specialists who can make objective assessments of the company's operations. They must be able to do this without management's prior permission.

One clear way that committees can hold a CEO accountable is through an annual review of performance. (We will explore this process in greater detail in Chapter Six.) An effective evaluation process is an act of leadership on the board's part. Such a process should include establishing goals for the annual performance of the CEO as well as systematically evaluating how well these goals have been accomplished. Goals need to include both the personal development goals for the CEO and the organizational performance targets that the board deems as critical for the year. The results of this annual review should be directly tied to determining the total compensation level of the CEO. The evaluation process itself is best controlled by the compensation committee.

The membership composition of committees is critical in determining the amount of influence independent directors can have over the operation of the corporation. One committee that should be composed entirely of outside directors is the compensation committee. Beyond the compensation committee, the committee that selects new directors (usually a nominating or corporate governance committee) should also be predominantly, if not exclusively, made up of outside directors. The norm has long been for the CEO to be a very active participant in the selection of new directors. Even where the CEO is not a member of the nominating committee, he or she often selects the new directors, and the committee then in effect rubber-stamps these choices. In the absence of a clear majority of outside directors on this critical committee, there is a great danger that the CEO and other internal board members will indeed pick and retain only those directors with whom they feel "comfortable" or "safe"—undermining the balance of power an effective board possesses. From the standpoint of best practices in corporate governance, the nominating committee members should themselves establish specific criteria for filling any board vacancies. These criteria should then be submitted to the full board for approval before a search is undertaken. Although the CEO is consulted during the process, the committee needs to make the final judgment on nominations, which are then voted on by the full board.

There is, however, one potential downside associated with a nominating committee composed only of a few outside directors. By placing selection in the hands of these few directors, they can profoundly shape the makeup of the board. This can result in problems if this group has very strong biases about "appropriate" directors. One relatively easy way to overcome this problem is to set term limits on committee memberships and to rotate all the outside directors in and out of the committee.[12] It should also be made clear that the committee's role is to make recommendations to the boards and not to make decisions on its own.

Conclusion

Strong committee leadership is where the greatest progress has been made to date in terms of corporate governance practices that provide a counterbalance to the CEO's power. It is in such committee leadership that we can expect progress to continue, given the hurdles facing the adoption of the roles of nonexecutive chair and lead director. We do feel, however, that boards make certain important trade-offs when they rely solely on committees to provide board leadership. For example, leadership is splintered across a number of individuals. No single director has overall responsibility for the board and for ensuring that its range of activities is both well coordinated and meeting high standards of corporate governance. Under a system reliant on committee leadership, there may be no central ombudsman to give the full board a collective voice. Given their more narrow focus around specific responsibilities, committees can at best only shape portions of the overall agenda. All these factors suggest that strong committees are only a partial solution to building truly effective board leadership. Such committees need to be complemented by other leadership roles. A nonexecutive chair, despite some trade-offs, can play a vital role in counterbalancing the power of the CEO. To a lesser extent, lead directors can serve as the voice of the directors by acting as both ombudsmen and facilitators of the governance process. All these roles have a central goal: that of putting the board's leadership in the hands of directors rather than in those of the CEO.

PRINCIPLES AND PRACTICES FOR EFFECTIVENESS

Principle: The CEO and independent board members should share the leadership of boards.

> **Practice:** Appoint a nonexecutive board chair who is not the prior CEO.

> **Practice:** In the absence of a nonexecutive chair, appoint a lead director who is an independent board member.

Principle: Independent board members should regularly meet without company executives present.

> **Practice:** Have all outside board members arrive early for formal board meetings and meet for several hours among themselves.

Practice: Schedule an opportunity for outside board members to meet on their own for an hour after the board meets to discuss their reaction to the board meeting and to identify issues that they feel need to be addressed in the future.

Practice: Ensure that outside board members regularly hold scheduled virtual meetings by telephone or videoconferencing.

Principle: Outside directors should be able to call special meetings of the board and place items on the board's regular agenda.

Practice: Identify a lead outside director who works with the CEO to develop the board's agenda and who can call special meetings of the board.

Principle: Independent directors should control the compensation committee as well as the corporate governance committee or whatever committee selects and evaluates directors.

Principle: There should be enough meeting time so that key strategy and governance issues can be discussed thoroughly.

Practice: Schedule monthly full-board meetings with the opportunity to cancel them if there is not sufficient business to warrant a meeting.

Practice: Schedule an annual multiple-day board meeting to review key strategic issues and the overall business strategy of the organization.

CHAPTER FIVE

INFORMATION FOR HIGH PERFORMANCE BOARDS

Timely, valid, comprehensive information is essential to the effective functioning of boards. Without it, directors cannot fulfill any of the responsibilities that have been discussed throughout this book. The information that boards require can be obtained in part through the directors themselves and their outside contacts and relationships, so a critical consideration in selecting board members is their access to information. Boards can also commission studies to answer questions they may have about the organization's operations or about changes in the business environment. In many cases, however, the most useful, "real-time" information is the information gathered by the organization itself and provided to the board as a part of the normal management processes of the organization. Two difficulties with this body of information are its sheer volume and the possibility that it has been slanted to support a particular viewpoint.

The quantity and types of information provided to boards must be carefully considered. Boards exist to govern, not to become immersed in managing company operations; so information must facilitate corporate governance, not micromanagement. All the same, there is a tendency for directors to micromanage. One way to limit micromanaging is to provide directors with only the information they require for boardroom decisions. For example, the information that goes to a company executive is usually not the information needed by the board. In most cases, it is too detailed, too specific, and too time-consuming to absorb. Boards need information that provides insight into the overall effectiveness and general direction of their corporation; they don't need detailed operational data.

In addition to the right information, boards need information that is packaged and delivered in a timely and useful manner. As we will discuss later in this chapter, there are key processes that an organization can use to be certain that its board gets information in a manner that makes it both useful and timely. Also important, the board's varying responsibilities demand different kinds of information.

At the same time, directors must realize that the information they receive can be too highly packaged and subsequently filtered. One of us had an opportunity to sit in on a conversation led by a division president who was preparing his staff for a boardroom presentation on their unit's performance. This executive explained to his staff members, "The board is interested in only two things: market share and costs. We are here to make them feel good about these." He then coached the group *not* to share certain types of information because he was concerned that it would generate too many questions from board members. It became apparent that he had learned from prior interactions the issues of greatest interest to the company's board. In turn, he carefully restricted the information the directors would receive. In essence, executives quickly size up board directors' preferred types of questions and areas of interest, and tailor information around these. This already narrow band of information is further restricted by the limited time available in boardroom meetings. In the case just described, the forty-five-minute period originally allotted to the operating unit's board presentation was cut to five minutes. One can only imagine what types of important information the directors never heard.

The other information problem facing boards is that much of a board's information is generated from within the firm. Rarely do boards solicit or commission external data gathering. For example, on global issues, boards are heavily dependent on internal company sources for information. Nearly half (46 percent) of directors in the 1999 Korn/Ferry survey reported that they "often" or "very frequently" received information pertaining to global issues from the firm's managers or employees. In contrast, only 12 percent of boards reported that they "often" or "very frequently" heard about global issues from consultants or global agencies or customers and suppliers, and even fewer (9 percent) regularly received information on these issues from investors or advisory boards (3 percent).

In the sections that follow, we will address these information-related challenges that boards must address in order to ensure their effectiveness in providing both counsel and oversight. Specifically, we will examine what types of information boards require to assess company and CEO performance, information needs as they relate to the specific roles of boards, the amount of information needed to make accurate assessments, and issues concerning the timing and availability of information.

The Performance Information That Boards Require

Boards need information on a variety of issues. In determining the types of information boards require, it is useful to distinguish between lag and lead indicators of organizational performance. *Lag indicators* essentially inform an organization about where it has been with respect to performance. In this category fall the typical accounting and financial results. These measures are critically important because they are reported to the general public and are of major concern to investors. At the same time, the information they provide usually arrives too late for a board or for management to prevent problems. In the ideal case, boards should be able to anticipate problems and take action in advance of a crisis. It is therefore particularly important for boards to get information based on *lead indicators,* which indicate where the organization is going and which anticipate potential problems and performance failures. Lead indicators, although by far the most difficult to develop and interpret, are of enormous value.

Closely related to the issue of lag versus lead indicators is the development of more comprehensive measures of organizational performance. Recognizing that traditional accounting measures capture only one aspect of the performance of organizations, there has been a movement to develop a *balanced scorecard* of corporate performance.[1] This has led some companies to broaden their measurements to include internal business processes, customer processes, and organizational learning. This is a very positive development in terms of providing boards with not only more comprehensive measures of corporate performance but also measures that are likely to be indicators of future performance. In essence, the developers of the balanced scorecard approach argue that organizations need to measure the entire value chain of their organization. Doing so makes particular sense in traditional businesses, because the value chain influences the end performance state of the organization and is therefore relevant to the board's understanding of how the organization is operating.

During the same time that the balanced scorecard approach was evolving in the United States, work was beginning in Europe on an *intellectual capital* model. It focuses more on knowledge management than does the balanced scorecard approach and therefore seems to be particularly appropriate for organizations built on knowledge work. Skandia AFS, the Swedish financial services company, provides an interesting example. It has developed a measurement package called Navigator, one of the more sophisticated and comprehensive uses of the intellectual capital approach. Since 1991, Skandia has combined measures of past performance (financial results), current assets, and the future (investments in development and renewal). Current assets are broken down into three types of intellectual capital: customer capital, human capital, and organizational capital. Organizational capital, for instance, consists of such items as databases, trademarks, and core processes that build Skandia's distinctive capabilities. Skandia AFS has not only translated these broad forms of capital into concrete measures that are embedded in a companywide intranet-based knowledge management system, known as Dolphin, but it also reports them to the public in its annual report.[2]

Despite the efforts of leading firms such as Skandia, at this time there are no established set of national or international measures for boards beyond traditional financial and accounting measures. Nonetheless it is clear that organizations are beginning to develop and use many other measures to assess their performance. The results of these measures will increasingly be reported to shareholders and others who are involved with the organization. These developments potentially can increase the effectiveness of boards by providing them with much better information about how the organizations they govern are actually performing and how they are likely to perform in the future. Thus it is important that boards actively encourage their companies to develop new measures.

The Responsibility-Related Information That Boards Require

It is best to think about the information needs of the board as they relate to the board's specific responsibilities. In the ideal case, a board would make specific information assessments with regard to the following areas: strategic direction and its implementation, development and evaluation of the CEO, development of human capital, legal and ethical performance, crisis management, and resource procurement.

Strategic Direction

One of the most important areas of board influence is the strategic direction of an organization. Although boards are not usually positioned to develop the details of the company strategy, they are expected to approve and potentially influence it. Of all the domains in which boards operate, however, strategy is perhaps the most difficult for which to specify the exact types of information boards require. Boards clearly need a mix of lag and lead indicators as well as a mix of internal and external information. They need to know, for example, about the current performance not only of their organization but also of their key competitors. With respect to the performance of competitors, it is very helpful to know the relative effectiveness of competitors and their core competencies and organizational capabilities. Boards also need lead indicators of changes in the market, the economy, and the workforce. Lead indicators are particularly important in establishing strategy; the challenge is to find the right lead indicators for the type of business the organization is in.

Information on an organization's emerging core competencies and its existing capabilities can be especially critical in helping boards decide whether an organization can actually execute a proposed strategy. External lead indicators that suggest how competitors will respond are also important. Measures of the core competencies and capabilities of competitors can be very useful for this purpose. In technology businesses, it is particularly important to gather information about what the expected rate of change in core technologies is likely to be. In some of these cases, outside board members who are technology experts can add value beyond what is known by members of the organization.

In a recent study of high performing companies in rapidly changing markets, the research showed that certain types of information were far more helpful than others in strategic decision making.[3] For example, the senior teams of the high performers avoided accounting-based data because it tended to lag behind the realities of the business. Instead they used extensive real-time information from a wide variety of sources—such innovation-related metrics as sales from new products, the number of new product introductions per quarter, and the length of time required to launch products. They also looked at average transaction sizes per client and shifts in customer segments. They tracked competitors' new product moves and exits from products, and technical developments within the industry. Similar, though more summarized, data might be extremely useful to assist the board in their strategy processes.

Boards also require up-to-date information about strategy implementation. Strategies often fail not because of the concepts behind them but because they are poorly executed. In rapidly changing businesses, tracking the effectiveness of strategy implementation is more than ever an imperative. Without such information, it is impossible for boards to know whether the company's strategy is a good or bad one. These same data are needed by the board to ascertain the effectiveness of management. One drawback with this type of information, however, is that there is a danger of the board becoming too involved in the implementation of strategy. Its doing so can lead to the board shifting from a governance role to a management role. Thus, although it is important that the information the directors receive about strategy implementation help them understand what the critical strategy implementation issues are and how well execution is progressing, this information must not be at such a detailed level that it encourages directors to become involved in hands-on "fixing" of problems.

Whether a board can distinguish between a strategy's failing because it is poor strategy or a strategy's failing because it was poorly implemented depends very much on the quality of the information the board receives. In order to make this distinction, boards typically need both process and outcome indicators. Measures and standards that can be used to determine success need to be established by management and the board when the strategy is first approved and scheduled for implementation. Often the best lead indicators of a successful strategy are data that are gathered from within an organization. These could range from employee survey data to various operational data concerning time to market, quality, and costs. When internal data can be compared to targets and benchmark data, it is possible to see whether the strategy is being successfully implemented.

Other useful lead indicators could include customer satisfaction and supplier data. Customers are often extremely good judges because they see whether the promised changes of product and services are actually visible. Often their initial reactions to new products and new services are good indicators of long-term success and so represent data that are critically important to boards. Oftentimes suppliers are in a particularly good situation to assess the implementation of a new strategy because they are so closely involved in elements of the implementation process. Ultimately, of course, the test of strategy implementation is its impact on accounting and financial data, but again this tends to be lag data.

Development and Evaluation of the CEO

Boards are in a unique position to evaluate and facilitate the development of the CEO and, in some cases, other executives. They are also potentially well situated to gather the kind of data that is needed to carry out these activities effectively. In the normal course of activities, however, boards may not get complete information about the performance of the CEO. Although CEO performance and organizational performance are closely intertwined, they are not necessarily the same. Many times the CEO's performance is actually a lead indicator of the organization's performance. Thus it is particularly important to collect lead data on the CEO's performance. In order to obtain this type of data, boards need to specify proactively the kinds of data they want.

What kinds of data should ideally be collected to assess CEO performance? Perhaps the best way to answer this question is to think in terms of the now popular 360-degree performance appraisal. In a 360-degree appraisal of the CEO, performance and competencies data need to be gathered from subordinates, peers, outsiders, and the board itself. For example, with respect to subordinates, data on the CEO can be gathered from employees throughout the organization as well from the CEO's direct reports. In the case of most employees, the best way to gather data is through a survey that assesses (1) the degree to which the strategy of the organization is understood, (2) whether leadership in the organization is perceived as effective, and (3) whether employees are getting the type of business information they need in order to do their jobs.

In the case of direct reports to the CEO, useful data can be obtained through surveys or interviews on the management style, competencies, skills, and knowledge of the CEO. Individuals outside the organization—such as members the investment community, suppliers, regulators, and other stakeholder groups—can often provide valid data about how the CEO is perceived in their communities and how effectively they perceive the CEO to be performing. Finally, board members themselves can contribute considerable information about the CEO's performance based on their exposure to the CEO in board meetings and through information they may gather in their activities outside the board. As we will discuss in Chapter Six, this same data about the CEO should also be used for the purpose of establishing rewards.

Development of Human Capital

The board's responsibility for the evaluation and development of company talent cannot stop with simply assessing and developing the CEO. An effective board positions itself to look at the entire senior management of the organization and to be involved in facilitating their development. Thus the board needs information about the competencies and capabilities of senior managers, and it needs to facilitate the development of these individuals so that they are capable of filling the most senior positions in the organization. The board should play an active role in succession planning and in monitoring the internal supply of senior management talent. It should also determine if the correct investments are being made in developing management talent for the future.

There are a number of approaches that can be used to provide information to boards about the capabilities of senior management. Regular talent reviews and presentations by senior managers to the board are one useful vehicle. These can be supplemented by informal contact between board members and senior management. These contacts can take place at dinners and social events scheduled around board meetings as well as during visits by the board to operating locations in the company. Particularly useful are retreat settings where boards can review strategy for a day or two and simultaneously have an opportunity to interact with a number of the senior members of management.

In the case of companies that are highly dependent on human resources for their competitive advantage, it is critical that board members go beyond reviewing talent at the senior management level. They need information on the organization's human resources that are critical to its core competencies and organizational capabilities. For example, Microsoft currently has one of the highest market valuations of any U.S. corporation but very few physical assets. The company's major assets are its people and its management systems. A responsible board in this case cannot simply look at the physical and financial assets of the corporation; it also needs to stay informed about the human assets at multiple levels.

One major problem in giving the board information about the human assets of an organization, however, is that doing so may encourage managing, rather than governing. This problem can be minimized by giving directors only indicator data with respect to the general human resources of the organization. Such indicator data should include information on the high-potential pool for specific management levels along with turnover rates, particularly turnover among individuals who are identified as critical human assets. Data should also include the results of employee satisfaction surveys, recruitment activities, and job offer acceptance rates. These kinds of indicators can provide the board with a good sense of how the organization is doing in attracting and retaining talent.

It is also useful for boards to have information about the amount and kind of training and development taking place in the organization. Unfortunately, there is no well-established way to report information on the value of training and development that individuals in organizations receive. In the 1960s, there was a movement in the field of accounting to create a human asset model that would allow organizations to systematically account for and value their investments in training.[4] For a variety of reasons, this approach never caught on. Today there is no broadly accepted approach to determining the financial value of training and development experiences. Thus the best a board usually can do is to look at spending levels and at information that might be available on the effectiveness of training.

Legal and Ethical Performance of the Corporation

To monitor the ethical and legal behavior of senior management and of the corporation, the board must have lag data concerning legal and ethical problems. Important lag indicators include lawsuits, complaints filed with various government bodies and agencies, and newspaper stories that report on company problems. These should automatically and immediately go to the board. What is particularly crucial in monitoring the legal and ethical performance of a corporation, however, is the development of lead indicators and preventive measures and programs. It is far less disruptive and dysfunctional for a board to prevent and uncover problems early on than to respond to outsider groups who discover them in advance of the board.

One effective way for boards to get lead information is to look at surveys of customers, vendors, and employees with respect to ethical behavior. Surveys should include questions that focus on the manner in which employees, customers, and vendors are treated by the organization and the degree to which the organization is seen as fair and ethical in its behaviors. The organization can also conduct regular audits, not only of its financial transactions but also of its human resource transactions, its sales behavior, and its relationship to its vendors. Audits are a critical way to turn up information before problems reach the formal complaint stage.

Boards should also create a safe communication channel that allows individuals both inside and outside the firm to call the board's attention to any unethical and illegal behavior on the part of the organization. This can be done through a secure telephone line, website, or mailing address that goes directly to an outside board member who is typically the head of the audit committee or, if there is one, the nonexecutive board chair.

If a legal or ethical problem has been identified, the board must have the ability to independently gather information about it and monitor its resolution. Often this is best accomplished by hiring outsiders who gather the information and report directly to the board. In order to do this, boards should have information on hand about outside resources that are available, as well as the power to hire and retain these outside resources.

Crisis Management

It is impossible for organizations to anticipate exactly what crises they will face. Nevertheless, in the best of all worlds, boards would identify the three or four most likely problems that could arise, and from these they would develop information scenarios about how to respond to them. Such likely crises would include takeovers, mergers, and disruptions in the senior management ranks. Ideally, a board would already have information on board members who might have the time to work on particular problems that come up. It is also helpful if board members receive ongoing information that assesses the possibility of acquisitions, takeover efforts, and other external events that may affect the organization.

Once a crisis has occurred, boards clearly need information about how to respond to it. As is the case with legal and ethical problems, boards typically require having data gathered by individuals who are not regular employees of the organization. They therefore need up-to-date information about the external resources that are available to them, and they must also have the ability and authority to contract for outside help.

Resource Procurement

Critical to a board's effectiveness in fulfilling its role in resource procurement is information about both the organization's needs for resources and the availability of external resources. Boards need to actively review data that indicate what resources the organization is likely to need in the future. The need for this review may be obvious with respect to finance, but it is less obvious and often equally important for boards to focus on the procurement of human talent, vendors, and suppliers, as well as to actively search for organizations with which to network.

With the growing importance of joint ventures and partnerships to secure competitive advantage, boards need to be particularly sensitive to opportunities for the organization to form links with other organizations in order to improve their market position. Boards can do this only if they have good, up-to-date information on the direction of the business as well as on the current business environment. Regarding the latter, one of the reasons individuals are selected for board membership is that they bring information about the environment to the boardroom. However, their information often needs to be supplemented by reports that are specific to the industry and include competitors of the organization.

The Amount of Information That Boards Require

Determining the right amount of information to give to board members is not an easy task, but it is an important one. With too little information, there is the risk that directors will be unable to accomplish their major objectives; too much information often is the equivalent of no information. When we interviewed board members, we frequently heard the complaint that all too often they were inundated by information. At times they were so overwhelmed that they had trouble sorting out and determining the important indicators. There is, of course, no easy solution to this problem. To some degree, boards need to trust management to identify the information they should receive and to package it accordingly. At the same time, there are some things that boards can do themselves to manage the flood of information they receive.

At a basic level, information can be classified into two types: regular indicator data and exception data. Information that is regularly shared on a predetermined schedule—earnings, financial information, various kinds of surveys, and the like—fall under the regular indicator category. The board needs to specify clearly what regular indicator data it needs in order to do its job. The category of exception data includes information that is reported only when it deviates from the normal or healthy. Data about ethical problems and jumps in quality problems clearly fall into this category, as does information about the loss of key human resources, problems with buyers or vendors, and exceptional customer complaints. To a significant degree, the board is dependent on management to sort this information and to make judicious decisions about what information to share and what not to share. If a significant level of trust does not exist between the board and management, then the board may have to get its information concerning problems directly from outside auditors and from individuals inside the company who are directly responsible for collecting the information.

Timing of Information

The timing of when boards receive information is another important consideration. Board members clearly prefer to get information at least a week before meetings. Board members repeatedly reported to us that they felt a great deal of boardroom meeting time was wasted when it was consumed by individuals simply reporting on operating results and events. Their strong feeling was that this kind of information should be provided several weeks in advance of the board meetings so that the board members could review it and come prepared to discuss it during the meeting time. Board members clearly prefer to use board meeting time for discussion, not for reviewing information.

There are a variety of reasons why board members do not get adequate information in advance of meetings. Perhaps the most common is that management simply does not have it ready. This reason is becoming increasingly less acceptable. The Web is revolutionizing the way board members can get information about corporate performance. The entire company's business model and results can be put on the desktop of every director. At Motorola, for example, the company's website for board members gives them access not only to important sources of board data but also to Motorola University and other information warehouses in the company. Directors can go to the site and improve their understanding of both the company and its products. With the development of high-speed financial information processes (for example, virtual closings that provide instant end-of-period financial data), directors can get nearly unlimited amounts of information, including almost immediate information on financial performance. Being able to do so increases the possibility of their taking quick action when financial problems exist. It may also finally eliminate the need to send out the extensive books of financial data and reports that go to board members shortly before board meetings.

The principal problem with Web-based financial information, however, is that it can allow and encourage board members to micromanage the company. Because the entire business model of a corporation can be made available to board members, it is possible for directors to get very detailed information about business and employee performance. In addition, they can obtain this information as quickly as the senior management of the organization. The risk is that some board members will react to the information too hastily and in a way that represents management behavior rather than governance behavior. Probably the best way to avoid this outcome is not to withhold the information from board members but to reach an agreement with them as to the type of discussions and actions in which it is reasonable for board members to be involved.

Even with advanced information technology and sophisticated internal financial accounting systems, board members will still be getting more lag data than lead data. The major difference is that they will get lag data faster, in greater volume, and at approximately the same time as senior management. New information systems also can make it possible for directors to perform online inquiries and data analysis that will give them much better insight into the issues of strategy implementation and performance.

A second reason why boards do not get sufficient information in advance of meetings is that management may fear having a true discussion. By filling meeting time with presentations, management can limit the opportunities for the board to get into discussions that the management wishes to avoid. Other times, management may be afraid that board meetings may lead to micromanaging by the directors. In a few cases, the CEO does not want the board to act as either a governing or managing body. The best resolution to the governance-management dilemma, however, is not to have management controlling the meeting and filling it with information; instead, it is to establish clear boundaries as to what constitutes governance and what constitutes an invasion of the management's responsibilities on the part of the board.

A final issue relating to timing concerns the actual duration of meetings. Short meetings lessen the board's power to influence the business strategy of the organization. Time after time, board members reported to us that they preferred to have at least one annual long off-site meeting. They argued that this kind of meeting is a particularly good opportunity to get information about strategy and to become familiar with the key management people in the organization. They pointed out that short board meetings provide little opportunity for real discussion, and as a result they decrease the amount of contribution that boards can make to complex strategic issues. To address this problem, some organizations we studied held a yearly strategy retreat, during which the discussion focused solely on the strategic direction the organization was planning to take. Board directors particularly valued these retreats.

Availability of Information

Table 5.1 presents interesting results from the 1999 Korn/Ferry survey on the frequency with which boards get different kinds of information. The results indicate that board members relatively frequently receive information that is relevant to key strategy issues. They get benchmark data, institutional indicator data, and economic data. Less often provided is information from two major stakeholder groups: suppliers and employees.

The 1999 survey by the NACD also confirmed that directors infrequently receive information about a company's human resources.[5] For example, only 50 percent said they received information on employee training and turnover. Slightly more than 50 percent received employee satisfaction data, and less than 60 percent received information on customer satisfaction. Clearly these are important information gaps. For the capital-intensive corporations, receiving little information on human resources may be appropriate, but it is certainly not appropriate for organizations that are highly dependent on their human resources and on their suppliers.

These studies are suggestive, not definitive, because they ask about information in only general terms. But they are probably accurate in indicating that boards tend to be more focused on investors than on other stakeholders. They also focus more on operational and financial results than on relationships with customers and suppliers or on the condition of human resources.

The studies are probably also accurate in reporting that boards particularly seek information that is relevant to business strategy. Our interviews with board members and CEOs clearly were dominated by the desire of boards to have a major say in business strategy. It is hard to argue with strategy being an important issue, but it may be somewhat overemphasized, in part because of the membership of a typical board. Boards are predominately composed of CEOs and executives from other firms, and strategy represents an area in which many are reasonably well grounded and quite comfortable. Thus they prefer and enjoy discussions about strategy more than discussions about legal and ethical issues, CEO succession, and management of human resources.

Table 5.1. Frequency with Which Boards Receive Information.

Type of Information	Mean
Benchmarks of company performance	3.82
Input of institutional investors	3.28
Relevant national and global economic indicators	3.22
Detailed scenarios of threats/opportunities	3.22
Key process benchmarks vis-à-vis other sectors	2.80
Measures of organizational climate	2.68
Input of consultants commissioned by board	2.68
Input of major suppliers	2.05

Note: 1 = Never; 5 = All the time

Source: Data from Korn/Ferry survey, 1999.

Conclusion

In this chapter, we have highlighted the areas of information that boards need in order to be truly effective. Our experience tells us that most boards fall short in the quality and, somewhat less frequently, the quantity of information in these areas. These shortcomings in turn hinder both the quality of their decisions and their power as a governing body. In addition, the data far more often tend to be lag indicators of organizational performance rather than leading indicators. This in part explains why boards appear to be slow in their responsiveness to problems. They have few early warning sources.

At the same time, boards and management face an essential dilemma. On the one hand, too much information to the board can overwhelm directors, an issue about which many directors complain. It can also encourage micromanaging. On the other hand, too little information can hinder the board's ability to make wise decisions and can limit the directors' capacity to foresee emerging problems. Boards themselves must proactively seek out a broader range of information and rely to a greater extent on leading indicators and outside, objective sources of data. If they are to provide true leadership, they need to move away from their historical reliance on standard financials, lagging indicators, and information provided by management.

PRINCIPLES AND PRACTICES FOR EFFECTIVENESS

Principle: Boards should have comprehensive information on corporate performance.

> **Practice:** Ensure that the board receives and reviews customer satisfaction data, employee satisfaction data, and corporation image data with respect to the company's position in the community, with its vendors, and with its customers.

> **Practice:** Provide the board with accounting reports as well as economic analyses that include economic value-added numbers and such operational measures as productivity, quality, rejects, and cycle times.

> **Practice:** Provide board members with opportunities for regular site visits to company locations so that they can observe firsthand how the organization operates.

> **Practice:** Ensure that the board has an opportunity to meet with major suppliers of the organization.

> **Practice:** Create opportunities for board members to interact with customers and, if possible, to use and experience the company's services as a typical customer would.

Practice: Provide a convenient and secure channel for disgruntled employees, vendors, and customers to communicate directly to the board. One channel can be a phone number that provides direct access to board members so that individuals can report cases of fraud or misbehavior on the part of the organization and its executives. A second channel can be a mailing or e-mail address that employees can use to directly communicate with outside directors regarding their concerns about how the company is operating.

Practice: Identify a lead outside director as the individual to whom employees, customers, vendors, and communities can report actions that they feel violate the corporation's standards. This director should be highly credible and trustworthy.

Principle: Boards should regularly review information on the development plans for the corporation's executives.

Practice: Have key executives make regular presentations to the board so that they are familiar with how the board operates and so that board members can become acquainted with them.

Practice: Have a succession plan in place for the corporation and review it at least annually with the board. This plan should include executives who are the backups for all the key positions; it should also include the planning and development activities for at least the top fifty executives in the corporation.

Principle: Boards should have timely, easy access to appropriately detailed information about corporate performance.

Practice: Provide information to board members well before board meetings.

Practice: Provide Web-based access to financial and other company performance information.

Practice: Have board members agree on the amount of detail they need to receive with respect to key performance indicators.

Practice: Have one board meeting a year that focuses on extensive information and discussion concerning the business environment, company strategy, and competitors.

CHAPTER SIX

EVALUATING THE CEO

One of the most important governance practices to emerge in the last two decades is the performance appraisal of the CEO. Whereas annual employee appraisals have long been a common practice in most U.S. corporations, CEOs have traditionally been exempt from such reviews. Since the 1990s, however, there has been sharp upswing in the use of formal CEO evaluations. The results of the 2000 Korn/Ferry survey indicate that approximately two-thirds (64 percent) of the *Fortune* 1000 now employ a formal CEO evaluation, with CEO evaluations even more common (83 percent) among the very largest firms (those with over $20 billion in annual sales).

Several forces have driven the greater use of CEO appraisals. One is the increased focus on the critical roles that CEOs play in corporations. The management literature is awash with books which argue that leadership at the top of corporations is critical to implementing strategy, creating successful corporate transformations, and so on. Reflecting this perception, CEO compensation levels—in particular, the wealth generated through stock options—have increased dramatically in the last decade. In turn, calls for greater CEO accountability have risen. Given the importance of senior leaders and their rising pay levels, natural pressures to formally judge a CEO's performance have increased. These pressures to justify how CEO pay is determined are particularly strong in the United States, where the rise in top executive pay has been particularly sharp.

From the standpoint of the governance movement, formal evaluations are seen as one practice that has the potential to make boards much more vigilant and proactive in their relationship to the CEO. At the very least, boards can establish predetermined, tangible objectives by which the CEO's performance can be tracked on a regular basis. Thus evaluations can serve as early warning systems for boards, allowing them to deal more effectively with poorly performing CEOs.

Another force has contributed to the popularity of formal CEO evaluations. Over the last decade, performance management systems have become increasingly more sophisticated and popular.[1] For example, there has been a dramatic expansion in the use of 360-degree feedback and of bonuses that are based on measures of individual performance.[2] As these practices have become commonplace, it has become harder and harder to justify why the company's most important employee—the chief executive officer—is not subject to a performance evaluation. Reinforcing this trend, research suggests that the inclusion of the CEO in a company's evaluation process has a positive influence on the overall effectiveness of the company's appraisal system. In essence, CEOs can role-model good appraisal behavior, and their performance accountability sets a standard for others.

The challenge in performing a CEO evaluation, of course, is to do it well. It is not enough to ask a few evaluative questions or to set performance targets that are checked off every year. In companies where CEO appraisals work well, specific, clearly defined objectives are set by the board and the CEO, and steps are followed to overcome the common shortcomings of performance appraisals. Evaluations require a special commitment from the CEO and from board members. Without the right practices and commitments in place, an evaluation can easily become a mechanical event during which everyone simply goes through the motions; worse yet, it can become a practice that creates a major rift between the board and the CEO.

In the discussion that follows, we will first examine the specific benefits of doing formal appraisals of the CEO's performance. Next, we will walk through the steps that make for an effective CEO evaluation process, drawing on our research. Finally, we will consider the implementation challenges that boards must address to ensure that evaluations produce the expected results.

The Benefits of Formal Appraisals of the CEO

What we found in our analysis of individual directors' ratings of their boards is that CEO appraisals do indeed have a positive, independent effect on board members' ratings of overall board effectiveness. For example, according to the 1999

Korn/Kerry survey, boards with CEO evaluations rated their overall board effectiveness significantly higher than did boards without such evaluations (4.16 versus 3.77 on a 5-point scale, with 5 being the most favorable).

In our case studies of companies successfully using CEO evaluations, we found positive outcomes in four areas. Appraisals were described as (1) heightening performance accountability and the link between performance and rewards, (2) clarifying strategic direction, (3) fostering the development of the CEO, and (4) promoting better CEO-board relations.

The outcome most expected from a CEO evaluation process is greater accountability for performance. And indeed we found that with a system of formal, mutually agreed-on targets in place, it appears to be far more difficult for a CEO to find "excuses" for poor performance. Having well-defined targets also makes it easier to determine CEO pay. When pay levels are tied to predetermined objective measures of performance, there is little doubt about the level of achievement needed to attain a certain level of bonus or stock award.

By specifying a set of strategic targets at the start of each year along with quantifiable measures for each, the CEO and the board develop a clearer focus on the company's strategic goals. This focus can then cascade down through the organization so that goals and responsibilities at multiple levels support the strategic direction of the organization. As one CEO explained, "The appraisal process has created basically a centerpiece of performance expectations that all board members have an opportunity to comment on and then cast in concrete. There is very little wiggle room on the board's behalf to say, 'We didn't want you to be doing what you are doing; we wanted you to do something else.' As a result, we have a very tight agreement in terms of what my emphasis ought to be for the coming twelve months."

Just as important, the board now has in place the basis for an early warning system. The measurable targets set by the CEO become benchmarks for board members to determine whether the CEO is meeting, exceeding, or failing to meet his or her own goals and those of industry peers. For such a set of metrics to provide an early warning, they must be monitored on an ongoing basis, not just examined once a year when it is time to assess the results of the appraisal.

Appraisals can also contribute to the chief executive's ongoing development. For many boards, this is the main purpose of adopting a formal appraisal process. One of the problems that comes with the power and prestige associated with the chief executive position is that CEOs rarely receive candid feedback. When they do get it, it is typically from a select few directors with whom they have a close personal relationship. Adoption of a formal appraisal process can increase the level, candor, and detail of the feedback CEOs receive, with particular attention to areas for personal development.

A final benefit of formal CEO evaluations is that they can improve relations between the CEO and board members. For example, we found that going through the process of establishing targets fosters greater dialogue, especially around the firm's long-term strategy. Board members felt that formalizing the evaluation process helped establish a healthy balance of power between the board and the CEO. With the proper procedures, appraisals increased the board's independence and control over the CEO and the compensation process. Once institutionalized, formalized evaluations are also likely to serve as an important constraint on future successors of the CEO who might be more reluctant to share power with the board.

Steps in Conducting an Effective CEO Evaluation

In all the boards we studied that were effectively employing CEO appraisals, board members had an opportunity to discuss proposed approaches to the appraisal and often participated in the design of the process. It is important, at a minimum, to discuss the range of possibilities and to get board members' feedback before choosing a particular design. Directors' comfort with the process and sense of shared ownership in its design help the board in its transition to a formalized procedure. Having ensured board participation in the process, there are typically three steps in an effective evaluation: (1) establishing evaluation targets at the start of the fiscal year, (2) reviewing performance midcourse, and (3) assessing final results at year-end.

Establishing Targets

Setting targets at the start of the company's fiscal year, the CEO and his or her direct reports need to work with the board to develop the annual strategic plan. Together they establish key short-term and long-term objectives for the coming year. Beforehand, the CEO should draft an initial set of both quantitative and qualitative objectives and send them to his or her direct reports for their comments. This is one of several opportunities the CEO's subordinates should have to influence the shape of the firm's annual goals. In reality, it should already be a mutual process, as some of the CEO's objectives themselves should be derived from his or her reports' own operating plans. This is also an opportunity to assign clear responsibility in the organization for key objectives. For example, senior managers at this stage should learn for which of their CEO's performance objectives they will be held accountable. In this way, the evaluation process ensures that the objectives set at the top align with operational and tactical goals further down in the organization. Once these objectives have been defined, the CEO can "translate" them into a set of personal performance targets that specify how his or her progress will be measured against each. These targets should include the usual financial and budget objectives, as well as strategic and personal development objectives. The CEO and the board should also set performance targets relative to the performance of competitors.

One of the problems we found in a number of CEO appraisals was a heavy reliance on standard financial performance measures, with limited consideration of other measures. As we discussed in Chapter Five, there needs to be a blend of quantitative and qualitative performance measures and a blend of financial and other measures. In many ways, financials are the most visible and easily tracked measures, but not always the most important. One CEO put it quite nicely: "[In some ways,] numbers are the least important . . . because the directors all know the numbers. Hell, we know if we have done well. We had a great year, our stock is at all-time highs. So the directors know the numbers. . . . What about other discussions [that should be part of an effective evaluation]: strategy, ability to carry out a vision, understanding of a global program?"

Once the objectives are set, they are then presented to a committee of the board—normally the compensation committee or a board governance committee, ideally composed solely of outside directors. In essence, this presentation is a "pre-review" of the objectives before the full board review. It provides an opportunity for the committee members to assess and, if necessary, to amend the CEO's targets. It is also the time to establish what financial rewards will result from meeting the targets. It is here that gaps between perceptions held by the CEO and those of the outside directors should surface and be resolved. This is a critical phase, and the committee members must work collaboratively with the CEO to ensure that the targets are realistic yet challenging. If directors simply rubber-stamp what is presented to them, they can undo whatever good intentions exist. When the CEO and the committee members reach final agreement on the objectives, the targets are presented to the full board for further discussion and final approval.

Involving both the board and the company's senior management in setting the CEO's performance targets achieves at least two outcomes. One, as we have already mentioned, is that the evaluation becomes a powerful tool for focusing management throughout the firm on clear and well-defined goals. The second is that the organization has achieved rigor in its performance standards for the CEO and for the corporation. The established objectives are the product of a thoughtful and comprehensive goal-setting process.

Reviewing Performance Midcourse

The next step in the evaluation process is to conduct one midcourse review (or several periodic reviews). Here the aim is to assess how well the CEO is achieving his or her objectives. This review is an opportunity for the board to assess areas where the CEO is meeting or exceeding agreed-on goals and where there are problems. It also encourages directors to act before major problems develop and to ensure that the objectives are relevant. Such a review is particularly important—and may need to occur quarterly—in companies where products and market conditions change rapidly. For example, if the CEO has reached a particular milestone for one of the objectives, he or she could highlight the achievement at the next board meeting. At the same time, often shortcomings can be identified at an earlier stage. A number of the boards we studied skipped the midcourse review or else held only an informal review. We feel that the absence of such reviews undermines the evaluation process. Some form of progress check is essential if the process is to remain well integrated with the company's business objectives and if year-end surprises are to be avoided.

Assessing Final Results

The final stage of the CEO evaluation occurs at the end of the fiscal year, when the CEO's actual performance is measured against targets and compensation is determined. This step often begins with a written self-evaluation by the CEO assessing how he or she has performed over the year. In a number of companies, this final step is combined with the goal-setting process for the next year. For example, at Dayton Hudson, one of the companies most frequently cited as a leader in corporate governance, both the chief executive's self-assessment of the past year's performance and his targets for the coming year are presented to the executive committee of the board at its March meeting.

One effective design is for the CEO to prepare a written self-assessment of the previous year's performance against objectives and a set of written objectives for the coming year. These are circulated among all the board members, who in turn send individual written comments to the chairperson of the governance committee. The committee prepares a written summary of the directors' feedback and provides the CEO with a copy to review. A few weeks later, the governance committee meets with the CEO to review the upcoming year's objectives, provide feedback, and suggest modifications. The very next morning, there is a full board session where the CEO hands out a summary of his or her plan and holds a general discussion. Though he or she discusses the prior year's performance, the majority of this meeting is spent on the coming year's objectives. Board members then have until the end of the month to provide additional feedback or suggest changes.

In the next month, a general board meeting is held that focuses on the prior year's results, and directors sign off on the upcoming year's plan. Because objectives set at senior management levels tend to build on prior years, it makes some sense to combine the assessment of the prior year with objective setting for the coming year. It is also a time-efficient process. At the same time, it is important that boards see each of these activities as distinct. If they are too "combined," there is a risk that one may receive a disproportionate amount of attention in a single board meeting.

Ideally, in the final performance review stage, board members receive a short questionnaire to assess the CEO's performance against key objectives. Exhibit 6.1 provides a list of the areas that should be covered.[3] We discovered a good deal of variation in the appraisal forms that were employed: some used open-ended questions, others used rating scales, and still others used a combination of the two. We recommend a combination. Rating scales make for easier comparisons over time and among board members' evaluations, and they clearly highlight wide variations among directors' perceptions. Open-ended questions provide a flexibility to consider additional factors overlooked by fixed scales and targets.

To ensure confidentiality in the assessment process, directors can hand off their evaluations to a trusted independent source, such as a consultant or the legal counsel to the board. This individual compiles and summarizes all the comments to provide general feedback that also preserves the anonymity of individual directors. The report is then made available to the compensation or governance committee for their review with the CEO.

In many companies, the appraisal is kept informal by using only oral feedback among directors. The trend is toward written feedback, however. For example, in the 1996 Korn/Ferry survey, only 28.3 percent of the respondents provided formal written feedback to the CEO. By 1999, this number had climbed to 42 percent. Our analysis of the 1999 Korn/Ferry data indicates that directors consider the evaluation process to be more effective when directors give the CEO written as well as verbal feedback. For example, boards with written CEO feedback rated CEO evaluations on average 10 percent more effective than those without it. Committing thoughts to paper encourages a certain clarity and deeper reflection on the CEO's performance. It also gives CEOs feedback that they can review after the meeting. Finally, written appraisals ensure that every director is heard. Oral feedback can usefully follow the written, taking place either during full board meetings or in one-on-one or small-group meetings with the CEO.

The next step is to have the board's compensation committee make its recommendation using the CEO's self-assessment and pertinent outside information. Following this, a meeting of all outside directors should be held to discuss the CEO's evaluation results and approve a final compensation package. An effective evaluation process can and should make the link to compensation a straightforward one. For example, at the outset of the evaluation, the compensation committee should assign rankings to the CEO's objectives for the year and translate these priorities into weightings of how much each objective contributes to overall performance. These can be averaged together to produce a single numerical ranking. This number is tied to a compensation scale that determines the CEO's pay for that year.

Exhibit 6.1. Sample CEO Evaluation Areas.

Strategy Formulation
The CEO has been effective in developing a long-term, sound strategy for the company that meets the needs of shareholders, clients, employees, and other corporate stakeholders; the CEO has in place processes that encourage effective strategic planning.

Strategy Implementation
The CEO has been effective in ensuring that company strategies are effectively implemented and that benchmarks have been met; the CEO has made timely adjustments in strategies when marked conditions and other forces demand a change.

Financial Performance
The company's overall financial performance has been competitive overall relative to industry peers; the company is making strong progress toward meeting its long-term financial goals; the CEO has managed well the impact of external market factors on the organization's financial performance.

Controls
The CEO has ensured that the company has strong auditing and financial control processes in place; the CEO fosters a culture of ethical behavior for the firm through effective compliance programs at all levels of the company; the CEO proactively ensures that the company complies with all of its legal obligations for this year.

Leadership
The CEO has exercised an appropriate level of leadership for the organization; the CEO has effectively communicated a vision, management philosophy, and business strategy to the company's employees; the CEO has actively sought to motivate and inspire employees to realize the company's vision; the CEO is an effective role model for the organization.

External Relations
The CEO effectively communicates the company's financial performance and future prospects to the investment community; the CEO is visible and proactive in representing the company in both community and industry affairs; public relations issues involving the CEO this year have been handled in a manner that builds good will for the company and is sensitive to various stakeholder concerns.

Succession
An updated plan for CEO succession was developed this year; the CEO has ensured that potential candidates have had adequate exposure to the board; key developmental assignments were made during the year that are consistent with the succession plan; there is an effective plan for developing candidates for senior management positions for the long-term success of the organization.

Board Relations
The CEO has kept the board fully informed of all important aspects of the company; sufficient and appropriate information has been distributed to board members throughout the year to effectively assess company strategies, their implementation, and other performance outcomes; the CEO has demonstrated sound knowledge of board governance procedures and has followed them; there is an effective balance between the CEO and the board; board members are able to initiate contact with the CEO whenever necessary; the CEO encourages candid debate and challenges in boardroom discussions; the CEO exercises the appropriate measure of board leadership.

Choosing the Right Objectives

A very important part of the CEO evaluation process is finding the right objectives to measure and setting targets that reflect realistic and high levels of performance. Objective-setting is critical because it helps define the scope and nature of the CEO-board relationship, as well as the level of detail with which the board will be involved. As we have mentioned elsewhere, objectives that are too focused on day-to-day managing can encourage inappropriate micromanagement by the board. Thus the objectives should be primarily concerned with defining the right performance and leadership behaviors, rather than the specifics of how these outcomes are achieved. For example, a specific advertising campaign is more of an operational issue best left to management and not to a CEO evaluation. In contrast, a multibillion-dollar oil exploration project in China is a major strategic issue that needs to be evaluated.

The challenge in setting objectives is to assess and accurately measure the most important aspects of corporate performance for which the CEO is ultimately responsible. An assumption behind many pay-for-performance plans is that the CEO's performance and the corporation's performance are synonymous. In reality, this is often not the case. Thus an effective evaluation uses objectives that focus on behaviors and actions that the CEO can control directly. It should also employ measures that adjust for changes in the industry and economy so that the CEO is neither punished for an unexpected downturn in the economy nor rewarded excessively for an exuberant stock market. In addition, the evaluation needs to include assessments relative to peer firms. In one of the more thorough evaluations we investigated, the chair of the governance committee explained

> Clearly we look at the numbers, how are we doing for the year. But the nature of this business is that if you have a war, the price of our product will go up. Our numbers will go up. You don't want to reward the CEO for those exogenous factors that move prices and our short-term business around. We look at our results on absolute terms for which we have our own standards as to what is good performance in any year. And then we always look relatively to the other major players in our industry. If they are doing even better, we say, "Well, we are doing well, but everyone does well in this environment."

Where the CEO is also the chairperson, evaluations should separate the performance targets for the two roles. In over 85 percent of large U.S. companies, the same person is both CEO and chair. Yet each role has different objectives, so evaluations should not overlap. If a formal evaluation of the board is done, it is best to include the assessment of the chairperson's role as part of the board appraisal process rather than have it subsumed under the CEO evaluation. Thus we will discuss the specifics of chairperson appraisal in the Chapter Seven, which covers evaluation of the board.

Setting an appropriate number of objectives is also a crucial part of an effective evaluation. Too few, and performance is likely to be centered completely around financial indicators. Too many, and the CEO and the senior management team risk losing a clear focus and diluting the importance of each target. The result of too many targets may be the functional equivalent of not having set objectives at all. The "best-practice" companies we studied set from five to ten objectives.

As mentioned earlier, it is important to ensure that the objectives are not just financial ones. Many companies have built their CEO's compensation package around annual financial objectives and stock market performance. Although naturally these objectives are important, they fail to capture important effectiveness issues that are not so easily measured. It is critical for the CEO and board to take the time to carefully review "big picture" qualitative objectives that can affect the company's long-term performance. For example, such issues as succession planning, involvement in lobbying efforts, involvement with trade associations, communications within the company, board relations, union relations, and leadership are all potentially critical qualitative areas of CEO responsibility that may need to be assessed, depending on the company and its strategic priorities. Such targets as return on equity and company profitability can only marginally and indirectly capture these important activities. In some cases, they may work against these activities by producing a focus on short-term results.

Measuring and Scoring the Objectives

Especially in the case of qualitative objectives, a board must be able to measure them in some concrete fashion that shows whether or not the CEO has indeed met his or her targets. For example, leadership might be measured with internal employee surveys and 360-degree feedback questionnaires along with outside analysts' assessments. Improvements in product quality can be measured using internal and external reject rates as well as customer satisfaction surveys.

In general, all available external sources of information are valuable. They can be more objective and reliable than internal sources. We found, however, that all too often boards relied almost entirely on the information from the CEO's self-evaluation and the company's financial reports. Although the CEO's self-evaluation should be a vital part of a performance appraisal, it is not enough. When individuals are in a position of being judged on their performance, certain biases may crop up that influence how they rate themselves. It is critical that self-assessment data be balanced by other information. Ratings from customers, institutional investors, and employee satisfaction surveys, as well as comparisons of the CEO's performance against leaders both inside and outside the industry—all are useful sources of information.

A desirable step, which very few boards take, is to carefully define at least three levels of performance for each measure—poor, acceptable, and outstanding. These levels become the benchmarks for different pay packages. They also help the board and CEO develop a shared understanding of the performance standards and can provide the groundwork for an early warning system if the CEO's performance is poor.

Scoring is always a difficult issue in evaluation. Some companies employ a numerical score; others prefer letter grades, such as A, B, or C; still others have categories, such as "outstanding," "excellent," or "satisfactory." In our opinion, the type of rating system is not a critical determinant of appraisal success. No scoring method is always right; which one is optimal depends on the situation. It is important, however, always to use some scoring approach and to avoid vague written or oral "feedback" that makes it impossible to deliver a clear message. An established, agreed-on scoring method can also help to avoid the upward creep in CEO ratings and salary. It is easier to say no or to cut a bonus in a tough year when objective measures of performance are agreed to and used as the basis for determining rewards.

Key Hurdles Facing CEO Evaluations

Board members' attitudes toward the CEO appraisal process and the role that the CEO's own behavior plays in the evaluation are shaped in large part by the CEO. Time and time again, board members told us that the CEO's attitude and behavior are the critical lynchpins in any evaluation procedure—and that both are relatively easy to read. Directors are able to discern whether evaluations are a serious process or simply window dressing for public relations. For example, if the CEO shows defensiveness toward critical but constructive and accurate feedback, it sends a message about the level of candor that he or she will tolerate. Similarly, if the CEO manipulates the goal-setting process so that the goals are easy or unimportant, the whole appraisal process is thrown into question. Sometimes manipulation is meant to be a harmless way to engage directors. For example, one CEO told us in interviews how he "managed the evaluation numbers around compensation" so that the directors would feel more involved in the process: "We tweak them up, we tweak them down . . . but they [compensation committee members] always want to play with the numbers a little bit. So I always make a few mistakes so they can play with something. They've got to have some form of input, or they go crazy."

Repeated defensiveness by a CEO can stifle honesty and constructive challenges. The evaluation then simply becomes a mechanical yearly ritual that adds little value. Similarly, if a CEO controls all phases of the evaluation, he or she establishes a low level of trust and credibility. Ideally, the board should assume responsibility for the evaluation process, entrusting leadership of the assessment to independent directors or to the board chairperson (when there is a separate chair).

The majority of the CEOs whom we studied wanted the evaluation process to be done effectively because they felt that it made their job easier and that it was an important part of the corporate governance process. In these cases, the issue of who on the board provided leadership for the assessment process was not critical. Leadership is critical, however, in those cases where the CEO is either resistant to the appraisal process or needs to be removed or replaced because of a poor performance appraisal. Power is the critical issue here. For this reason, the evaluation is likely to be effective only if there is leadership on the board by an outsider or a group of outsiders. Chapter Four describes the possible ways to provide outside leadership on a board. From the standpoint of CEO appraisals, the chair of the compensation committee or corporate governance committee often takes on the role of leading the evaluation of the CEO. There is always a question about whether being the committee chair is a sufficiently powerful position if the CEO either resists the evaluation or resists actions that are suggested by the evaluation. A lead director or nonexecutive chair may be in a better position to force action.

When evaluations of the full board are coupled with the CEO evaluation, the effectiveness of the CEO evaluation is higher. In our research, we find that board members participating in both types of evaluations rate their CEO evaluation activities as significantly more effective than do those without board evaluations. There is no single explanation for why simultaneously conducting a board evaluation makes a board more effective at doing the CEO evaluation. It may well be that when boards are evaluated they are simply more effective and as a result are better at evaluating the CEO. Their evaluation may also bring more credibility to the CEO evaluation: they are subjecting themselves to the same kind of process to which they are subjecting the CEO, thus they have more credibility as evaluators of the CEO. Another simple explanation is that they may learn something from their own evaluation that helps them conduct a more effective CEO evaluation.

The research on performance management consistently shows that performance appraisals are more difficult to conduct when they affect an individual's pay.[4] It also shows that unless performance has an impact on an individual's pay, pay is unlikely to be a motivator. We therefore recommend that pay actions be directly tied to the outcome of the performance appraisals of CEOs. The alternative is simply to tie CEO pay to such classic financial indicators as profit, return on investment, economic value added, and stock price performance. There are a number of reasons for taking this approach, but they are beyond the scope of our discussion here. We are not arguing that financial indicators should not be used—indeed they should be one of the determinants of the CEO's compensation—but another important determinant should be the results of the performance appraisal process.

CEO compensation has become extremely controversial in the last decade. Part of the problem has been that boards have lacked principles and guidelines concerning how much to pay CEOs. In many cases, the issue is not so much what to pay for as it is how much to pay for various levels of financial performance. There is no objective way to determine what CEOs should be paid. Boards therefore need to have a few key principles on which they can rely to establish the pay of the CEO and members of the senior management. Examples of useful principles and practices are presented following the Conclusion in this chapter.

Conclusion

CEO evaluations, if done carefully, can create a new dynamic for the CEO-board relationship. They can serve as a means for the board and CEO to hold each other accountable for clearly defined performance expectations, while avoiding the dangers of board involvement in day-to-day management. Evaluations can also provide the CEO with candid feedback and targeted development areas to improve the operations of the board, to enhance his or her leadership, to clarify the respective roles of the two parties, and to ensure that the CEO consistently focuses on his or her responsibilities.

It may still be too early to assess the ultimate success of formal CEO evaluations. Many U.S. firms adopted these appraisals in the last decade, a time of unprecedented profitability and stock market growth for corporate America. When times are good, it is easy to conduct evaluations and make everybody feel positive. The real test comes during bear markets.

The key to effective governance in general, and evaluations in particular, may lie with an emphasis on *continuous improvement*. Like any procedure that is used repeatedly, evaluation formats can become stale and lose their effectiveness after several years of use. For this reason, a periodic review of the CEO evaluation procedure itself is necessary. Most boards we studied performed such a review and found that doing so improved the process. They would ask these kinds of questions: Does the board have sufficient information to effectively evaluate CEO performance? Is communication throughout the entire process effective? Is there a correct balance between the board's policy role and the CEO's operating role?

Are the right measures being used? How can the process be improved? In addition to reviewing the process, varying some of the evaluation objectives and formats every year or every few years keeps the process from becoming routinized and losing its overall effectiveness. The CEO of one company put it very nicely when he said, "These processes need to be renewed. They have to reflect living situations and in turn be open to change in the future. It needs to be a living process."

PRINCIPLES AND PRACTICES FOR EFFECTIVENESS

One of the clearest ways that outside board members can influence corporate performance is by influencing the CEO. This influence process needs to be multifaceted, but one part of it should be an annual review of the CEO's performance. A summary of our analysis suggests that the following principles and practices should be a part of formal evaluations of a CEO's performance by his or her board.

Principle: There should be an annual evaluation of the CEO's performance.

> **Practice:** Begin the annual evaluation cycle by having the compensation committee set the CEO's performance standards for the year. End the year with a systematic evaluation of how well these goals have been accomplished and use them for determining the cash compensation of the CEO.

> **Practice:** At the beginning of the evaluation cycle, establish regular reviews of the CEO's performance standards using midyear or more frequent targets.

> **Practice:** In choosing performance measures, include a mix of qualitative as well as quantitative targets—including, for example, succession planning, leadership skills, lobbying efforts, internal communications, and relations with unions.

> **Practice:** Use comparative assessments—for example, they should be made vis-à-vis key industry players and should reflect overall economic conditions.

> **Practice:** Include separate measures for chairperson and CEO roles when these positions are held by the same person.

> **Practice:** Limit performance objectives in a single year to five to ten priorities. Carefully define three categories of performance for each objective: for example, poor, acceptable, and outstanding. These levels in turn need to become the benchmarks for differing pay packages.

> **Practice:** Weight each target based on its perceived importance to the success of the firm.

Principle: Independent directors should control the CEO evaluation process.

> **Practice:** Staff the key committee involved in CEO appraisal only with outside directors.

> **Practice:** Outside directors should provide a written report to the CEO at the end of the year on how effective they perceive his or her performance to have

been during the year. This assessment needs to rely on information beyond the CEO's self-evaluation data. For example, it might include data from such sources as customer and employee satisfaction ratings, industry surveys, institutional investor information, and so on.

Principle: CEO compensation should be determined by organizational and individual performance.

Principle: The pay level of executives should be higher than that of business competitors only if performance is higher than that of competitors and lower if performance is lower than that of competitors.

Principle: Individuals throughout the organization who contribute to the organization's performance should experience the same general types of pay changes that senior managers experience.

Principle: Senior managers should be held accountable for performance in the same way that others in the organization are held accountable for their performance, and there should be no special deals or exceptions to company programs for senior managers.

> **Practice:** Make profit-sharing stock ownership plans that cover the senior executives more broadly available throughout the corporation.

> **Practice:** Gather survey data on senior executive compensation that gives good information about what business competitors earn. Target CEO compensation at the 50th percentile while allowing for significant variance depending on performance.

> **Practice:** Consider indexing stock option strike prices and other forms of variable compensation to a comparative performance number that is based on how other companies in the same industry perform.

> **Practice:** Use both cash and stock in compensating CEOs; tie the amount of at least one of them to the results of a performance appraisal.

> **Practice:** Avoid repricing options and creating special stock and earning opportunities for only a select few of the senior managers.

CHAPTER SEVEN

EVALUATING AND REWARDING THE BOARD'S PERFORMANCE

A formal performance evaluation of the board and of individual directors is one potentially effective way to respond to the demand for greater board accountability and effectiveness. An evaluation that is based on predetermined, tangible objectives by which a board's performance can be tracked offer one way to measure board performance. More important, evaluations offer the prospect of creating more powerful boards that can deal effectively with poorly performing CEOs and major crises that a company might face.

Feedback about the performance of individual board members can help them enhance their skills as directors and motivate them to be more effective board members. Evaluations can provide an ongoing means for directors to assess their performance. They can also provide a basis for determining whether a board member should be reappointed and how much he or she should be paid. In the absence of formal reviews, members are all too often informally evaluated in a hit-or-miss fashion that provides neither good feedback nor valid data.

Despite the potential of board evaluations to enhance board performance, the results of the 1999 Korn/Ferry survey indicate that whereas approximately 70 percent of the largest U.S. companies have adopted a formal CEO evaluation, only a third of them evaluate the performance of the entire board. Individual director evaluations are even rarer and more controversial, occurring in only 20 percent of the firms surveyed.

CEO evaluations are widespread, and they are also reasonably well understood and accepted in large U.S. companies. Quite the opposite is true with respect to board and board member evaluations. Many companies are not clear on how to conduct them, and as a result they are hesitant to use them. There are a small number of companies who are leaders in this area, however; they are performing evaluations well and reporting positive results.[1] Because we believe such appraisals can enhance corporate governance, we will focus on what we have learned from these pioneers. We begin by discussing the benefits that boards can expect from employing formal appraisals, and then turn our attention to the mechanics of a well-designed evaluation process. We close with a discussion of evaluations of individual directors.

Benefits of Board Appraisals

In our research, we have found that board appraisals, if conducted properly, produce a number of positive outcomes. In addition to the obvious benefit of greater board accountability, we found four areas of performance improvement: (1) more effective board operations, (2) better team dynamics and communication, (3) greater clarity with regard to member roles and responsibilities, and (4) improved CEO-board relations.

Soliciting feedback and reflecting on the board's performance through a formal process encourage boards to pay greater attention to how they actually operate and in turn are very helpful in identifying ways to improve the board. As a result of such a process, suggestions and concerns about boardroom activities emerge more often and more constructively from board members. For example, directors told us that meetings became more streamlined, better materials were provided by management, directors had greater input into meeting agendas, and greater attention by the board was given to long-run strategy. By focusing on the board as a team and on its overall performance, directors also became much more aware of and concerned about teamwork. Because the board's appraisal process usually involves input from every member, we found that both communications and overall levels of participation improved.

Evaluations of group performance usually encourage a more thorough examination of an individual's and a group's responsibilities and roles.[2] Board evaluations are no exception. We consistently found that they fostered clarity and understanding about each director's roles and responsibilities. Greater clarity about committee responsibilities was an additional outcome, particularly in those cases where evaluation of the committees was a formal part of the overall appraisal process.

A fourth benefit of the evaluation process as described by directors included the improvement of their candor and relations with the CEO. This outcome was particularly true at Texaco, where former CEO Al DeCrane instituted informal, one-on-one meetings with every outside director as part of the evaluation process. Said DeCrane of the evaluations: "If directors and the CEO agree on a specific set of targets, then you get better focus, which in turn leads to better feedback to the CEO."

Adoption of the combination of formal board and CEO appraisals also ensures a healthy balance of power between the board and the CEO. It institutionalizes a process that is difficult for an incoming CEO to dismantle if he or she is less disposed to share power with the board. At the very least, an established board evaluation process can make it more difficult for a new CEO to dominate a board and to avoid accountability for poor performance.

In many respects, boards are like fire departments, in that they need to be constantly on standby, and when called upon they must perform effectively. One board chair observed that in good times, corporate governance is "largely irrelevant," but in bad times, it is crucial. In order to perform effectively during a crisis, boards of directors need the good processes, procedures, and relationships that are developed, assessed, and improved as the result of effective board appraisals. The challenge is to conduct them in a manner that produces the intended outcomes.

Conducting an Effective Evaluation

Our research suggests that an effective board evaluation requires the right combination of timing, content, process, and individuals. We found that board evaluations customarily occur on an annual basis, although in a few firms they are performed every other year. From our perspective, the board's performance is so important and so potentially dynamic that it makes sense to conduct an evaluation annually—especially if there is director turnover or if the organization's industry is volatile.

The board evaluation process should start at the beginning of the company's fiscal year. Directors need to agree to a set of objectives for the group and then assess the board's performance against these targets at year-end. When setting out to define the right objectives for a board's performance, it is best to engage the entire board in the process. Typically, a nominating or governance committee designs an initial set of objectives that it feels covers the essential responsibilities of an effective board. These objectives should be stated so that accomplishments can be measured. The objectives and measures are then presented to the full board and CEO for discussion and debate. The board then produces a final list of evaluation criteria.

In setting objectives and measures, it is important that the board focus on the right number of areas. Too few, and essential responsibilities may be overlooked. Too many, and there will be little sense of the board's priorities. One good approach is to combine a stable set of basic performance objectives with a changing set of development- or improvement-oriented objectives. The stable performance objectives should cover the basic functions of boards (which were discussed in Chapter One) as well as some measures of group effectiveness.

For development, it is generally best to pick two to five areas that the board needs to improve over the coming year. For example, one year a board might choose to focus on improving its new director training, board committee composition, assessment of senior management talent at the division level, and team building. Typical initiatives could include holding more presentations and forums to interact with division managers, developing a two-day information seminar for new directors that includes site visits to operations, formalizing a matrix for assessing the capabilities of committee members, and holding a special session on team building with an expert adviser during the board's annual strategy retreat.

At the year-end review, it is quite reasonable to add to these developmental objectives a checklist of outcome measures. The five-factor board effectiveness model described in Chapter Two serves as a valuable guide to what should be covered. Problems in any of the five areas (information, knowledge, power, rewards, and time) become the developmental objectives for the next year. For example, a set of questions might assess the quality and quantity of information that the board receives on its business issues and whether this information is received in a timely manner. Does the board get up-to-date information on the competition, on key strategic issues, on acquisition targets? How well are new directors brought up to speed on company issues? Are there multiple information sources—outside stakeholders, the directors' own observations, and customer and employee surveys? Are board members receiving beforehand the appropriate information to ensure that they come to meetings well prepared to debate crucial issues?

In our research, we observed a variety of different approaches to measuring how a board performs. Several firms have their directors provide written responses to short questionnaires, using a simple rating system like that in the Motorola example shown in Exhibit 7.1. Other companies have an individual member of the board—frequently the chairperson of the nominating, governance, or compensation committee—interview each director face-to-face or on the telephone, using open-ended questions. In both cases, a summary of the findings is prepared and then reported to the board. A few companies simply hold an open-ended full-board discussion.

One company we studied circulates a questionnaire to all its directors. Written responses are then handed into the nominating committee with the names

Exhibit 7.1. Board Evaluation Form.

The following survey is a tool to help you think about the performance of the board of directors as a group. It is intended to enhance the board's overall effectiveness. The results will be discussed at a future board meeting. Please indicate to what extent you agree with the following statements concerning the functioning of the board of directors as a whole. Circle the response for each item.

The following questions refer to the board of directors.

The board of directors:	Strongly agree	Agree	Neither agree nor disagree	Disagree	Strongly disagree
1. Has an appropriate level of involvement in CEO succession	1	2	3	4	5
2. Has in place appropriate processes to assess the CEO	1	2	3	4	5
3. Has sufficient information for the CEO evaluation	1	2	3	4	5
4. Spends an appropriate amount of time discussing the long-range future of the company	1	2	3	4	5
5. Proposes changes in company direction	1	2	3	4	5
6. Has a vision and a mission that is understood by all board members	1	2	3	4	5
7. Is prepared to deal with unforeseen corporate crises	1	2	3	4	5
8. Has appropriate structures and processes to help evaluate company strategy and objectives	1	2	3	4	5
9. Effectively inquires into major performance deficiencies	1	2	3	4	5

of directors removed. These responses are compiled into a single document showing close to verbatim responses to each question. The nominating committee reviews the results and prepares a report that identifies areas for improvement. This
report, along with the responses, is then circulated among the directors, and a portion of one full-board meeting is spent addressing the feedback.

Texaco takes a very different approach to board appraisal. After the board
defines its nine objectives and primary responsibilities, the nominating committee
then analyzes the minutes of all board meetings to determine how the time was
allocated relative to these priorities. This information is provided to the board
members as the basis for a discussion of board effectiveness. "We look back each
year and say how did we do on each of these nine points and did we do enough,"
observed Texaco corporate secretary Carl Davidson. "It isn't intended to come
out with a report card. It is rather an objective listing of what we spent time on
and a subjective assessment of how well we did in paying attention to our key
responsibilities."

Based on our analysis of the elements of the evaluation process that directors
consider most effective, it appears that board evaluations need to include the following steps. First, board members must agree on the performance measures and
objectives. At the end of the year, a lead director or respected counselor to the
board then distributes to every board member a questionnaire that has both numerical ratings for activities and open-ended questions. This is followed up with
a confidential one-on-one interview. The results of both are presented to the board
in summary form and without attribution to individual members, unless a director specifically requests that his or her name be used. At this time, all other performance data are presented to the board. A full-board discussion follows. This
group discussion revolves around the areas identified as needing improvement.

This arrangement of appraisal steps has several advantages. First, the scores
on the questionnaires help the board members rank themselves along a series of
dimensions. Directors can also see where they have differing viewpoints on the
same activity. The interviews allow for greater detail, and topics can surface that
are not covered by a questionnaire that measures formal objectives. As one executive involved in designing his company's board evaluation explained, "If I were
to do it again [redesign his company's evaluation], I would do a telephone interview with directors [along with the questionnaire]. You can get more richness of
data than you get out of a questionnaire. You get the softer or convoluted issues
that don't fit well into an agree-disagree type of scale."

The report itself must be presented in a balanced way, highlighting the areas
where there are divergent ratings or viewpoints. The selection of the presenter is
crucial. Although it is best to use a respected outsider, the chair of the compensation or nominating committee, or a counselor to the board, the personal char-

acteristics of the individual are just as important as his or her role. Effective individuals are good listeners and communicators and are trusted by board members. They should also be seen as independent of the CEO and the company's senior management.

An essential element that is missing from the board evaluation process as currently practiced in virtually every company is data obtained from outside the corporation. It is particularly important to have this kind of data when assessing board performance against the performance of competitors. Institutional investors, market analysts, suppliers, major customers, and regulatory bodies are all potential sources of valuable outsider information. There is evidence that institutional investors, in particular, want to be asked for their views of board performance.

Our analysis of the Korn/Ferry survey also indicates that directors view the evaluation process as significantly more effective when boards receive feedback from company stakeholders. In addition, it might be useful to have independent group process experts observe board meetings and give feedback on how the board's performance might be improved.

Once an effective board appraisal is up and running, there is a strong argument for regularly reexamining the process to see how it can be improved or varied to avoid its becoming stale. Dayton Hudson is a good case in point. It began a board evaluation fifteen years ago, with a very formal process; annually each description of the board's and the committees' responsibilities was reviewed paragraph by paragraph to determine whether the board was meeting its obligations. "There was a point in our history where that was useful and productive," recalled one director. "Over time it got stilted, and we felt that it was more important that we have good communication than that we have a specific format."

In the last decade, the Dayton Hudson board has continued to set aside a block of time each year to review its governance procedures and evaluate its effectiveness, experimenting with a variety of different formats. For example, during the takeover boom in the 1980s, the board did a case study of another firm that had been through a hostile takeover, examining how its board dealt with this process. In other years it has sent out written surveys to the directors, asking them to assess the information the board was given and to suggest how the process could be improved. In 1998, the board circulated its extensive, publicly available corporate governance guidelines and asked the directors whether any amendments were needed. The critical lesson here is that boards must vary their evaluations on an annual or biannual basis by changing questions, formats, and their focus. If they do not, the process runs a very high risk of becoming mechanical and its information relatively useless.

It is likely that the first try with a formal evaluation will produce less useful results. Board members want to preserve the collegiality of the group and so tend to be more reserved during the initial experiment with conducting an evaluation. They test the waters with responses that are more supportive than critical or challenging. One director whose firm has used board evaluations for a number of years described his board's first evaluation experience: "I can tell you that during the first time around there was a propensity to be superficial in the feedback. I don't mean that negatively. . . . I think it had to do with unfamiliarity with the process. In the second round, we then dealt with the board's functioning and what changes do we really need to make. The basic lesson is that you have to clearly communicate an expectation of wanting honest feedback, and then the confidentiality of the process [to make these assessments work]."

Evaluating Individual Directors

Perhaps the most controversial issue in the area of board appraisal is whether individual directors should be evaluated. A 1997 Russell Reynolds survey on corporate governance showed that investors feel strongly that boards need to be more aggressive in weeding out underperforming directors.[3] Yet formal appraisals of individual directors have, until recently, been relatively rare. The Korn/Ferry survey data from 1999 indicate that only 19 percent of the boards of large firms do individual appraisals. In our interviews, we found considerable opposition to these evaluations because of several concerns.

A number of directors and CEOs felt that collegiality might be undermined if a performance spotlight was turned on individual members. One board in our study, which had carefully considered implementing a peer assessment, backed off at the last moment for this very reason. The company officer who designed the assessment process told us, "There was a concern it might cause disharmony in the group. It was that primitive notion of what creates more effective teams. 'Effective' teams, in this case, are where you skirt issues of difficulty, of personal differences. It's more like 'We want to be able to have a drink together and like each other' as opposed to 'If we confront ourselves on real issues, we'll deepen the relationship.'"

Other boards worried that an evaluation process might drive away good board members who felt they had already "proven" themselves and would find an evaluation "insulting." At a time when there is heavy competition to attract top directors, appraisals could prove to be a potential deterrent to signing up good candidates. One CEO we interviewed reported that when he proposed a director evaluation plan to his board, he met strong resistance. Board members told him it "wasn't worth it" to be on his board if they had to go through an evaluation.

It is also difficult to determine who should evaluate a director. Peers are the most obvious source, but they often lack sufficient information to make an accurate assessment of other directors' performance. Boards have relatively little time together, and what occurs in the meetings may not be the best gauge of a director's contribution. Said one corporate secretary, "Not every board member is contributing actively and asking questions at board meetings. A lot of people are very quiet, but they still are very effective. They operate in different ways. We've got a board member who hasn't said ten words at a board meeting, and yet one of the other directors said getting that guy on the board was a real home run. It's what goes on in sidebar conversations, at dinners, telephone calls between meetings, that kind of thing which may really matter."

Some directors felt an individual evaluation could even promote counterproductive behavior, for example where individuals simply want to create an impression of being involved and to look like active contributors: "I think it leads to the wrong kind of responses, encouraging individual board members to talk when there's no need for it," said one director.

The board chair is another obvious source of evaluation data about the performance of board members. He or she typically has the most complete information about how board members perform. When the board chair is also the CEO, however, there is a major danger with having the board chair be the predominant or only evaluator of board members. There is a great risk of putting too much power in the hands of the CEO, thus making it difficult for the board to take effective action when there are problems with the CEO's performance. In essence, this situation puts individuals who are being evaluated by someone into the position of having to do an effective evaluation of that person. In organizations where the chair is not the CEO or where there is a lead director, the problem is less severe. The lead director and the nonexecutive chair can reasonably carry out this activity without tipping the balance of power too far toward the CEO. Particularly if data from the board members and from a lead director or nonexecutive board chair are combined, the evaluation process can produce a reasonably good picture of individual performance can be developed and a proper power balance maintained. In cases where the CEO is also the board chair, the best approach is to have the evaluation conducted by a committee of independent directors who feel they are not bound by the evaluations that are performed by the CEO.

Because each board member brings a different set of competencies to the board, it can be difficult to establish criteria for how members should be assessed. For example, using a universal set of evaluation criteria overlooks the different ways in which members contribute. As one board member commented to us,

> We have several directors who are very knowledgeable in the technology issues this company deals in. But they may not be at all, or nowhere near, expert in financial matters. And some of our directors have a strong financial background,

and with acquisition and takeover issues they will play a much greater role than others. You have other directors who have a stronger background in personnel management and can deal more expertly with issues about employment benefit plans or when diversity issues come up. Different directors contribute in different ways at different times. A uniform evaluation cannot capture these different contributions.

Research on team effectiveness clearly supports the idea that when individuals are interdependent, as they are when they work together on a board, it is important to place the main emphasis on evaluating and rewarding the effectiveness of the group overall.[4] Otherwise, individuals tend to optimize their individual performance rather than contribute to the team's effectiveness. Thus the primary appraisal focus should be on the performance of the board at the collective level rather than at the individual level.

Despite the aforementioned problems with individual appraisals, we believe there is an important role for some form of individual appraisal as one component of the overall board evaluation process. Certain issues of group and individual effectiveness simply cannot be addressed without evaluating individuals. Without a formal, ongoing appraisal, board members are typically replaced for performance reasons only in extreme circumstances (for example, criminal misconduct, conflict of interest, active disruption, very poor attendance and participation record); if they are replaced, they are rarely given an early warning and a chance to improve. In most cases, boards wait for poorly performing directors to retire; occasionally they fail to renominate these directors when their term is finished. Although it appears from our research that underperforming directors are relatively rare, it would seem to be a sound practice to identify such individuals through a formal assessment process so that the board can initiate corrective action.

Considering that the average size of boards is decreasing and that the demands and rewards for serving on boards are increasing, companies need more from directors than simply regular attendance and questions posed at meetings. Individual assessment is a good way of making performance expectations clear. Support for this view is provided by our analysis of the Korn/Ferry survey data, which showed that in companies where individual directors are evaluated, directors rate the board's overall effectiveness significantly more positively, although the impact on perceived effectiveness is smaller than it is with the adoption of either CEO or full-board evaluations (see Table 7.1).

There may be less opposition to individual appraisals than suggested by the objections that were raised in our interviews. The 1999 Korn/Ferry survey found that 73 percent of the respondents favored them. This widespread support is a

Table 7.1. Directors' View of the Impact of Various Evaluations on Their Board's Effectiveness.

Significance of evaluating the following:			*On the board's effectiveness in:*
The CEO	The Board	Individual Directors	
Extremely significant	Significant	Significant	Governing, overall
Extremely significant	Very significant		Shaping long-term strategy
			Bolstering the company's image in the community
Very significant			Managing during a crisis
Extremely significant	Extremely significant		Planning for top management succession
Extremely significant			Anticipating possible threats to company survival
Extremely significant			Balancing interests of different stakeholders
Extremely significant	Significant		Monitoring strategy implementation
			Building networks with strategic partners
			Enhancing government relations

critical issue, because it is impossible to conduct effective individual appraisals without the support of directors.

Motorola recently began an individual self-assessment. It grew out of boardroom discussions focusing on its full-board evaluation. Guided by the essential question, What does the board add to the management of the corporation? the discussion turned quite naturally to, What does each individual member add? This questioning led to a self-assessment exercise that is conducted annually.

In Exhibit 7.2, we see the types of questions on which each Motorola director assesses himself or herself. The process is for the individual's use only; it is not shared with other board members or any committee. What it provides is a simple discipline and structure for each director to reflect on his or her own performance.

Exhibit 7.2. Board Self-Assessment Form.

The following survey is a tool to help you think about your own individual performance as a member of Motorola's board of directors. It is intended to be used for self-reflection only and you will not be asked to share the results with anyone else. Please indicate to what extent you agree with the following statements which relate to your behavior as a member of Motorola's board of directors.

Circle one response for each item (1, 2, 3, 4, or 5)

The board of directors:	Strongly agree	Agree	Neither agree nor disagree	Disagree	Strongly disagree
1. I devote an appropriate amount of time to the issues and the needs of Motorola to be able to make informed decisions.	1	2	3	4	5
2. I feel comfortable with my understanding of Motorola's critical technical issues.	1	2	3	4	5
3. I spend sufficient time with the materials and the CEO to understand the long-range planning issues.	1	2	3	4	5
4. I initiate contact with the chairman when appropriate.	1	2	3	4	5
5. I understand Motorola's industry and markets.	1	2	3	4	5
6. I challenge the strategy and direction of Motorola when I think it's necessary.	1	2	3	4	5
7. I am able to remain objective, even in the face of the most difficult decisions.	1	2	3	4	5
8. I often speak my mind during meetings, even if I believe my views differ from those of the other directors.	1	2	3	4	5
9. I have personal contact with Motorola's senior management.	1	2	3	4	5
10. I am fully prepared for board meetings.	1	2	3	4	5

It is also an effective device for making a gradual transition to a peer-based evaluation.

Although individual self-assessments are quite helpful for personal reflection and are not threatening, they have some shortcomings. One is that they reflect only one perspective—others may see a director's performance quite differently. A second is that individuals have biases in their self-image. For example, some of us are particularly tough on ourselves—rarely giving ourselves an excellent rating even if we deserve it. Others of us can see few or no flaws in who we are or how we act.

Compaq has adopted a different approach to evaluating individual directors. The chairman, the CEO, and the head of the board's human resource committee meet once every three years to assess each director on criteria that are very similar to those used by Motorola (as shown in Exhibit 7.2); they also examine the extent of each director's stock ownership. The process, which was conducted for the first time in 1996, is designed to identify any directors who are not carrying their weight on the board. Compaq's chairman, Ben Rosen, explains: "If we found someone who was not working out, this formal process might make it easier to solve the problem. Fortunately, that hasn't been an issue for us." A written record of the evaluations is kept by the board secretary; the individual results, however, are not shared with anyone, including the directors.

If a company wishes to take a bolder, potentially more effective step, it could introduce a peer evaluation process in which board members assess one another. This assessment, combined with individual self-assessments and the CEO-chair-board assessments, should provide the most balanced assessment. The evaluations can be collected by a trusted adviser or outsider who summarizes the results and provides each board member with a summary of their peers' ratings and comments—ensuring the anonymity of all respondents, following the best practices now common in 360-feedback processes. The appraisal results could then be provided to the committee charged with director nominations to identify underperforming directors.

A useful way to begin the evaluation of an individual director is to conduct the first appraisal in a way that provides performance evaluation information only to the individual being appraised. This approach gives each individual a chance to improve his or her performance before a second appraisal is done, the results of which are shown to the board chair, to the chair of the corporate governance committee or nominating committee, or both. Once a standard appraisal process is in place for individual board members, it should become an important influence on the nominating committee's decisions with respect to board membership. That committee needs this kind of data in order to make valid decisions about who should and should not continue on the board.

Pay and Board Performance

Historically, board members have been paid a flat fee for membership on the board and an additional amount for attending particular meetings. They have also received a number of benefits, including retirement programs. Recently there has been a definite trend toward eliminating retirement pay. In the 1999 Korn/Ferry survey, only 15 percent of the board members reported receiving retirement pay, and 35 percent reported having had their retirement plan cancelled. There has also been a substantial increase in the degree to which board members are compensated in stock, leading to a significant upward trend in total compensation to directors in a number of corporations. For example, in 1998, directors at Sun Microsystems received an average of just over $400,000 in compensation. At Compaq, the dollar number was $362,000, while at Pfizer it was $258,000.

Director pay is ballooning precisely because companies are looking more and more to stock options and stock grant programs. One estimate is that in the five years from 1993 to 1998, pay for outside directors jumped 70 percent. Paying directors with stock began to become popular in the mid-1990s in the United States, and it has since become standard practice in most companies. In 1999, 98 percent of large companies included stock as part of their compensation package for directors. At some companies, compensation comes only in the form of stock. For example, outside directors of General Mills can receive all of their compensation in stock instead of receiving their $50,000 annual retainer.

The extensive use of stock-based compensation for board members raises a number of important questions. The first, and perhaps the most fundamental, is whether it is in fact a desirable practice. On balance, we believe it is. It is one way to deal with the issue of motivating directors to behave in ways that are in the best interests of an important stakeholder, the shareholder. Admittedly, the line of sight between board performance and share price is relatively weak, but it still exists. For example, there is evidence that board members who hold stock are more willing to make "tough decisions" than those who do not. The reason for this is obvious: when they fail to deal with poorly performing CEOs or other difficult issues their company faces, they are losing not just company money but also their own.

A second question concerning stock compensation regards what kind of stock vehicle should be used. A strong argument can be made for using both stock options and stock ownership. If executives are paid only with options, there is a danger that because they have none of their own money invested in the company, they are not truly aligned with shareholders. This can be a particular problem if the stock price falls significantly below the exercise or strike price for the options; in this situation, shares lose their motivational value. Thus a strong case can be made that board members should own stock in their corporations. Ownership can come through restricted stock grants or through requiring board members to purchase stock. If the latter approach is used, the company may need to make loans to some board members in order to enable them to purchase stock.

If cash compensation is combined with stock-based compensation, much of it should come in the form of variable compensation. Specifically it should be tied to the profitability and financial performance of the company. Fixed compensation that is paid simply for someone's being on a board does not make a great deal of sense in a world where it is important to motivate board members and where shareholders are demanding board accountability.

Despite the growing popularity of stock and stock-based compensation packages, they are not without a downside. There is a clear danger that board members may become myopic and overly focused on short-term stock price changes and financial results, losing sight of the other stakeholders in the corporation. They may fail to make decisions that are in the best interest of all stakeholders. There is also some risk that the board will optimize the short term in order to make directors' stock valuable at a time when they can cash out. This risk can be significantly reduced, of course, if the stock vehicles are structured such that they require long-term performance effectiveness.

Another potential problem associated with stock-based compensation is that boards may end up having a conflict of interest. Typically, directors are the ones who initially approve and propose stock-based plans to the shareholders. This means they are effectively determining their own compensation, and as result they may end up overcompensating themselves by creating plans that simply make payouts that are too large. This tendency argues strongly for boards establishing guidelines concerning how much compensation board members should receive. A key to creating effective guidelines, of course, is to be sure that stock grants to board members are in line with practices at competing corporations.

What about tying directors' pay to assessments of board performance or of directors' individual performance? These approaches are clearly possibilities in organizations where board assessment processes are in place, but neither is generally a good idea. The more defensible of the two is to pay board members based on the performance of the board. Teams and groups tend to perform most effectively when they are evaluated and rewarded as groups. Thus a case can be made for rewarding board members based on the effectiveness of the board. In order to reward groups for their effectiveness, however, objective measures are needed that separate the team's performance from the performance of the organization of which they are a part. In the case of boards, this is very difficult to accomplish. The measures of board performance that can be obtained are often not objective enough to warrant their use as a basis for compensation. Therefore, it is typically better simply to reward boards based on the performance of their overall organization.

The idea of rewarding individual board members based on their performance is even less defensible than the idea of rewarding the board for its collective performance. Individual performance on boards is particularly difficult to measure, and thus it is hard to create pay-for-performance systems at the individual level. In addition, individual pay for performance tends to decrease the teamwork and cooperation that are critical in making any board effective. Therefore our recommendation is clear: do not reward individual board members for their performance, and do not reward the board for its collective performance.

Conclusion

As the pressure mounts on publicly owned companies to improve their corporate governance practices, we are likely to see more and more firms adopting formal board evaluations. The future is less clear in the case of individual director evaluations because of the significant resistance to them. They are likely to be widely adopted only if institutional investors demand them—something that could quite possibly happen.

We do think, however, that formal board evaluations, like other recommended corporate governance practices, are no panacea. Companies can simply go through the motions to satisfy the investment community. As the chairman of one company that recently instituted both a board and individual director evaluation admitted, "I don't think it's important. It's important to others, but it's not important to good corporate governance. It's just that there are surveys [best practice surveys of corporate governance by business magazines and associations] . . . and we wanted to have the evaluations on our checklist of good governance practices." Even evaluations performed at companies that do take them seriously do not provide an assurance against trouble. In the last decade, Texaco's board has been a leader in the adoption of best practices in corporate governance, yet these practices did not help the company avoid a well-publicized racial harassment incident and the damage this caused to the firm's reputation.

What evaluations can accomplish, if done correctly, is to create a positive dynamic for the CEO-board relationship. They can provide a means for the board and the CEO to hold each other accountable for clearly defined performance expectations, while avoiding the dangers of board involvement in day-to-day management. Evaluations can also improve the operations of the board, clarify the respective roles of both the board and CEO, and ensure that both consistently focus on their responsibilities. Perhaps the clearest and most consistent benefit we observed is that board appraisals encourage directors and the CEO to devote more time and attention to long-term strategy. This outcome in itself is significant enough to justify the implementation of board appraisals.

PRINCIPLES AND PRACTICES FOR EFFECTIVENESS

Principle: Regularly review the performance of the board.

> **Practice:** Once a year, conduct a formal evaluation of board performance. Summarize the data from director evaluations and feed the findings to the full board. Report summaries should include developmental areas for the coming year along with performance feedback. A full-board discussion should follow feedback.

> **Practice:** Focus the board evaluation on four to seven developmental objectives at the beginning of each year as part of the board's performance goals. Establish measurable target outcomes for each.

> **Practice:** Have all board members provide data on how they feel the board performed. In order to improve the process, discuss these data at a board meeting and, if appropriate, agree on ways to improve board performance.

> **Practice:** As part of the evaluation process, gather systematic data from key stakeholders (for example, investors) on how the board has performed. Feed these data back to the board so that they will have multiple sources of evaluation to look at as they discuss their performance.

> **Practice:** For the year-end evaluation, employ an assessment questionnaire for director self-evaluations of board performance (using a blend of open-ended questions and questions with numerical ranking scales) and face-to-face confidential interviews conducted by the lead director or by the chair of the nominating or compensation committee.

> **Practice:** In addition to the board's developmental objectives, create a separate checklist of issues covering the five key attributes of board effectiveness (information, knowledge, power, rewards, and time). Identify tangible outcomes and procedures in each area of board responsibility to ascertain whether the board's needs are being met with regard to each attribute.

Principle: Perform an annual evaluation of the performance of all individual board members.

> **Practice:** Annually conduct an assessment of individual director performance. This can be done through a combination of self-assessments, peer evaluations, and a board committee review. The results of these individual assessments should be fed back to each director with suggested areas for improvement and action steps.

> **Practice:** Make performance appraisal results available to whatever committee is charged with nominating individuals to the board so that poorly performing board members can be replaced.

Principle: The amount of board member compensation should be based on the amount received by directors of other comparable corporations.

> **Practice:** Survey comparable corporations and, after determining what they pay, create a total compensation package that is of comparable value. Put enough upside potential in it so that if the corporation outperforms its peer

companies, the total compensation package for directors will in turn be more than those of their peers.

Principle: The total compensation of board members needs to be clearly and substantially tied to changes in long-term shareholder value.

Practice: Require that board members have substantial stock ownership in the corporation.

Practice: Grant board members the same types of options that are granted to members of senior management.

Practice: Be sure that stock option grants cannot be exercised for several years so that they encourage board members to take a long-term view of corporate performance.

Practice: Be sure that at least 50 percent of an independent board member's compensation is in the form of stock.

PART THREE

BOARDS IN THE FUTURE

CHAPTER EIGHT

GOVERNING IN THE AGE OF THE INTERNET

Boards must prepare themselves to face a series of governance challenges if they are to have legitimacy in the twenty-first century. These challenges are the product of the most significant disruptive technology of our era: the Internet. Just as the printing press enabled the transition from individual, hand-lettered manuscripts to mass publications, so too the Internet has dramatically reduced the barriers to the flow of information. Just as the telegraph transformed world commerce and communication by reducing the time required for news and messages to traverse the world from weeks down to hours or minutes, the Internet is rapidly increasing the speed of global communication and transforming the level of global competition.

The Internet is creating virtual markets in almost every sector by allowing, for the first time, real "many-to-many" communication. It is simultaneously transforming the individual exchange of information by enabling the instantaneous and virtually no-cost exchange of digital data in all forms. Either of these advances in information exchange would represent a major discontinuity for existing firms and the corporate boards governing them. But the joining of both a new publication vehicle and a new communications vehicle in a single medium is truly revolutionary, giving rise to an unprecedented array of new business models and creating immense amounts of wealth in a short period of time. Although many of these fortunes may prove to be transitory as the speculative bubble bursts, the long-term implications of this new medium should not be underestimated. If past history is any guide, many of the consequences will be unanticipated, and hence they pose an even greater challenge for those charged with governing corporations in this new era.

In many respects, boards are much better positioned to cope with the challenges brought about by the Internet and other major changes than they were a generation ago. As we have seen throughout this book, the boards of large U.S. companies are far more active than they were in the past. They are more powerful, thanks to a higher percentage of independent directors and to outsider control of key committees. They are also more careful in monitoring the performance of their firms and top managers. Thanks to this combination of factors, boards today are better prepared to take decisive action when threats or new opportunities arise.

At the same time, boards may find themselves in a trap. As boards and their companies have evolved more and more successful designs for maximizing shareholder value in the old competitive context, they may actually be condemning their firms to failure in a new marketplace where the rules and players have changed. There is now a convincing body of research on cycles of innovation which demonstrates that the firms that were dominant in one technology almost inevitably fail to be the leaders when the next technological breakthrough emerges.[1] This is not because they are unaware of the new technology; often it is developed by their own researchers. It is not because they were poorly managed; these firms are often widely admired and emulated for their management practices. On the contrary, it is precisely because these firms were so successful in designing their entire governance and resource allocation mechanisms to maximize the satisfaction of customers in their existing markets that they often fail to react quickly to a disruptive technology. Their governance mechanisms are so well aligned around current market conditions that they find it virtually impossible to adapt to a new technology with new customers; this inflexibility eventually threatens to undermine their market position. This pattern applies not only to technology-sensitive firms but to any organizations whose product or service markets are likely to face major disruptions due to the Internet.

Current and Future Challenges

Thus boards of existing corporations face the challenge of satisfying existing customers and shareholders while simultaneously attempting to facilitate the transformation of their organizations to preserve for the longer term the value their companies have created. To help prepare boards for this delicate balancing act, we first examine the series of challenges they will face in the future. Some of these are a direct result of the Internet, though in many cases the Net has simply taken an existing trend already facing boards and their firms and intensified it. We then apply our framework for board effectiveness to this new set of challenges. We explore how firms can enhance their knowledge, information, time, motivation, and power to "Net-enable" their board of directors.

Speed

The single characteristic that most distinguishes successful Internet firms from traditional organizations is speed. The CEO of one Internet firm is fond of saying that an Internet year has thirty-one days and is getting shorter. One manager we interviewed who had recently joined Amazon.com from a bricks-and-mortar firm commented, "You know that things are going to happen more quickly when you join, but you have no idea how much faster until you're actually living it day to day. That is the hardest thing to get used to. Knowing that there are ten things you could be doing that would add real value, but you just don't have the time for them. Even with the things that you do have time for, you don't feel you have the time to do them really well."

Boards neither can nor should get involved in the frenzy of day-to-day operations in the "24/7" world of e-commerce. They must, however, adapt their ways of operating to cope with the accelerated pace of major strategic decisions in this new environment. Cisco Systems, for example, was making acquisitions at a rate of nearly one every two weeks in 1999; Sun Microsystems recently split one business unit into three, made two significant acquisitions, and undertook a second major reorganization—all in a span of eleven months. In such a rapidly evolving competitive environment, boards' traditional approach—setting annual targets, working with three- to five-year plans, and meeting four to eight times a year to review progress—appears increasingly obsolete. Boards that continue to operate in this way will at best be rubber-stamping management's strategic decisions and will have missed a crucial opportunity to add value at the top level of the firm.

Globalization

The globalization of the world economy was well under way before the Internet became a prominent commercial and business medium in the mid-1990s. The Internet has simply accelerated the globalization trend. The case of a single hypothetical customer at Amazon helps illustrate how much more global markets are becoming. Punkaj, a software programmer in Bangalore, is able to log onto U.S.-based Amazon's website and order a book at 30 percent off the U.S. list price for his cousin in Manchester, England, and have it delivered the next day by regular British mail. He is so impressed by Amazon's efficiency that he decides to put his family's business—selling fresh, vacuum-packed spices—on Amazon's zShops online shopping mall, where these products can potentially reach a global customer base of more than seventeen million people. Using the profits from this enterprise, he expands his collection of antique porcelain through Amazon's online auctions at Sotheby's and direct Internet contact from other individual collectors.

Even this example understates the impact of the Internet, considering that consumer business on the Internet is relatively small compared to the even more rapid growth in Web-based business-to-business transactions. Although it is estimated that "e-tailing" will grow by more than 50 percent annually from 2000 to 2004, from a base of $60 billion, this is likely to be dwarfed by the growth in e-business, which the Gartner Group projects will increase exponentially from $145 billion in 1999 to $7.3 trillion in 2004.[2]

The amount of attention corporate boards devote to global issues, however, appears to lag behind the globalization of U.S. firms' business and the competitive pressures they face. More than half of boards had had at least one board meeting outside the United States in 1999, but more than two-thirds reported that their directors rarely or never paid visits to company sites outside the country. Fewer than half (47 percent) of the directors in *Fortune* 1000 firms surveyed in 1999 reported that they "often" or "very frequently" participated in discussions about "their firm's global strategy and/or organization," and a much smaller percentage devoted time to developing or evaluating managers outside the United States or to building strategic global customer or supplier partnerships or joint ventures (see Table 8.1).

Changing Basis for Corporate Value: The Growth Imperative

The value of a firm's stock has always been driven by two underlying factors: the company's profitability and cash flow (or return on capital) and its rate of growth. At least in its early phases of growth, the Internet appears to have significantly altered the balance between these two factors. Because of the Net's tremendous growth potential and the belief that there are first-mover advantages for those firms who can establish a strong identity on the Net, investors have attributed huge valuations to dot-com stocks, including those with no profits or with limited prospects of making money in the near future. In a few years, extremely young companies have eclipsed in value some of the world's largest and most well known companies. At the end of 1999, for example, America Online (AOL) was worth more than AT&T, and Yahoo's stock market cap was roughly equal to the combined value of Ford and General Motors. AOL's subsequent acquisition of

Table 8.1. Global Activities of U.S. *Fortune* 1000 Boards.

"How frequently does your board spend time on each of the following activities?"	Never or Rarely (%)	Often or Very Frequently (%)
Participating in discussions about firm's global strategy and organization	22	47
Identifying and evaluating global trends and events critical to the firm	24	37
Monitoring and evaluating firm's international initiatives	28	42
Developing and overseeing global management development programs	54	16
Evaluating firm's management capabilities in nondomestic markets	43	21
Managing and developing relationships with global partners, including suppliers, customers, strategic alliances, and joint ventures	55	17

Note: N = 990

Source: Data from Korn/Ferry survey, 1999

Time Warner marked a dramatic affirmation of the shift in how firms are valued. AOL was able to capitalize on the growth potential embodied in its share price to purchase one of the world's most well established and valuable media companies.

Even after the bursting of the initial Internet stock market bubble, the explosive growth of this new form of business is likely to have a lasting impact on the way firms are valued. For small firms in other sectors, the Internet made it much more difficult to attract venture capital in the latter half of the 1990s, as even their most optimistic scenarios for future growth paled in comparison to those of their dot-com counterparts. This situation applied even to such previously attractive high-tech areas as biotechnology. At the same time, there is now much greater pressure on established companies to identify new growth opportunities while also continuing to meet the profit forecasts for their existing businesses. Without growth and the higher price-earnings multiple that it brings, the boards of these organizations risk losing control of the organization's fate by becoming takeover targets.

One sign of the shifting shareholder emphasis from profitability to growth has been the significant decline in the dividends that large firms pay out to investors. In 1990, virtually all the firms in the S&P 500 were paying some dividends (97 percent of the total market cap). By 1999, this figure had fallen to under 75 percent.[3] At the same time, the size of dividend payouts has decreased significantly from just under 4 percent of the stock price in 1990 to approximately 1 percent in 1999. Although there are many possible reasons for the relative decline in dividends, one factor that may have contributed to this trend is directly related to the reward practices of corporate boards. The stock options that account for an increasing percentage of the compensation packages of directors and top executives increase in value with an appreciation of the firm's share price. These individuals do not benefit from dividend payouts.

In response to this growth imperative, organizations are adopting strategies that add to the burdens of those governing the organization. One approach has been to grow through mergers and acquisitions. Compared to internal growth, this method offers a much more rapid and certain way for a mature organization to increase sales. The number and value of mergers have been growing at a record pace, reaching an unprecedented $1.5 trillion in 1998 and then more than doubling to $3.4 trillion in 1999. This is despite a large body of evidence suggesting that the initial price premium and problems of integration mean that a majority of such deals fail to create value for shareholders of the acquiring firm.[4]

A second strategy has been to attempt to turn an existing firm into a generator of new businesses, including e-businesses, using an internal incubator model. The hope is to leverage the resources of the existing firm, such as expertise, support services, capital, and brand recognition, to enable the new enterprise to come to scale more rapidly than a stand-alone start-up. This strategy poses severe challenges from a governance perspective, however. Research suggests that if new start-ups are to grow, they require fundamentally different governance mechanisms—resource allocation systems, reward practices, and so on—than those suitable for existing firms. In addition, the resources that a large firm brings to new initiatives often come at a cost of lost speed as well as higher overhead, which the new enterprise cannot afford.

High Levels of Uncertainty: New Business Models and Changing Rules of Competition

Boards may feel that they do not need to focus on the new economy if their firm is not actively pursuing a dot-com strategy or does not yet face a strong Internet competitor. For those who are not yet actively involved in the Internet, there is a great danger in ignoring the medium. The Internet is changing the basic rules of competition in a number of fundamental ways. First, it is blurring the traditional boundaries between sectors: Amazon was originally perceived as the world's first and most successful online bookstore. Within three years, however, it had (1) added a diverse array of product lines (for example, toys, electronics, tools, videos, and Christian merchandise); (2) taken major ownership stakes in other successful online businesses (homegrocer.com, pets.com, drugstore.com); and (3) broadened out from e-tailing to offer online live and asynchronous auctions, a search engine to other Web shopping sites, zShops (an online mall open to any vendor), its own credit card, and even a line of branded Amazon bags. Amazon's goal, as stated in its 1998 annual report, is "to become the best place to buy, find and discover any product or service available online." The Internet is giving rise to other new business models that are also likely to place significant pressures on the way traditional firms are governed. Among these are the following:

- Virtual markets, or business-to-business exchanges, in nearly every sector, such as steel, plastics, and chemicals, where thousands of buyers and sellers can come together.[5]
- Name-your-own-price sites, such as Priceline.com, where individuals can decide what they want to pay for anything from an airline ticket to groceries; suppliers then decide if they are willing to accept the offer.
- Heavily discounted or free product and service offerings, such as personal computers or Internet access, in exchange for information about the consumer that is then marketed to advertisers. Some sites are even paying individuals who access the Web through them.
- Smart shopping tools that do an automated search for the lowest price available on a particular good or service.

The combined effect of all these new business models is a substantial increase in the level of price competition for all firms, not just those on the Net, as well as more information and power in the hands of consumers.

Greater Mobility of Key Knowledge Assets

"People are our most important resource." This claim is increasingly common in the annual reports that boards produce, yet the rhetoric often fails to match the reality of how firms treat individuals. Employees are often the most cynical audience of all, hardened by multiple waves of downsizing and frequent corporate restructuring.

For an increasing number of companies, however, it is unquestionably true that human capital, rather than physical or financial capital, is the key to their competitive success. This is particularly the case for new high-tech and knowledge service enterprises that have been the key drivers of the new economy. The value of Microsoft or Amazon is not accounted for by its physical assets but rather its intangible assets—its people and the knowledge that they have created. As one successful venture capitalist put it: "There is no shortage of ideas—I've never seen such an explosion of new business opportunities. And there is no shortage of finance—venture capitalists are lined up to give money to entrepreneurs with good ideas. The main constraint on growth is people. Finding enough good people to execute these ideas and turn them into viable businesses is the key constraint on growth."

The boards of today's knowledge-intensive enterprises face an essential dilemma. At the same time that they are increasingly dependent on knowledge workers to create value, these knowledge workers are also more mobile than ever before. Unlike the investments that firms make in new information technology or brand identity, the resources devoted to attracting and then developing key talent can literally walk out the door at any time. The mobility of talent can be a particular problem in acquisitions, as the board at Sears found to their dismay; Sears acquired Kidder Peabody only to find that many of the key assets of this firm—its investment advisers—had left, along with its key customers. The competition for top talent, and the accompanying turnover rates of key personnel, is particularly intense in the United States, where the economy has been operating beyond what most economists define as "full employment" for several years. Demographic trends suggest that labor markets for top executives and technology talent are likely to remain tight throughout the advanced industrialized economies for the next several decades. As the baby boom generation reaches retirement, the rate of labor force growth in Japan, Western Europe, and North America is projected to be significantly below the rate of economic growth through 2015, creating a major shortfall in key talent areas.

The explosive growth of the Internet has fueled the mobility of knowledge workers in two ways. First, the opportunities the Internet is creating for individuals to generate large fortunes in short periods of time are making it difficult for established organizations to retain their top talent. Companies that just a few years ago were considered by top graduates to be the most desirable places to work, such as McKinsey & Co. and Anderson Consulting, have cut some of their most Internet-savvy employees to start-up firms. Even Stanford Business School, a key training ground for new Internet-ready managers, is finding it harder to attract the best new students. Applications declined by 7 percent in 1999 as individuals sought to take advantage of the early potential of the Internet before the window of opportunity for these new business models closed.

Second, for the much wider pool of talent already in organizations, the Internet is making it much easier to determine the true market value of their skills. Online recruiting agencies are able to reach into firms to target key talent, and the proliferation of Internet job sites has greatly facilitated individuals' ability to identify employment alternatives. Organizations risk losing their key performers if they do not provide rewards and internal opportunities for career development that are as exciting as the external alternatives.

Some consultants and futurists have gone so far as to argue that the Internet spells the eventual demise of the large firm. Tom Malone and Robert Laubacher coined the term e-*lance economy* to describe a scenario in which electronic and personal networks bring together highly skilled freelancers or small, employee-owned and -controlled units to combine specialized skills to complete projects.[6] Once the project is completed, these cellular or network organizations can then disband or reconstitute themselves, depending on the success of their partnership and the requirements of the next task. Although this may sound more like science fiction than a near-term economic reality, in fact this scenario already exists in some large and growing segments of the economy. Such networked forms of organization are already the norm for many of the individuals working in project-intensive sectors ranging from construction to moviemaking to information technology. Malone and Laubacher cite the example of Topsy Tail, a fashion accessories firm that generates $80 million in sales with just three employees.[7] These individuals focus on identifying market opportunities and the new products to fill them. All other parts of the value chain are then outsourced to strategic partners. What the Net does is make it easier for individuals scattered across wide geographical distances to identify each other and connect their specialized expertise into a team, to complete the work virtually, and then to deliver it in a way that it is not apparent to the end user where it was developed.

Nevertheless, it seems unlikely that such examples and the move toward more knowledge- and project-based work signal the end of the large corporation. Indeed, at the same time that there has been a general trend toward growth in employment among small firms and the self-employed, we have been witnessing the emergence of ever larger and more powerful multinational corporations driven by the pressures for global consolidation and growth discussed earlier. For those charged with governing these larger organizations, the e-lance scenario holds an important lesson. If they cannot devise ways for the firm's most vital assets—its knowledge workers—to feel that they have a stake in the success of the enterprise and a say in how it is run, then they are likely to lose these highly mobile assets to start-ups or competitors who do. This suggests the need for finding new ways to make employees and other knowledge partners true stakeholders in the organization. (We discuss ways to increase stakeholder involvement in the following section and in Chapter Nine.) Boards can no longer pay attention simply to the development of the CEO. They must become deeply attentive to the organization's broad set of human resources.

Net-Enabling the Board

The Internet not only poses many new challenges for corporate governance, but it also is a powerful tool that can potentially be used to Net-enable boards. In the following section, we use our framework for creating effective boards to identify what changes are needed to prepare boards to take full advantage of the Net.

Knowledge

As noted in Chapter Three, the knowledge that boards contain is largely determined by the members they select. In many respects, it is difficult to imagine a group less well suited to forming a strategy for the Internet Age than the board of a typical large U.S. corporation: a large homogenous group of mostly white American males who grew up and entered the workforce prior to the advent of the personal computer. Some have never surfed the Web, and many still rely on their assistants to handle their e-mail. Although this group is usually rich in managerial expertise, the expertise is typically associated with bricks-and-mortar firms and the types of organizations and decision making in which they engage. Thus these directors' knowledge may predispose them against the types of risks and new business models associated with the Internet.

Most boards outside the high-tech sector do not need to add individuals with in-depth knowledge of the technical workings of the Internet. Nor do they need to replace all their senior directors with members of Generations X and Y. But they will increasingly need to ensure that several of their members have a clear understanding of how the Internet is changing the dynamics of their industry and the array of strategic options open to their firm. This expertise could come from a director who is a CEO or senior manager at an Internet firm (although the pace at which these dot-com firms are operating means their CEOs' time for sitting on boards is likely to be in short supply) or from others who are actively working in the dot-com world (for example, venture capitalists, consultants, academics who are researching the Internet). These individuals will need to quickly bring the rest of the board members up to speed on Internet developments. They must frequently update them through presentations from external experts, senior managers, and visits to dot-com firms, and ideally by encouraging each member to spend time on the Internet as a routine part of his or her board responsibilities. (We discuss this further in the next section.)

The challenges facing firms in the rapidly evolving marketplace of the twenty-first century suggest two other areas in which boards will need to add capabilities. The first need is to enhance the diversity of viewpoints on the board, and in particular the board's global perspective. Although U.S. boards have become significantly more diverse in the last twenty-five years, in 1998 only 13 percent of all the boards of *Fortune* 1000 companies had even a single director born outside the United States.

While increasing the pressure on boards to become more global, the Internet and other advances in communication technology also make it easier for boards to enhance their global capabilities. As we noted in Chapter Three, one of the greatest obstacles to increasing the foreign membership on boards has been the travel requirements for directors to attend frequent meetings. Although not a complete replacement for face-to-face meetings, videoconferences are soon likely to be of sufficient caliber to replace some in-person full-board and committee meetings, thus making it easier for firms to recruit directors from around the world. By supplementing these meetings with regular e-mail discussions and exchanges of routine information among directors, it may be possible to make board meetings far more productive.

Our analysis suggests that a second key knowledge area for the future is significantly underrepresented on existing boards: an understanding of organizational design and transformational change. Recruiting other firms' chief executives to serve as outside directors may provide some of this knowledge. these individuals are unlikely, however, to have all the expertise required to handle the broad array of challenges that boards will routinely face, such as assessing the organizational fit of key mergers and acquisitions, creating an internal context that is a fertile ground for new ventures, and redesigning or outsourcing key processes so that they can be delivered via the Web. Indeed, in recognition of the need to rapidly add this array of organizational expertise if they are to sustain their growth into more mature and profitable enterprises, many of the most successful dot-com start-ups have been recruiting top managers from more traditional firms to join their boards and executive teams.

To ensure that the knowledge of the board is fresh and closely aligned with the firm's changing strategic needs, it is likely to be necessary to change the membership of boards more frequently than has been common among most firms. Cisco Systems, for example, has adopted a policy of regularly replacing one or two directors on its ten-member board. Observed Cisco chairman John Chambers, "We have to invigorate the board and churn it every year. The speed at which change is evolving applies to the board makeup as well."[8]

Information

Just as boards can take advantage of the Internet's ability to improve communications among its members, so too can they become more effective by tapping into the wealth of information contained on a firm's intranet and the World Wide Web. Motorola, for example, is enabling all its directors to access electronic courses through Motorola University, an inexpensive means of increasing their knowledge about the firm and its markets. Because of the wide array of potentially relevant topics for the board and the limited time of its members, however, there is a very real danger that use of the Internet will lead to information overload. Thus it is vital that the board Web tools distill the key data directors require to provide financial and strategic oversight without overwhelming them with the immense amounts of operational information that a corporation generates. The following sections describe some of the key kinds of information that boards may wish to gather and distribute electronically to its members.

Key Performance Indicators. A growing number of firms are using a balanced scorecard approach to monitor not just the short-term financial performance of the organization but also the extent to which the firm is building longer-term capabilities and meeting the needs of key stakeholders (customers, suppliers, and employees).[9] Rather than just gather these indicators in reports for each board meeting, organizations can create an electronic dashboard that the directors and top managers responsible for running the corporation can consult on an ongoing basis.

Internal Communication. Many boards have already attempted to improve their legal oversight and compliance function by establishing an 800 number that concerned employees can call to raise any issue. Such a number can be usefully supplemented by creating a widely publicized e-mail address or website link where employees can send suggestions or voice concerns that they may be reluctant to share with management. For such a system to work, of course, employees must be assured that all such e-mail will be treated as strictly confidential. Thus the board may want to contract with a trusted outside organization to act as a clearinghouse for such communications.

Employees are likely to be far more willing to share their thoughts with the board's directors if the board first takes advantage of the Internet's potential to build a two-way conversation with employees. Currently most directors are invisible to employees. Company intranets, however, provide a low-cost and rapid way to share appropriate information—such as long-term strategy, celebration of key successes, rationales for major acquisitions or divestitures—with a firm's entire employee base. Some firms are already making good use of this capability, although more commonly it is the top managers, rather than board directors, who have taken the lead. For example, when Sun Microsystems was considering moving its corporate headquarters to a different site in the Bay Area, it used its intranet system to survey its employees' views on the new location. The responses indicated that the firm might lose a number of important personnel if it chose to move, leading to a decision to keep the original headquarters site. Likewise, when Charles Schwab grew concerned in 1999 that the tremendous growth in the brokerage share price of the firm he had founded was leading some key employees to retire early, he began a very personal electronic dialogue with the firm's employees to seek their input on how the firm could address the turnover issue.

External Viewpoints on the Firm. The ease with which the Internet can search for specific information makes it an ideal tool for boards to monitor how their firm is perceived by the outside world. Boards can gather a constant stream of information on their firms by conducting automated searches of analyst reports, the general press, and specialized industry and technical publications. Internet chat rooms (such as those hosted by Vault.com) that are visited by current or former employees and customers can provide a more variable, but potentially valuable, source of information that is not filtered through a company's bureaucracy or top management.

Individual directors may wish to tap some or all of these sources to create a search process that gathers and summarizes key information and posts it on a website for the board. Ongoing monitoring of the Web can provide a useful early warning system for issues relevant to the board and allow the board to take steps to quell rumors that can spread like wildfire on the Web, affecting the share price and employee morale. Shareholder activists are already becoming much more sophisticated at using the Internet to link individuals and institutions who own a firm's stock and using their votes to put pressure on boards that they do not consider to be acting in shareholders' best interests. Furthermore, the Web is likely to raise problems that will fall under the boards' legal responsibilities, as one firm recently discovered when an overzealous employee posted in a Web chat room false information purported to be from the company, which resulted in a suit from investors.

Proactive Scans of the Environment. All the aforementioned approaches could greatly enhance the information boards use to govern firms; but most of them are reactive, simply more effective ways to monitor the internal and external performance of the existing enterprise and to improve the links between the board and the organization's stakeholders. Boards are, however, in a unique position to add value by looking further into the future to identify key trends or events that pose potential threats or opportunities for the enterprise. Their independence, diversity of backgrounds, and legal mandate position boards well to play a more proactive, external scanning role.

At a time when the Internet and other technologies are evolving so rapidly and unpredictably, it may seem odd to be arguing for more emphasis on long-term strategic planning, a process that historically has had relatively limited success in forecasting future events. However, a number of tools have recently been created that could help boards perform this proactive strategic role without their attempting to predict the future. New firms, such as Evolving Logic and Thinking Tools, have developed exploratory modeling systems that harness the tremendous gains in computer power to move beyond traditional scenario planning. Rather than examine a few possible future scenarios, none of which is likely to prove correct, these systems have enabled such organizations as Ford Motor to build models of the key drivers of their business and to map thousands of possible futures. The intent is not to come up with the single most likely scenario but rather to identify what factors are the most significant drivers of success or failure. From there, such tools can create an ongoing system for tracking these key drivers, which then forms the basis for making strategic decisions. Hewlett-Packard has built a similar Web-based tool, named Cassini. It simplifies the capture of the market data that underlie future scenarios and creates a process for routinely updating this information in a form that is easily interpreted by high-level decision makers. Although such tools clearly do not provide all the answers for boards seeking to guide organizations through an uncertain future, the process of creating the models and regularly examining key future trends can itself enhance directors' understanding of the key drivers of the business.

Time

The combination of new strategic challenges and the demands for accelerating decision-making speed posed by the Internet is likely to force boards to reexamine both how they operate and the time requirements for individual directors. The time bind will be further exacerbated by the move to fill more outside director slots with CEOs of other firms—individuals who typically have little, if any, time to spare. The next sections look at a variety of strategies that boards can adopt to cope with these time pressures.

Delegating Tasks. There are inevitable limitations on what can be accomplished in meetings of the whole board, particularly if the size of the board grows to accommodate more diverse stakeholders. Thus we may see greater task specialization and more work delegated to committees. Such changes are already evident, for example, in the case of Motorola, where the full board meets only four times per year. Despite the rapid pace of change in its high-tech markets, the board is able to add value to the firm's strategy and maintain its oversight because much of the work is performed outside of full-board meetings: in committees, teleconferences, and one-on-one interactions between directors and top managers.

Creating More Time for Strategy. If boards are to rely more heavily on delegation of tasks, then they need to have subgroups responsible for all the key board roles. Currently almost all boards have such committees for their legal roles—audit and compensation—and three-quarters of large U.S. firms have a nominating committee. Few boards, however, have established specific groups charged with oversight of strategy, or specifically the firm's e-commerce strategy. Strategic issues are typically discussed in meetings of the full board, and as a result they easily get crowded out by more pressing immediate concerns or routine business. Some boards have addressed this problem by having annual retreats specifically devoted to strategic discussions. A useful supplement to such an approach may be to choose a group of inside and outside directors who have the greatest understanding of the firm's industry, markets, and technology and to form a strategic planning committee to focus on these issues throughout the year.

Increasing the Board's Capacity. Outside directors of the largest U.S. firms reported spending over 150 hours per year on a single firm's board-related activities in 1999, which according to the Korn/Ferry survey appears to be as much time as anyone working another full-time job can possibly spare. One way to provide additional capacity for the board is to hire a small staff dedicated to serving the board. Although these individuals would not be able to substitute for the ultimate authority of board members, they could, like the clerks for the Supreme Court, gather, analyze, and prepare briefs for key boardroom decisions. As is the case with Supreme Court clerks, these positions would be ideal for existing high-potential staff, who would gain a broad exposure to high-level strategic issues.

Another approach is to have one or more outside directors designated to play leadership roles in coordinating the activities of the board; there would be a corresponding increase in their hours and their compensation. These roles are, of course, those that chairpersons or lead directors currently play, but such positions still exist in fewer than 30 percent of large U.S. firms.

The future may bring greater specialization of roles and time commitments among directors. This would represent a partial move away from the current norm of equality and joint decision making among directors, but it would be a recognition of the very different strengths these individuals bring and of the differences in their time availability. Some active CEOs, for example, bring significant strategic and networking value to a company yet have only limited time to devote to the board. In contrast, recently retired individuals who have both the time and capabilities to serve as active directors may be underexploited by the board. In the future, the number of individuals in this latter category is likely to increase; demographic trends suggest there will be a large group of highly experienced baby boomers with relatively long, healthy life expectancies. These will be joined by a large cadre of talented younger executives from high-tech industries who have accumulated enough wealth to retire early from their full-time jobs but who are likely to continue to want to remain active in the business community.

Rewards and Motivation

The main trends in rewards for directors of U.S. public corporations are clearly in the direction of more closely aligning directors' interests with those of shareholders: abolishing director pension programs, increasing the percentage of rewards

that are in the form of stock grants or stock options, and requiring or strongly encouraging directors to own a significant amount of the firm's stock. (Some governance expert groups, such as the National Association for Corporate Directors'
Blue Ribbon Commission on Director Compensation, have advocated a target of
directors owning ten times the annual board compensation in stock.)[10]

The other main change in rewards to directors is the significant increase in
overall levels of director compensation to reflect the greater demands being placed
on these individuals. Twenty-five years ago, a directorship was a mostly honorary
position with a commensurately low compensation; 83 percent of *Fortune* 1000 firms
paid directors in total under $7,000. In 1998, average director compensation had
increased to over $40,000; with stock options and grants, while many directors'
earnings in both large and smaller high-tech firms surpassed $100,000.

How do these trends in rewards fit with the new demands that boards are facing in the Internet Age? From the perspective of encouraging decisions intended
to maximize the returns to the corporation's owners, these practices are clearly
beneficial. They have brought director rewards in large public firms into closer
alignment with the reward policies of a typical high-tech start-up. (See Chapter
Ten for a discussion of the venture capital governance model.) These reward practices may also help encourage the board to respond more quickly to events that
may affect shareholder value and to push the firm's managers to seek opportunities for growth through internal innovation or acquisition. The general increase
in the level of director compensation—particularly, having a high percentage tied
to the performance of the firm's stock—also appears to be warranted given the
greater time demands, array of responsibilities, and legal liability associated with
being a director.

The same factors that make these practices attractive from the perspective of
shareholder governance, however, call them into question from a wider stakeholder
view. As we have mentioned elsewhere, the more closely directors' pay is tied to
the firm's stock performance, the less likely directors are to give equal weight in
their deliberations to the interests of employees and other stakeholders. Likewise,
those firms requiring directors to own a significant portion of stock may end up
with less diverse boards. For example, whereas such a requirement is usually not
an issue for CEOs or already wealthy individuals, it can represent a major financial risk for individuals who represent other parts of society (for example, those
who have been in public service, those in lower-paid professions, or academics).
Even when the stock ownership comes in the form of a grant of shares to the director, it presents a financial difficulty if the director is immediately liable for the
tax on the value of the shares though prohibited from selling the stock for the term
he or she serves as a board member. Others have questioned the wisdom of paying directors solely or predominantly in stock because of its potential impact on

director independence.[11] They note that accountants are prohibited from owning stock in firms they audit, yet the members of the board, for whom these audits are done, are now being encouraged to own more stock. Moreover, because the directors generally set their own compensation levels through the compensation committee, they run the risk of criticism for overpaying themselves and diluting the earnings of other shareholders if the stock price greatly appreciates. The director of a biomedical board we interviewed explained to us, "The same shareholders who used to criticize us for being paid totally in cash are now on our backs for overpaying ourselves, because the stock has done very well."

As in other areas of board design, the optimum approach to rewards for a board in the new economy is to strike a balance between the board's different roles and the constituencies the board serves. It is important that the board have at least some members who have a significant financial interest in the value of the firm's stock, so as to reflect one of the board's vital roles: that of representing the firm's owners. Where one or more directors, such as a venture capitalist, has such a stake, however, it is not clear that all directors need own stock. Indeed, a board may be considered to be more independent and attuned to wider societal concerns if not all directors have significant ownership stakes. For example, the traditional target of criticism for poor governance is a family-owned or family-dominated firm, where a high percentage of the directors are members of the family or have close ties to them (business colleagues, friends). Where the ownership of a large organization is so diffuse that no individual or institution has a major financial stake, it is probably beneficial to have a significant portion of directors' pay in stock. If the board is to maintain desirable diversity, however, the measure of that "significant portion" should be relative to each director's personal wealth, rather than a uniform standard applied to all directors. In addition, to avoid the appearance of bias, boards should tie their variable compensation to the achievement of a set of predetermined comprehensive objectives. Ideally these objectives would use measures of the interests of all the firm's stakeholders—for example, employee satisfaction, customer satisfaction, environmental and safety records—not just those of shareholders.

Power

The challenges that the Internet is likely to create for corporations suggest that boards need to have considerable power to represent a variety of stakeholders and to influence business strategy. Many of the changes in board power demanded by globalization and the Internet have been suggested in earlier chapters. For example, in order to respond quickly to rapidly changing global markets, boards need to be independent of management. They also need to represent a global stakeholder orientation, and they need the kind of decision-making processes that will lead them to make quick, effective decisions. Given sufficient independence, they may be in a better position than company management to challenge basic assumptions of the organization's business model that could be threatened by e-commerce. Without the power to engage in debate with senior management and to force them to deeply examine the organization's assumptions about e-commerce opportunities and threats, a board's independence can prove to be of little value. Ultimately, a key issue in the evolution of power at the board level involves creating the right balance of power among the various stakeholders in the organization. In Chapter Ten, we explore what form this balance should take.

Conclusion

We feel that the new and rapidly changing world of e-commerce brings both opportunity and danger for boards. On the one hand, the Internet will provide new sources of information and make old sources far more accessible. It may encourage boards to bring on new skill sets and in turn foster more adaptive mind-sets at the top of the corporation. It has the potential to open new markets and business partnerships. In other words, it presents great new opportunities for boards and the organizations they govern. On the other hand, the world of e-commerce will accelerate the speed at which boards must make their decisions. Many more of the decisions will be around highly complex issues that are in unexplored territories requiring great experimentation—putting boards beyond their comfort zones. The organizations they govern will face new competitors whose mind-sets, metrics, and infrastructure are better suited to an e-commerce world. In some cases, their companies will need to partner with competitors. There will be important shifts in how company talent is rewarded, not only at the executive level but also all the way down the line. Talent skilled in e-commerce will be highly desirable and therefore mobile. Boards will become more and more concerned about attracting and retaining talent throughout their organizations. As a result, boards will find themselves navigating complicated compensation issues. Although boards will have greater access to information from many more sources, they will have to become more savvy about assessing the quality of that information and where to direct their attention. In other words, this world of new opportunity is fraught with dilemmas and changes. Boards must be prepared to contend with the same reinvention pressures that their companies are facing. They must incorporate the very qualities characteristic of the Internet Age—speed, flexibility, new worldviews, and a deep appreciation for experimentation. If successful in their own transformation, boards can provide vital leadership for their companies in this new age.

CHAPTER NINE

TO WHOM ARE BOARDS ACCOUNTABLE?

Although today it is widely felt that a board's primary allegiance is to the company's shareholders, historically this has not always been the case. At different moments in the history of the modern corporation, the directors' allegiance has been focused elsewhere. In addition, a growing number of institutional investors, analysts, and advisory firms question whether a board and corporation can be truly effective by addressing the needs of only one of its many stakeholders. We share this concern. In this chapter, we will present a brief history of the shifting allegiances of boards and present our arguments in support of a *stakeholder* model of corporate governance, which we consider more appropriate than today's *shareholder* model.

The Shifting Tides of Director Allegiances

The roots of today's board of directors can be traced back to England, where grants from the Crown were necessary for the privilege of operating in a joint stock or corporate form. The charter model simply migrated with commerce to the American colonies. Under a charter, the early colonial business enterprises typically had governing bodies that consisted of a council of peers—predecessors of the modern board. Alexander Hamilton and Benjamin Franklin built upon the council idea to establish "boards of directors" for their eighteenth-century corporations. Hamilton's stated purpose for his directors was simple: "the affairs of the company are to be under the management of 13 directors."[1] As Lorsch and MacIver have pointed out in their seminal book on boards, this description is remarkably similar to the wording of the General Corporation Law of the State of Delaware, where many U.S. public corporations are incorporated today: "The business and affairs of every corporation organized under this chapter shall be managed by or under the direction of a board of directors."[2]

After the Revolutionary War, the right to incorporate was vested in the states as one of their sovereign rights by the U.S. Constitution. The charters themselves, however, could be very restrictive. For example, the state of Massachusetts issued a charter to Maine Flour Mills in 1818 with a $50,000 cap on the value of the total property the corporation could hold.[3]

In addition, charters were not available to anyone wishing to start a business, but rather were confined to Caucasian males. At some point, it became evident that this concentration of power in the political system led to wheeling and dealing and corruption. The state of New York first addressed the problem by creating in 1811 the first general corporation law for business purposes that essentially opened to anyone the privilege of doing business.[4] By the start of the twentieth century, such general incorporation laws had become largely universal, and numerous states even had laws forbidding the granting of special charters.[5] One component of these incorporation laws shared across all the states was the notion that the board of directors bore ultimate responsibility for the financial and legal activities of the firm. This mandate has remained largely the same to this day.

At the beginning of the twentieth century, directors' allegiances were clear. Directors were instruments of the owners. Most of America's large corporations were still in the hands of founding owners and shareholders, and directors were beholden to them. For example, in the year 1900, only 22 percent of the country's largest companies were in the hands of professional management.[6] By the 1920s, however, control of large corporations was shifting into the hands of professional managers. By 1929, 40 percent of the nation's two hundred largest nonfinancial companies were under the control of professional managers.[7] By the 1970s, the shift was almost complete. For example, in 1974, professional managers were in charge of 82 percent of the largest two hundred companies.

The advent of nonowning managers changed the nature of corporate decision making. Increasingly, personal aspirations related to power, image, career, and other motives began to intrude into the decision making. In addition, the concerns of company employees, local communities, nonprofit organizations, and other corporate stakeholders were influencing decision making as these groups pushed their companies to become more "socially responsible."[8]

The rise of the professional manager was also accompanied by an important shift in the allegiances of board directors. They were increasingly beholden to management rather than to shareholders. This change in allegiance was further magnified by the fact that directors were themselves more and more likely to be members of the same managerial class—often either CEOs or retired CEOs. As a result, directors began to share in the broader agendas of management. At the same time, paradoxically, a challenge to directors' allegiances was being laid in place. As more and more of the control of corporations moved into the hands of professional managers, the ownership stakes held by companies' senior leadership started to decline. In 1938, for example, CEOs and their families at the nation's top 120 companies held an average of 30 percent of company shares. By 1974, this figure had dwindled to 4.7 percent.[9] Professional managers were now in control, but they were rarely substantial shareholders in the companies they were running.

The shareholding issue would rise to paramount importance during the 1980s, when several powerful forces coalesced to produce massive shock waves in corporate boardrooms and to realign directors' alliances. Among the more influential of these was the evolution of the junk bond market and the appearance of takeover entrepreneurs such as T. Boone Pickens and Carl Icahn. Like the multiple strands that make up the length of a rope, two other forces—the rapid growth of the global economy and the growing number of shares held by institutional investors—intertwined with the takeover movement to destabilize the status quo of U.S. boardrooms. These three forces spurred on many of the governance initiatives we see today.

The takeover movement of the 1980s proved to be a primary catalyst because of its direct challenge to the allegiances of directors. To whom did they actually report: to management or to the owners? In contrast to the early twentieth century, the "owners" were now no longer founding entrepreneurs, their families, or a handful of individual investors, but rather external shareholders.

The ground for the takeover movement had been laid earlier by the rise of global competition, starting in the 1970s. The more intense competitive environment began to reveal the flawed and outdated strategies put in place by professional management in many of America's largest companies. As a result, many corporations who were household names entered an extended period of profit decline, which naturally produced sliding stock prices. Eventually the blame for these declines would be placed at the doorstep of senior managers, clearing the way for the takeover movement of the 1980s.[10] The arrival of global competition, in essence, eroded the control of professional managers throughout American boardrooms. Peter Drucker's comments echo popular sentiments of the time: "What made the takeovers and buyouts inevitable . . . was the mediocre performance of enlightened-despot management, management without clear definition of performance and results and with no clear accountability to somebody."[11]

As Michael Useem has also pointed out, solutions to resolve these performance problems were varied and depended largely on the proponent.[12] Incumbent senior managers wished to remain incumbent and so sought reform through internal measures, such as downsizing the workforce. Corporate raiders were skeptical about the incumbents in the first place, doubting their capacity to bring about genuine performance improvements. Though self-serving, Carl Icahn's comments, a leading raider of the time, captured their sentiment: "We're supporting managements who produce nothing. Not only are we paying those drones to produce nothing, but we're paying them to muck up the works."[13] At this point, another set of players was gaining power: leveraged buyout firms like Kohlberg Kravis Roberts; and institutional investors, such as pension funds, insurance companies, and nonprofit endowment funds.

While only a minority of publicly traded firms were converted in leveraged buyouts to privately held, owner-managed companies, the threat was enough to spur governance reform. The buyouts of the late 1980s—$5.4 billion for Beatrice in 1986 and at that time an eye-popping $24.9 billion for RJR Nabisco in 1988—convinced many of the chieftains and boards of large corporations that their size was no longer protection from being "put into play."[14] While such defensive tactics as golden parachutes and poison pills were invented to protect incumbent managers, there was also a simultaneous move toward empowering boards. Notions that company CEOs should undergo formal appraisals by the board and that a greater percentage of directors needed to be from outside the firm gained popularity as ways to improve company performance and to show action on the board's part.

As leveraged buyout activity was accelerating, institutional investors were simultaneously growing in power as large volumes of shares came under their control. For example, pension fund shareholdings would almost triple in size from $891.2 billion in 1981 to $2,266.8 billion in 1988.[15] The ten largest funds alone would control more than $500 billion in assets by 1990.[16] CalPERS, for example, controlled assets of more than $57 billion; CREF held $35 billion in assets. Their vast shareholdings made it increasingly difficult for these funds to move easily in and out of stocks if performance slumped or if they disagreed with a company's policies and management. Finding buyers other than other institutional investors who could digest tens of thousands of shares at any given moment was extremely difficult.

By the late 1980s, the investment environment also appeared somewhat limited. Domestic opportunities were well exploited, and only a handful of international opportunities were seen as attractive.[17] Finding the door closed to a quick exit by divestiture and a lackluster investment environment, pension and other institutional funds began to alter their strategies. Why not apply direct pressure to company CEOs and their boards for performance improvements?

The controller of New York City in 1992 commented on the investment strategy of the New York City Employees Retirement System (with assets of more than $40 billion at that time): "We are long-term investors. We can't get out of these companies. We want to break up the concentration of power at the top, create more accountability, provide checks and balances."[18] The chief investment officer of CalPERS similarly announced: "We realized we don't have the option of voting with our feet. The only course available is to see [that] companies are effectively run."[19] This approach became more and more feasible as institutional holdings in individual companies grew. For instance, by 1990, institutions owned on average 50 percent of the shares of the nation's one thousand largest publicly traded companies; they often held more than 50 percent of the highly visible, blue chip stocks—for example, 71 percent of Digital, 52 percent of General Electric, 59 percent of Johnson and Johnson, and 83 percent of Intel in 1991.[20]

With their concentration of shareholding, institutional investors—especially the large public pension funds—began to demand a broad range of reforms across the corporate landscape of America. Shareholder activism accelerated. Among the most visible players at the time was Dale Hanson, the head of CalPERS. In the case of W. R. Grace and Company, Hanson publicly expressed his deep concern to J. Peter Grace, the CEO, that the company was one of the poorest-performing shareholdings of CalPERS. Moreover, he pointed out that Mr. Grace's compensation was out of line with the firm's performance by some "82 percent over market."[21] He informed Grace that a resolution would be submitted for shareholder vote to amend the company's bylaws to establish a board-level compensation committee composed of independent directors. To avoid potential embarrassment, the board voluntarily accepted the CalPERS proposal without the measure ever going to the shareholders for a vote. Successes like these encouraged greater activism.

Publicly traded companies sensed the need to be seen as proactive. Suddenly, companies were undertaking significant actions in the interests of shareholders, such as raising dividends, cutting engorged corporate staffs, paring administrative costs, eliminating unprofitable operations, focusing on fewer businesses, and adopting new governance structures. Aside from the individual company initiatives, investor organizations formed to give a collective voice for the pension funds. Among the more prominent of these were the Council for Institutional Investors and the United Shareholders Association.

These forces of the 1980s created paradoxical outcomes for boards. On the one hand, they realigned directors' primary allegiance toward the shareholders. During the 1990s, if one were to ask most directors, "To whom are you accountable?" the vast majority would say "the company's shareholders." On the other hand, the takeover movement created a shift in the legal environment that now allows directors to define their constituents far more broadly than as simply the company's external shareholders. Again we must raise the fundamental question: To whom then should boards be accountable? The answer depends on how directors, management, and the company conceptualize the role of the public corporation.

The Public Corporation: Property or Social Entity?

Throughout the twentieth century, there have been two distinct but conflicting conceptualizations of the public corporation, each of which has had direct implications for directors' allegiances. One is the *property conception;* the other is the *social entity conception.*[22] Under the property conception, the corporation is the private property of the owners or shareholders. Directors, in this case, are agents of the owners, and it is their role to dutifully advance the financial aims of the owners.

Throughout the nineteenth and early twentieth centuries, the property conception was the dominant conception of the corporation. As Allen notes, a pivotal case heard by the 1919 Michigan Supreme Court, *Dodge* v. *Ford Motor Co.*, epitomized this viewpoint. In their capacity as shareholders, the Dodge brothers had sued the Ford Motor Company, arguing that the corporation did not have shareholder welfare as its principal concern. The impetus for the suit was a decision by Henry Ford to suspend indefinitely dividend payments and instead to reinvest some $58 million in company profits so that the company could lower the price of products and expand the company's business. Whereas Mr. Ford had argued that the purpose of a corporation was to produce good products inexpensively, to provide employment, and only "incidentally to make money," the Dodge brothers argued that the shareholders were the owners of the enterprise and that they were entitled to a portion of the accumulated profits. The Michigan Supreme Court sided with the Dodge brothers and ordered Ford to restore the dividends. Underlying its decision, the court highlighted a principal assumption: "A business corporation is organized and carried on primarily for the profit of the stockholders. The powers of the directors are to be employed for that end."[23]

In sharp contrast, the conception of the corporation as a social entity treats the organization as an institution with multiple constituencies. The corporation is no longer simply a private entity responsible solely to its owners, but rather it is "tinged with a public purpose."[24] This opposing conception of the corporation first appeared in the late nineteenth century with the emergence of the modern business enterprise run by professional managers. The "owners" (public shareholders) of the modern corporation were increasingly outside investors who could and did easily and at little cost move funds from company to company.[25] In addition, they were fragmented, which simply reinforced the fact that it was easier to sell than to intervene when top management was ineffective. As control of the corporation shifted toward professional managers, their expertise and freedom to act were soon seen as critical ingredients in shaping the success of the modern-day business enterprise. The aim of shareholders—to maximize their investment—began to take a back seat to the seemingly longer-term aim of management—to create value. Although the contributors of capital were due an attractive rate of return on their investment, there were also other constituents to serve—customers, employees, and the community. No longer were directors solely beholden to shareholders; instead they had to balance with management the frequently conflicting claims of the corporation's many constituencies.[26] The duties of the board of directors went beyond "assuring investors a fair return, to include a duty of loyalty in some sense to all those interested in or affected by the corporation."[27]

From the perspective of the boardroom, the difference between the property conception and the social entity conception is very significant. Each conception provides the fundamental decision-making framework for the activities of boards, and the two alternatives can call for very different board decisions in many situations. For example, in the case of a hostile takeover offer, a board operating from the property conception might quickly and easily decide to accept the offer. In contrast, a board guided by the social entity conception might quickly and easily reject the offer because of its potential negative impact on stakeholders other than investors. Thus the question of whether the property conception or the social entity conception is the correct one for a board is not merely the object of an intellectual debate but a critical issue that profoundly shapes the decisions boards make.

Margaret Blair has advanced an interesting alternative perspective to this governance debate, arguing that it is ill conceived to frame the issue as a choice between shareholders versus stakeholders.[28] The stakeholder advocates have failed, she contends, because they have failed to articulate a clear set of legally defensible criteria that could consistently guide corporate directors in weighing the interests of a broad set of groups when making key decisions for the corporation. In the absence of such criteria, directors of U.S. boards have generally adopted the owners' best interests as the key guidelines for their decisions. Blair contends, however, that the common interpretation of the property conception of the board's role is misguided because, as discussed in our Introduction, it rests on the mistaken assumption that shareholders are the sole "owners" of the corporation.

From the time the modern corporation was created, the law has recognized that those who hold equity in a firm do not have unlimited property rights over that organization; rather, the corporation is granted a charter to operate for the benefit of the wider society and its shareholders. Because the equity holders are deemed to hold the "residual risk"—receiving their payout only after all the company's employees and debtholders are paid—then the best way to ensure an adequate flow of investment capital has been to entitle shareholders to the profits of the enterprise and control of the board to ensure that their financial interests are safeguarded. This corporate governance model may have been a relatively good fit for corporations of the Industrial Age, where the owners of a company contracted with workers and suppliers for the raw materials and the low-skilled labor that they used to produce finished goods. In other words, this was a world in which contracts for mostly generic inputs were easy to specify, physical capital was the scarce commodity, and the owners of this capital bore the risk.

This same model, however, appears to be an increasingly poor fit for many of today's corporations. As argued in our Introduction, employees are major stakeholders in organizations because they are a scarce resource and the critical corporate asset. In addition, as firms increasingly specialize in their areas of core competence, they are relying more heavily on close partnerships with suppliers to provide key elements of their product or service.[29] Such partnerships have been shown to operate most effectively when both sides make investments dedicated to the relationship, in both physical and human capital. For such network-based, knowledge-intensive organizations, it is clearly no longer accurate to claim that the equity holders, whose shareholdings are often part of a diversified portfolio, bear all the risks associated with operating a corporation. Rather it is all those groups who make personal and resource investments that are firm-specific who should be considered the stakeholders, or shared owners, of the enterprise.

Although the property and social entity conceptions of the corporation have coexisted without a great deal of debate for most of the twentieth century, the takeover movement of the 1980s pushed directors toward the property conception.[30] For example, when most, if not all, of the shareholders wished to sell control of the company, whose interests were the directors to promote and protect? How could a board member turn down a hostile cash tender offer when investors saw it as a wise return on their investment? Accustomed to serving the CEO, directors soon found themselves in conflict over their allegiances. The takeover environment had created a situation where it was extremely difficult for directors to convince shareholders that realizing an immediate, substantial profit on their investment was a bad idea. The property conception had regained the upper hand. After all, how could directors turn down a significant financial gain for investors using arguments that future returns might be better?[31]

In the 1980s and 1990s, however, the tug-of-war was intensified when there was a sharp divergence between the decisions of the court and shifts in the marketplace. Setting the precedent, the Delaware Supreme Court in the Time Warner case decided that corporate directors could indeed take actions that prevented shareholders from realizing an immediate high premium offer if those directors were acting in pursuit of goals aimed at the corporation's long-term welfare.[32] In essence, the judgment implicitly recognized the social entity conception. Following this decision, legislative acts were passed in twenty-eight jurisdictions in the late 1980s that in one form or another authorized boards to weigh the interests of all stakeholders in their decision making.[33] The states of Connecticut, Indiana, and Pennsylvania were especially clear in stating that directors were not obligated to give a controlling effect to any one constituency or interest. As Allen points out, this in essence eradicated the notion that "maximizing the financial interests of shareholders . . . is the core duty of a corporate director."[34] This position argues that directors and senior managers must walk a tightwire between their responsibility to investors in the form of stock market performance and their social responsibilities to the employees and community.

Despite this reality, the concentration of power in today's institutional shareholders and the highly competitive global economy continue to exert an enormous pull on directors—reminding them of their obligations to investors. No similar pressures remind them of the obligation to other shareholders. It is not surprising therefore that despite the Time Warner case, we continue today to hear more about shareholder value than about social responsibility. The unfortunate consequence of this is that all too often boards do not take into consideration the impacts of their decisions on all stakeholders.

In many ways, even though the law in the United States is on the side of the social entity conception, recent economic events favor the property conception. Nowhere is this more evident than in the contrast between U.S. firms and those in Japan and continental Europe.

Corporations in Japan and Germany fared less well during the 1990s. They operate under a stakeholder model, essentially the social entity conception, which means they must balance their shareholders' interests against those of employees, suppliers, customers, and the larger community. What particularly distinguishes many of the firms under this model are lifetime employment and cross-shareholdings by customers and suppliers. Core workers, for example, are in large part protected by both social convention and by labor laws that make it difficult to lay off individuals.

In continental Europe, many of the employees of large public companies are legally guaranteed representation on "supervisory boards." In addition, often among the largest shareholders in Japanese and continental European companies are firms that are the company's suppliers, customers, or creditors (a key feature of keiretsus or cross-firm shareownership).

Many German companies have a sole long-term shareholder. In these countries, there has been an historical assumption that such characteristics conferred distinct advantages over American models of shareholder capitalism. For example, it was assumed that including employees in strategic decisions ensured their support in implementation. Lifetime employment was seen to encourage deeper employee loyalty and create stronger incentives to invest in learning longer-term job skills as opposed to simply acquiring skills that would carry employees to the next better job offer. Cross-shareholdings among suppliers, customers, and creditors were believed to foster better coordination of initiatives and greater investment in long-term payoffs. It was also assumed that such shareholders would devote more attention to working with company managers to resolve problems as they arose, rather than simply selling out or giving in to hostile takeovers.

Just as the U.S. model has not always produced the right governance behavior on the part of U.S. boards, the European and Japanese models have had their problems as well. In many cases, they have created corporations that are not able to change as rapidly as the business environment is changing in the era of the Internet, or to attract as much capital as they need in order to compete with U.S. firms. In addition, they have often been criticized for not providing truly effective vehicles for employees to influence the direction of their corporations. Thus, although they provide an interesting alternative to the U.S. model, it is not clear that they provide the best approach to creating boards that operate effectively from either a stakeholder or shareholder perspective.

Why the Stakeholder Model of Governance Is the More Viable

Well before it ended, the twentieth century had already been dubbed the American Century by many scholars. This reflects the triumph of the Americans in both world wars and the subsequent victory of the United States in the Cold War, capped off by the collapse of the Soviet Empire. Arguably just as significant as the military victories, however, was the economic one: the triumph of capitalism over communism and socialism. Leading the charge for capitalism has been one of humanity's greatest inventions: the modern corporation. Given its dominant place in our lives, it is easy to forget that this wealth-creating organizational form was a creation with a specific charter and legal standing. As is true of the technological discoveries that have shaped the last century—from the automobile to the splitting of the atom—the corporation has brought both great benefits and unintended consequences. Like nuclear power, the modern corporation is a powerful device that, once unleashed, is difficult for its inventors or governments to fully control. The challenge from a corporate governance perspective is to harness corporations so that they serve the best interests of society, rather than just those of shareholders.

With respect to corporate governance, the twentieth century may also end up being the American Century. Although the victory is not nearly as clear-cut as on the battlefield, American-style capitalism and the shareholder model of governance appear at the start of the twenty-first century to have triumphed over the stakeholder model of governance most closely associated with Japan and Germany. Evidence for the dominance of American-style shareholder governance was most clearly seen in the success of the United States in those industries most closely associated with the new economy: the knowledge-driven high-technology and service sectors. Evidence is present in the boardrooms of leading Japanese and German multinationals, where managers and investors have been slowly pressing for reforms of their governance arrangements to focus on the interests of shareholders over other stakeholders. Finally, in the boardrooms of large U.S. corporations, two decades of governance reforms had firmly entrenched the concept of "shareholder value," increased the independence of the board from management, and more closely aligned the interests of the board and the owners of the corporation.

We believe it is important, at this moment of triumph for the shareholder model of capitalism, to return to a question first posed by Karl Marx, the economic theorist most associated with the failed alternatives to a market economy: Does capitalism contain the seeds of its own destruction? Or, put more specifically in the language of corporate governance debates: Does focusing boards of directors on maximizing the returns to one group (shareholders) over the interests of other stakeholders in the corporation ultimately undermine the legitimacy of corporations' role in society?

We believe the risks of pursuing a shareholder-only vision of the board's mission to be twofold. First, for the companies themselves there appears to be a growing tension between, on one side, the increased role that employees, in particular knowledge workers, are playing in the overall creation of a firm's value and, on the other side, the move from stakeholder models of corporate governance (that give employees and others a voice in the boardroom) to an exclusive focus on the interests of shareholders. As we have discussed, an employee's stake in the company and its future may be extremely high today, unlike the situation of traditional shareholders and laborers of the past. As Margaret Blair has pointed out: "In firms where highly specialized skills are important, . . . employees may be as highly motivated as shareholders to see that the firm's resources are used efficiently. Moreover, employees of such enterprises exercise de facto control over many important decisions and, because of their inside knowledge of the business and their stake in its success, may be much better situated than distant and anonymous shareholders to act as monitors of management."[35]

Given the blurring of the traditional distinction between employees and owners, it is useful to examine the different components of "ownership" and how they are distributed within organizations. Owners are most simply defined as "those who have a rightful claim to property."[36] In the case of corporations, the law has defined four rights that come with ownership: residual control rights, an interest in the current and long-term profits of the organization, access to information, and decision making or control.[37] Together these rights serve as a means of safeguarding the value of the investments of those individuals who provide capital to firms yet who are not directly involved in management. An analysis of these ownership rights suggests, however, that employees in many firms today possess elements of all of them.

For example, in a growing percentage of large companies, as well as in high-tech start-ups, employees are typically given a high degree of control over their work, the financial and strategic information they need to make good business decisions, and rewards that entitle them to a share of their organization's success. Even residual control rights—the ability to deploy or sell a firm's assets after paying off the firm's creditors, which have historically distinguished investors' privileges from those of managers and employees—are inevitably a shared right in knowledge-intensive organizations. Although investors retain the right to sell off a firm's nonhuman assets, these assets are often worth only a small fraction of a knowledge-based firm's collective capabilities. Based on this analysis of the components of ownership and who possesses them, Rousseau and Shperling conclude that rather than refer exclusively to shareholders as owners, "it is often more appropriate to refer to financial investors, managers, and workers, since any and all of these may participate in the firm as owners."[38]

By failing to recognize these rights and investments, firms risk alienating their most valuable and mobile assets. One concrete illustration of how the short-term maximization of shareholder value may undermine the long-term prosperity of all the firm's stakeholders is seen in the impact of financial analysts' metrics on staffing decisions. Trying to maximize performance on measures such as revenue per employee or earnings per employee can encourage firms to use consultants, or temporary or contract labor, rather than full-time employees, even when the costs are higher and potentially valuable knowledge to the firm is lost.

The second risk of pursuing a shareholder-only vision is to the wider society. The combined forces of global capital markets, the Internet, and free-trade agreements are shifting the balance of power from national governments to transnational corporations. The efficiencies and increased competition in these global markets have helped generate economic growth. But if the firms that operate within these markets are held accountable to only one relatively small segment of society (the owners of capital), there is a danger that their actions may lead to greater inequality and a failure to maximize the welfare and well-being of the population as a whole. The concern, as symbolized by the protests at the World Trade

Organization (WTO) talks in Seattle in January 2000, is that global firms, responding to the constant pressure to maximize profits and the returns to global investors, will pursue strategies that sacrifice the environment, hold down wages, and call for low labor standards.

The ability of countries to regulate these firms, even if that is the desire of the majority of the electorate, is constrained by a collective action problem in the world marketplace. If one country pursues a governance regime that is less friendly to shareholders than that of other countries, then they risk losing the ability to attract the very investment from world capital markets needed to sustain employment and a growth in living standards. Conversely, governments that establish corporate governance regulations that are very favorable to managers or shareholders (or both) are likely to act as magnets for corporate headquarters. This has long been the case in Delaware in the United States, as it has been for the Netherlands in Europe. With governance laws that feature low corporate taxes and high tolerance for poison pills and other hostile takeover defenses, the Netherlands has attracted 57 percent of all multinational corporate headquarters in Europe.

Ways to Increase the Stakeholder Perspective

Given this potential for a race to the bottom in corporate governance, with countries vying to attract capital by lowering the regulation of firms, the key question becomes, Can companies be governed so that they recognize the interests of legitimate stakeholders, without undermining their primary function as creators of value? In the following sections, we explore the different options with respect to ensuring that corporations serve all the important stakeholders.

Enlightened Self-Interest

The most straightforward option is to retain the status quo. The argument in favor of this approach is that there is no need to change current U.S. governance arrangements, because the self-correcting mechanisms of the market and the enlightened self-interest of boards will ultimately ensure that all stakeholders are well served by corporations. The logic of this argument is as follows: boards recognize that an increasing percentage of the value that resides within corporations rests in the intangible assets generated by a firm's employees and by its relationships with key suppliers, other firms, and communities. As a consequence, boards will take steps to safeguard these assets by altering and structuring the relationships with these stakeholders in a way that gives them a direct stake in the success of the enterprise. Firms that take the lead in making these changes should outperform their competitors and grow in size at the expense of firms who concentrate solely on the interests of shareholders. Their successful governance models will be emulated by other organizations and gradually diffuse through the economy.

There is evidence that changes in this direction are under way. As firms focus on a few core competencies and increase the amount of outsourcing and the value of what they outsource, they are changing the nature of their relationships with other firms—for example, reducing the overall number of suppliers while building mutually beneficial alliances and supplier partnerships. These arrangements include long-term contracts, shared research, joint problem-solving efforts, and, in some cases, cross-firm shareholdings. The mutual dependency that such relationships create can in turn entail the development of new governance models to oversee the relationship.

Many knowledge- and service-intensive firms are likewise reforming their organizations to try to build stronger relationships with their employees. At the board level, as noted in Chapter Five, some boards have broadened the array of metrics that they track so as to include measures of employee satisfaction and development. Another sign of this trend is the lengths to which many firms are going in order to be recognized on lists like *Fortune*'s "100 Best Places to Work." The following are among the practices that are now common among these "employers of choice":

- High levels of employee involvement in decision making
- Flexible work schedules and other practices (for example, employer-subsidized child care, telecommuting, sabbaticals) intended to help individuals balance work and personal lives
- Heavy investments in ongoing development of employees' knowledge and skills
- Generous benefits and other perks (for example, free food, exercise facilities)

Perhaps the most widespread change is the increased adoption of reward practices that tie individuals' compensation to their organization's performance. This practice is most common in high-tech start-ups, where widespread use of stock grants and stock options for all or most employees and not just top executives is now the norm. Large corporations—for example, Pepsico, Chevron, and Bank of America—have followed suit, introducing stock option plans for all workers.

However, the large number of employee millionaires that stock option plans have created and the good press being generated by some exemplary employers should not be taken as representing a general shift toward treating employees as full stakeholders in the corporation. Only 16 percent of the largest U.S. firms included all employees in their stock option plans in 1999.[39] The growth of comprehensive employee stock ownership plans (those that cover all workers) has been very gradual among the largest U.S. firms, increasing from 28 percent of firms in 1987 to 33 percent in 1999.[40]

There are a number of reasons for doubting whether the enlightened self-interest of boards will, by itself, lead them to weigh the interests of employees fairly relative to the interests of the shareholders. One element of the current U.S. governance system that undermines a long-term focus on employee interests is the ease of acceptance of takeovers, whereby shareholders may increase their returns at the expense of other stakeholders by selling their stakes. There is some evidence to support the view of takeovers as a "breach of trust via the actions of new owners who bear none of the prior commitments of the old regime."[41]

A second reason is that many of the changes in the employment practices of U.S. firms appear to be more of a response to the tight labor markets of the latter half of the 1990s than they are to a fundamental rethinking of whose interests companies should serve. For example, the adoption of more employee focused practices has been concentrated in those sectors and regions where unemployment has been lowest. Although demographic trends suggest that tight U.S. labor markets are, in general, likely to continue for several decades, the first signs of a recession could lead to a significant shift in firms' relations with their employees.

Paul Osterman has illustrated the fragility of the enlightened self-interest approach by examining the recent employment records of some of the historically most progressive U.S. firms: for example, Levi Strauss, Xerox, and Corning.[42] In the face of growing competition and failure to meet shareholder expectations, these firms were forced to abandon the long-term relationships they built with their employees, laying off a large percentage of their U.S. workforce, while in some cases expanding employment in countries with lower labor costs.

The other difficulty with relying on market mechanisms to look after the interests of the employees is that the market inevitably rewards those whose skills are in short supply while penalizing those who have low levels of skills or whose skills have become obsolete. This is exactly what we have observed with the sharp rise in income inequality in the United States over the last two decades. College-educated knowledge workers have received the vast majority of all employee stock options and corresponding increases in wealth that firms have generated. In contrast, the majority of the workforce have seen their real incomes remain stagnant; the least skilled have even experienced a decline in real earnings. Lower-skilled workers have experienced persistently high levels of job insecurity, despite the longest period of sustained economic growth in U.S. history.

In two ways, the growth in wage and opportunity inequality has been exacerbated by the growth of the Internet and other new technologies. First, the spread of information technology has increased the premium associated with levels of education that provide the skills necessary to use existing technologies and create new ones. Second, the Internet has made it easier for companies to manage operations on a global basis, accelerating moves to locate work in countries with lower labor costs.

Proponents of the current governance system counter that it is not the role of firms to deal with societal problems such as income inequality. Rather, firms need to focus on maximizing the wealth they create; it is up to governments to raise skill levels and redistribute wealth. The problem with this perspective is that adoption of a shareholder-first model of governance make it increasingly difficult for governments to redistribute wealth, a progressive policy that is generally opposed by corporations and the owners of capital. What actions, then, should the government take? Maybe they should include changing the membership and structure of boards in order to make them more representative of the stakeholder perspective.

Legal Entitlements for Stakeholders

Governments can alter the laws of corporate governance so that employees and other stakeholders have enhanced rights in the boardroom. As noted earlier, boards in the United States can take into account the interests of employees and the community when making major decisions (such as selling the firm or relocating major facilities to another location). In practice, these precedents have had little effect, for two reasons. First, a high percentage of U.S. firms have chosen to incorporate in Delaware, where the governance laws are most favorable to the shareholders' interest. Second, even in states where stakeholder governance laws are in effect, the courts have determined that as long as boards include some discussion of the interests of all relevant stakeholders, they have the ultimate right to determine the relative weighting of each stakeholder's interest. Thus boards can weight decisions heavily in favor of shareholders and frequently do just this—hardly a surprising outcome given that board members usually are shareholders.

An alternative approach is to create a governance structure that provides the stakeholders with seats in the boardroom. This has been done in Germany and other parts of Northern Europe that have a two-tiered board system. There is a management board (roughly equivalent to the U.S. top management team) of insiders who are responsible for the firm's daily operations, and a supervisory board that includes outside directors, employee representatives, and other stakeholders, such as large banks who hold ownership stakes. These boards operate within a wider national regulatory regime that provides far greater protection for employee rights than exists in the United States. The following are among the elements of this protection:

- Legal restrictions on hostile takeovers
- Mandatory work councils for all firms with more than fifty employees, to give employees a voice in decision making
- More powerful unions that represent a much higher percentage of employees than in the United States and negotiate at both the firm and industry levels
- Guarantees of generous severance packages that make it costly to lay off workers
- Strict restrictions on hours worked and the use of temporary workers

The combined effects of these regulations and employee board representation have created a governance system characterized by high levels of consensual decision making. Typically, management consults and negotiates with labor over major decisions that have a direct impact on employees.

This Germanic or social democratic approach to governance has both strengths and weaknesses relative to the Anglo-American model.[43] One the one hand, it is well suited to the long-term product life cycles and investment demands of high-value-added manufacturing and capital goods sectors, where Germany has long been a world leader. It has helped encourage more cooperative, flexible labor relations within firms and wage restraint across firms, which have enabled Germany to create high levels of productivity, low inflation, and one of the world's highest living standards.

On the other hand, the relatively slow pace of decision making and the high regulatory burden make this governance model a much poorer fit for high-tech start-ups or service sector enterprises. In addition, the model privileges the interests of firms' existing employees over those who may be seeking jobs in the labor market, contributing in Germany's case to relatively high levels of unemployment (particularly for women and immigrants) over the last fifteen years.

The growing importance of high-tech start-ups and service enterprises to both wealth and job creation in advanced industrial countries has led to a significant reassessment of the success of the German and Japanese models in the last decade. Throughout the 1980s, these governance systems were heralded by many researchers as the model for success in the global economy.[44] By the end of the 1990s, however, these same governance arrangements were seen as a major constraint on the ability of Japanese and German firms to restructure and compete successfully. Leading firms were calling for reforms to adopt more "global" (read "United States–like") governance arrangements, including legalization of stock options, more rights for shareholders, and shifts away from cross-firm shareholdings. It is important, however, not to overestimate the pace of change in these stakeholder models or to assume that they will simply move toward an Anglo-American model of shareholder governance. There remain major differences in the institutional environments that are slowing any convergence to a U.S. approach to governance.[45] Among the most significant differences are the following:

- Few publicly traded firms in Germany. Germany had only seven hundred publicly traded firms in 1997, and just thirty-five of them accounted for 73 percent of total market capitalization. Overall, the value of the stock market accounted for only 31 percent of GDP in 1997 compared to over 100 percent in the United States and the United Kingdom.[46] German firms rely far more heavily on bank finance than public equity markets for raising capital.
- Lack of activist investors. Only 6 percent of German adults owned shares in 1998, compared to more than half of the U.S. population. A majority of shares remain heavily concentrated in banks, insurance companies, and cross-firm shareholdings, and there remains a far less active institutional investment community than in the United States.
- Continued broad public and regulatory support for "codetermination" (that is, stakeholder representation) in the governance of firms.

There are significant forces at work that are creating pressure for reform of the German and Japanese governance systems. Some firms (for example, Daimler Chrysler and SAP) have begun to seek alternatives to their national governance arrangements, listing themselves on the New York Stock Exchange to obtain access to capital and to leverage the demands of U.S. investors as a mechanism for driving change within their organizations. At the same time, individuals have gained increased access to investment opportunities outside their home country and have seen the growth of more U.S.-style mutual funds. Recent tax law changes are likely to encourage firms and banks to sell off their large stakes in other enterprises that are not closely related businesses. And although they are still a rarity, there have been a handful of incidences of hostile takeovers, such as Vodafone's high-profile and fiercely fought acquisition of Mannesman. At the same time, both the Japanese and German governments have provided funds and introduced new, U.S.-inspired laws to encourage the growth of a venture capital industry to foster the development of new enterprises. And they have encouraged the development of new stock markets, modeled on the NASDAQ, to make it easier for start-up firms to go public.

With the U.S. economy thriving and its main competitors moving toward an American governance model, it seems unlikely that U.S. policymakers will consider adopting elements of a Japanese or German stakeholder approach, nor is it clear that they should. Although the puncturing of the Internet-fueled U.S. stock market bubble may lead to another reassessment of the relative merits of the different national models, it is unlikely to lead to significant U.S. governance reforms in favor of employees or other stakeholders. First, the United States lacks the societal or regulatory supports, such as a strong union movement, that are necessary to provide employee directors with the leverage they need in order to be effective representatives of worker interests. Second, the existing laws governing campaign finance have led to a strong dependence on corporate financial support; thus it is very unlikely that such reforms could garner sufficient congressional support to become law.

Increased Power for Stakeholders

Osterman argues that the most plausible way to encourage U.S. firms to better serve the interests of employees and the wider society is not to rely on corporate responsibility or reforms of formal governance mechanisms.[47] Instead he argues for building "countervailing power" for these groups. Rather than increasing the direct representation of stakeholders in the boardroom, this approach relies on a more traditional concept of bargaining. If employees and community groups can more effectively organize and wield power, they can in turn compel firms to take their interests into account when making strategic decisions.

Some elements of the new economy support this view. As noted, the Internet has significantly shifted power to consumers, countering the threat that large firms will use oligopolistic power to raise prices. The Internet also offers a powerful organizing mechanism for individuals and community groups that can act as an effective balance to the greater global mobility of corporations. As Thomas Friedman observes, leading nonprofit groups such as Greenpeace and Amnesty International have already effectively harnessed the power of the Internet.[48] They have created global networks of individuals who share interest in a particular issue and who can wield significant influence on the environmental and employment policies and practices of multinational firms. The result is that firms who are seen to violate accepted standards, such as Exxon or Nike, risk losing global sales when they become the targets of campaigns from these nonprofits.

The move toward a more knowledge-based economy, combined with slow or negative population growth in the advanced industrial countries, has also significantly increased the employment options and hence the relative labor market power of the most highly educated individuals.

The difficulty for the countervailing power argument, however, is that although these trends have helped raise the earnings and improve the work conditions of highly skilled *individuals*, it has not helped build employees' *collective* power. In addition, it has not helped the lower-skilled individuals who are most vulnerable in the labor market. Further, many trends in the new economy—the shift from manufacturing to services, the greater mobility of the workforce, the threat posed by firms' ability to relocate to lower-wage locations, the increase in self-employment and teleworking, the adoption of employee-friendly policies by many antiunion firms—have contributed to the decline in the power of the traditional collective voice for workers: trade unions. Unions now represent fewer than 10 percent of U.S. private sector workers, and despite major new organizing campaigns, they have shown no signs of seriously reversing the more than thirty-year decline in their membership.

There are a few examples of promising models of collective employee organization that may offer a better model for the new economy. Working Today in New York City and Working Partnerships in San Jose, California, have successfully organized contingent workers by offering many of the same services (for example, access to benefits and health care, training) as the more progressive temporary staffing agencies. They are then able to negotiate with firms for work on behalf of these individuals. Although the restructuring of unions to emulate these examples might help stem the decline in organized labor, the difficulties of organizing the new workforce suggest that unions are unlikely to serve as the mechanism for a real increase in collective employee power unless there are significant reforms of labor laws in the United States.[49] Such legislation, however, is highly unlikely due to the same political dynamics that work against shifts toward a stakeholder governance model.

Transnational Regulation of Corporate Governance

The global reach of financial capital and the increasingly transnational scope of many firms are major deterrents to a single national government's attempting to reform corporate governance or to otherwise increase the power of employees and other societal groups. One potential way to redress this situation would be to create a global code for the governance of corporations, one capable of regulating firms wherever they are headquartered. In place of the current de facto migration to the U.S. governance model, such a code could combine the best features of the shareholder and stakeholder perspectives. For example, it might feature the American emphasis on open, annually and independently audited financial information, as well as the use of formal evaluations of management by independent directors to provide clear oversight of shareholders' interests. At the same time, it could include features from the stakeholder models to recognize the investment in firm-specific human capital that employees have made and their accompanying ownership rights. These features might include an entitlement to employee voice in certain strategic decisions (sale of the firm, major relocation, or site closures), the protection of employee retirement and other benefits, and the right to fair compensation if an employee loses his or her job.

On the surface, the most obvious institution to adopt such regulations would be the WTO. However, the wide divergence in the interests of its members makes it unlikely that the WTO could adopt any governance code that would have an impact on U.S. firms' decisions. At the 1999 meetings in Seattle, for example, the WTO was unable even to initiate discussions on basic guidelines to limit the use of child labor, much less to consider any other far-reaching reforms of the role of corporations. An alternative, more homogenous group to introduce such common governance rules would be the leaders of the G7 nations. Because trade among these seven largest industrial economies accounts for over 85 percent of world commerce, an agreement among them to enforce a common set of governance requirements on firms operating in their territories would in effect cover most of world output. There is currently no evidence of the G7 nations being interested in common corporate governance statutes; therefore, at this time there is little prospect of the development of an effective approach to transnational corporate governance.

Turning Stakeholders into Shareholders: True Employee Ownership

As we have noted, employee ownership is already widespread among U.S. firms. At the start of the 1990s, a group of one thousand large U.S. firms together accounted for 29 percent of the total U.S. stock market value in which employees owned a significant direct stake (a minimum of 4 percent and an average of 12 percent of equity).[50] Since then, employee ownership has grown dramatically as a share of the economy; firms that have driven the stock market boom have shared the wealth they created by distributing stock widely among employees. In 1999, 87 percent of the *Fortune* 1000 had stock option plans, including 10 percent that offered options to all employees.[51]

Employee ownership can take a variety of forms: purchase of company stock as part of a pension fund or 401k (often with a matching contribution from the firm), an ESOP, or an element of an individual reward package. From a governance perspective, however, employee ownership in large U.S. firms has, with rare exceptions, failed to translate into an employee voice in the boardroom. In the largest study of firms with substantial employee ownership, Blasi and Kruse found "no evidence that employee ownership leads to participative management" nor that it had an effect on salary distribution or employment security provided by the firm.[52] This is hardly surprising, as ESOPs were treated as a purely a financial device in 95 percent of these firms.

Many of the early ESOPs in the 1960s and 1970s were established as ways for a private firm's founder to cash out his or her stake in an enterprise without having to sell it to a large corporation. The intent behind the framing of the original ESOP legislation and behind the tax incentives that were in effect between 1975 and 1986 to encourage the establishment of ESOPs was to give workers a collective ownership stake in the enterprise. In practice, however, ESOPs have not lived up to this ideal. Many large corporations adopted ESOPs to take advantage of these tax incentives, and later ESOPs grew in popularity as a tool for combating hostile takeovers. Of the one thousand employee-owned firms that Blasi and Kruse studied, only four had employee directors on their boards.[53]

The voting rights associated with the stock held in ESOPs often have a long vesting period. Once the stock becomes vested, it is like a pension fund's shares voted by a trustee rather than directly by the workers. Employees can express their preferences to trustees through a process known as mirror voting, but, as Blasi and Kruse note, the Department of Labor's interpretation of how trustees should interpret these votes reads like a catch-22: trustees are instructed to focus on the best interests of employees as "shareholders only" and to disregard their expressed interests as workers.[54] Thus, if a majority of the employees' shares are voted for a position that is counter to the preference of other shareholders, the trustees can ignore it as unduly influenced by the employees self-interest as workers. In sum, ESOPs have, if anything, served to entrench management rather than to foster a stakeholder approach to governance.

One of the few sectors in which ESOPs have led to active employee participation on boards is the airline industry. Ironically, moves toward giving employees greater say in these organizations came out of adversarial labor-management relationships. For example, Northwest Airlines was near bankruptcy in 1993. As part of its restructuring process, the airline negotiated a deal with its unions that gave employees a 30 percent ownership stake and three board seats in exchange for $900 million in wage and work-rule concessions. The deal not only helped the airline return to profitability, but the subsequent employee voice in the governance of the firm led to innovations in how the airline operates. For example, a joint union-management committee gives workers a chance to bid on jobs that would otherwise be outsourced. United Airlines subsequently negotiated a similar agreement with its unions.

The limits of existing approaches to governance should not deter policymakers from considering employee ownership as a legitimate route for governance reform. Putterman offers a convincing retort to the critics of the theory of employee ownership, showing that if employee-owned firms are properly structured, there is no reason why they cannot be as efficient as firms with absentee shareholders.[55] And Blair makes a convincing case for employee-owned firms, pointing out that they

> Fit with the existing U.S. governance system
>
> Are potentially politically attractive to both the right and left
>
> Bring firms closer to the entrepreneurial model that has proved so successful
>
> Provide a powerful retention tool for firms in an era of tight labor markets
>
> Provide a potential basis for employee commitment in the absence of job security
>
> Foster greater alignment between employee and shareholder interests, encouraging workers to think more like owners
>
> Encourage investment in firm-specific and tacit knowledge

With increased employee ownership, employees could play a major role in the election of directors. This in turn could put employees or their representatives on more and more U.S. boards. All too often, employees are powerless when it comes to electing directors because they don't have a vote or because the election has only a single slate of candidates (or both). What is needed is not just employee ownership but the opportunity for employees to vote for directors in a truly open election.

Conclusion

In sum, we feel that boards today need to define their stakeholders more broadly. Whereas the 1980s and 1990s were the era of the shareholders, the twenty-first century needs to be characterized by a broader stakeholder model if governance models are to match the needs of the global economy and society. Our narrow conception of shareholders as the *investors* in a company does not reflect today's reality. Employees and suppliers are also making highly specialized, at-risk investments in firms. In a knowledge-based economy, these investments can be thought of as equal in significance to the equity that is purchased by stockholders. Corporate boardrooms must reflect this new world of multiple "investors" if directors are to truly lead their corporations into the future.

CHAPTER TEN

REDESIGNING THE BOARD: NEW GOVERNANCE FORMS

Does a one-size-fits-all approach to corporate governance make sense? Should all boards use the best practices we have discussed throughout this book? We think the answer is probably not. Given the increased diversity of organizational forms, it is important to consider alternative approaches to structuring boards that may be more effective under certain conditions. There is one form of board that has been particularly popular and effective recently: new ventures boards. Thus, before we turn to other new forms of boards, it is important to briefly review its characteristics.

Venture Capital Boards

The boards that oversee high-tech start-ups, including the firms that have created the Internet revolution, are structured and operate in ways that differ significantly from the governance practices of large corporations. Indeed, if one were to measure these high-tech boards against widely accepted best practices for governing public companies, they would receive a failing grade in the membership arena. They tend to have the following characteristics:

- A large number of inside directors. These high-tech firms typically have a much higher percentage of current or former employees on the board than the average *Fortune* 1000 firm (18 percent in 1999). This tends to be the case even after the firms have gone public and grown substantially in size. At the start of 2000, three of Microsoft's seven directors were current or former executives; half of Yahoo's six directors were insiders.

- Outside directors with close ties to management. Many of the outside directors on these boards joined as a result of a close business relationship with the firm, for example, through providing venture capital or legal or consulting services.

- Lack of diversity. These boards are typically much smaller than the average *Fortune* 1000 board (six to eight members, compared to eleven) and, as noted, tend to be drawn from within the close-knit high-tech community, which may underrepresent women, blacks, and Hispanics.

- Directors sitting on multiple boards. Large firms have been clamping down hard on professional directors, limiting the number of other boards on which their directors can serve. In contrast, on the boards of these small firms, some of the key outside directors, such as the venture capitalists, may hold a dozen or more directorships.

These characteristics have raised some concerns about both the ability of these boards to exercise independent oversight of management and their capacity to anticipate or cope with a major crisis, such as the Microsoft antitrust suit. These criticisms were muted, however, by the extraordinary financial performance of these firms throughout the 1990s. The unanswered question is whether these governance arrangements will prove adequate when an inevitable downturn occurs in the financial performance of these firms.

Whatever the future may bring, it is a mistake to judge high-tech boards by the yardstick of the best practices for established public companies. These venture capital boards are not a throwback to the bad old days of the 1970s, when weak corporate boards allowed managers of U.S. firms to underperform. If anything, they bear a closer resemblance to the governance arrangements of the early 1900s, when tycoons like Carnegie, Morgan, Rockefeller, and Ford built and ran the great companies of the day. As was true of these firms, there is little danger that the venture capital board will fail to represent the interests of the shareholders, because the boards of these new start-ups typically are the owners. The inside directors and venture capitalists who sit on the board together usually control a large majority of the firm's equity and take most of their compensation in the form of stock. A survey of twenty-seven Internet firms, for example, found that only 7 percent paid any annual cash retainer, and just 14 percent paid a meeting fee, compared with 95 percent and 81 percent, respectively, for bricks-and-mortar firms.[1]

Thus the directors of these boards have a strong shared interest in enhancing the value of the enterprise. Along with this shared interest, however, the venture capitalists rely heavily on several governance mechanisms to maximize the likely success of their investment. One such mechanism, for example, is that they appoint a separate chairman from outside the firm to run the board in the interests of the owners and to counteract the potential dominance of the CEO. According to one venture capitalist we interviewed, "This is the single most important factor in creating the right balance of power needed for effective governance. Our country has this separation of powers, why shouldn't companies?" Venture capitalists also hold one or more seats on the board and typically have a strong say in the appointment of outside directors. They also require a vesting period for the founders of the firm so that the vital intellectual capital does not leave before the enterprise is established.

Rather then spend their time on oversight, these venture boards concentrate on the other roles that boards can play: giving strategic advice and providing access to external resources. These roles are particularly crucial to start-up enterprises. For the advice and mentoring function, the initial board members are generally selected to complement the expertise of the firm's founders—for example, to provide marketing and financial expertise to individuals who have good product and technical knowledge. One of the first tasks of the board is to bring in other full-time managers to fill strategic competency gaps in the top management team. This often includes replacing the original founders or changing their roles because they do not have the skills necessary to take the firm to its next stage of development. For example, the board may have the founder make the transition from a line management role to a more strategic director role. The other key criterion for choosing board members at this early phase is that they bring personal networks. The start-up firm can use these networks to build partnerships for those key areas in which it elects not to build in-house expertise.

Net Keiretsus

As the more established venture capital firms develop a large portfolio of investments in related companies, some are beginning to conceive of their business as representing a new multifirm governance model. One interesting example is provided by Zone Ventures, which originated in Silicon Valley and has provided initial seed capital to a larger number of successful Internet firms than any other (roughly 150 as of 1999). This early venture capital model proved so successful that the founders decided to franchise it, setting up seven Zone Ventures scattered across the country, each raising its own capital to fund new start-ups. One of the benefits they offer to entrepreneurs, in addition to venture capital, is participation in the wider Zone network of firms.

The networks exist at multiple levels. Local networks, called Zone Clubs, are membership organizations that are open to entrepreneurs in the cities where Zone Ventures are based, including the managers of their portfolio companies. The club has quarterly meetings with a star speaker (750 people attended the Los Angeles meeting in September 2000), and smaller monthly meetings that focus on issues of common interest to Net businesses, such as branding on the Web, how to manage human capital, and so on. The second network consists of all the portfolio companies and provides them with opportunities to form partnerships and identify areas of common need. Out of these common needs, Zone Ventures then identifies new business opportunities. For example, Zone Ventures established a new, dot-com-focused public relations firm to service its portfolio companies and others through the IPO stage and potentially beyond. None of these firms had this expertise in-house, yet it is a competence that they would all need if they were going public.

This overall structure can be described as a Net keiretsu, a loose agglomeration of firms joined by a central firm with cross-ownership stakes. Like a Japanese keiretsu, this network organization could potentially wield far greater leverage than individual enterprises, for example, in bulk purchasing or creating shared benefits packages. In other respects, however, it would be the precise opposite of a traditional keiretsu, maintaining a very flat, cellular structure rather than a multitiered hierarchy. Each cell would retain a distinctive competency and the speed that comes with this specialization, and it would be free to do business with organizations within or outside the network. Employees would retain the benefits of a start-up model, with a clear line of sight between their efforts and their firm's performance, and with ownership stakes providing a strong incentive for their efforts. Another benefit of this model in terms of human capital is that it would enable entrepreneurs to repeatedly start new enterprises without leaving the wider network. By appointing members to the board of each firm, the venture capital firm is able to act as the focal point for the network, continuously seeking opportunities for potential partnerships that would leverage the capabilities of the individual organizations.

Recognizing the potential power of this governance model to combine the benefits of large and small organizations, many traditional firms are seeking to build their own Net keiretsus. General Electric, for example, already has two under way; GE Capital has taken investment stakes in more than forty-five e-businesses. NBC is serving as the hub for a network of media firms that are combining the Web with other forms of delivering news and entertainment. Intel already has one of the world's largest venture capital portfolios, with more than $12 billion invested in a host of firms with which it also has close business relationships. Other major technology and e-service providers, ranging from IBM and Hewlett-Packard to McKinsey & Co. and KPMG, are taking ownership stakes in start-up firms in lieu of fees. A similar pattern exists in the pharmaceutical and biotechnology industries, where large firms are increasingly taking ownership stakes and partnering with start-ups. The new firms provide cost-effective and cutting-edge new products and tools; the drug companies provide established processes for testing new products and then marketing and distributing them. In most of these cases, the large firm, at least initially, seeks a board seat and privileged access to the small firm to safeguard its investment, but avoids the problems that can arise when attempting a full acquisition.

Internal Venture Capital Boards

One of the ways in which established companies have attempted to overcome the barriers to the internal creation of new enterprises—particularly new businesses that potentially threaten their existing, already profitable products—is to set up the new ventures as stand-alone enterprises.[2] Like any start-up, however, these enterprises require different governance mechanisms than a large firm. Therefore, to increase the odds of their survival within the potentially toxic environment of the parent firm, some companies have established separate internal boards, modeled on venture capital boards, to both nurture and oversee the new business.

One promising example is Teradyne, a leading firm in the automated testing equipment market, which in 1998 had sales of $1.5 billion.[3] In 1998, the firm came up with a new tester called Integra, based on a new, low-cost technology. Although it was currently less capable than its high-end machines, Integra had the potential to deliver similar-quality tests in a few years for one-quarter the cost. To commercialize this new disruptive technology, Teradyne set up a separate unit for Integra; the unit prepared a business plan, was given a venture capital stake rather than a budget, and reported to a board of directors. "The idea was to think of it as a business from the start, not an R&D project," said Marc Levine, Integra's general manager.[4] Although the board was composed completely of Teradyne senior managers, the new governance structure enabled them to operate differently: "Being on the board let us jump out of the daily crap, which is the toughest thing for a division manager to do," said Edward Rogas, one of the internal directors.[5] The separate governance arrangements also gave the new enterprise the speed and freedom to make decisions—such as to outsource key components and not to worry about satisfying existing customers—that would have been impossible within the normal Teradyne structure. This enabled the new unit to reach profitability in just eighteen months, with projected sales of $150 million in 2000. At the same time, because Integra was not spun out initially, Teradyne retained the full value it created and was able to gain additional cost savings once it was ready to function as a full business unit.

Other firms, such as Hewlett-Packard, have attempted to create internal venture boards, but with mixed records of success. Observed one HP employee we interviewed: "These governance mechanisms can be much more effective at killing ideas that don't make sense than protecting the ones that do." One possible way to enhance the credibility of these internal boards—while also keeping the venture and the highly confidential information it often contains within the firm—would be to appoint one of the outside directors from the full board to serve on each significant new venture board.

An alternative strategy has been adopted by Proctor & Gamble (P&G) with its first e-business venture, Reflect.com, which offers consumers customized cosmetics over the Web. In order to give this the true feel of a start-up, P&G sought outside venture capital for the new business and created a separate board for Reflect.com, with two representatives from P&G, two from the venture capital firm, and two others on which they jointly agreed. This approach has the advantage of creating a truly separate governance structure for the new enterprise, but also implies that the parent firm must be willing to relinquish a greater degree of control.

Partnership Boards

A number of forces are propelling the growth in partnerships between companies.[6] Partnerships provide the means for firms to focus on a few core competencies and to minimize fixed assets. They can provide valuable expertise and shorten the time required to enter global markets and establish new international standards. They can offer a means to share risk or forge new capabilities by combining the learning from different organizations. For all these reasons, partnerships are an essential means of doing business in a networked economy. Thus, for the boards overseeing firms, developing effective mechanisms for governing partnerships will be an increasingly important capability.

In partnerships where two or more firms have made significant investments, such as joint ventures, the boards from each partner will have to come together to create a new and separate board to oversee the new enterprise. Corning has used this type of joint venture strategy as an integral part of its success for more than a century, including such partnerships as Dow Corning and more recently Corning Samsung, a partnership to extend Corning's fiber optic technology into Asia.[7]

Corning's board and top management have developed some simple yet important guidelines for how to establish successful governance of such partnering arrangements:

- Before entering into the marriage (a formal joint venture), have a courtship (that is, work as partners on a project); doing so allows both sides to explore not just the strategic fit but whether the organizations' cultures and leadership styles are compatible.[8]
- Structure the joint venture as a win-win arrangement in which it is clear what the expectations and benefits are for each side. A firm that enters a joint venture to try to extract the maximum value for itself at the outset may get a short-term win, but it is unlikely to develop long-term benefits from the relationship and may find it difficult to find partners in the future. At Corning, for example, most managers can recall a time when they were chastised for not searching for benefits for their partner.[9] Creating a win-win situation does not always mean that both sides should have an equal say in operating the partnership, however; indeed, because of the potential for conflicts, the failure rate of shared-responsibility partnerships is generally higher than that of partnerships in which one partner plays a lead operating role. In the case of the Toyota-GM joint venture to create the NUMMI plant in Fremont, California, it was in both partners' interests for Toyota to run the venture, because GM was seeking to learn lessons about the world-leading just-in-time Toyota Production System, and Toyota was interested in learning if its model would translate to a U.S. setting.[10]
- Treat the partnership as a learning opportunity; both sides should frequently reexamine how the partnership is progressing and adapt the new organization in accordance with lessons learned and changes in the competitive context.
- Don't stifle the child; the joint venture needs to be given sufficient freedom from the two (or more) parent organizations to develop its own business. This independence may be facilitated by bringing in a set of independent directors to join those appointed by each of the original partners.

The role of the corporate board in establishing such legal joint ventures is clear; however, in order to help leverage their key capabilities while protecting their intellectual capital, firms are also finding the need to create new types of "boards" or internal governance mechanisms to oversee less formal partnerships. Such new boards are particularly important in the case of the growing phenomena of "coopetition," whereby firms that are normally fierce competitors collaborate on a specific project. Boeing and Lockheed Martin, for example, are partnering on the development of the F-22 fighter; at the same time, they are the only two competitors for the Joint Strike Fighter (JSF). Because of the strategic importance of the JSF project to the future of the two businesses, it was vital for the firms to define at the outset how the cooperation on the F-22 project would be structured, what role each partner would play, and what information could be shared.

Even when not dealing with a direct competitor, firms may find they need to establish new governance mechanisms to ensure that they get the maximum value from each relationship. Hewlett-Packard, for example, is experimenting with the creation of an internal board to formulate a strategy and coordinate its multiple business dealings with Microsoft; energy companies have established similar mechanisms for governing their global relationships with key engineering supply firms. Although it is beyond the remit of the corporate board to become involved in each of these partnerships, it can play a useful role in setting guidelines for how the partnerships should be structured and in periodically reexamining the effectiveness of the most important partnerships.

Advisory Boards

A potentially well-established complement to the traditional board structure is the advisory board. However, many firms have introduced advisory boards only to see them fall into disuse. The CEOs and directors we interviewed often were critical of their advisory boards, seeing them as talking shops that wasted time and money. Although current practices generally fail to create effective advisory boards, if carefully structured and used strategically, advisory boards can offer a means to reconcile and relieve some of the growing demands on boards.[11] The following are some of the important benefits that an advisory board can provide:

• New market entry. Advisory boards are often used to provide the knowledge and local contacts a firm requires to enter new markets around the world. These local networks can be particularly important in many Asian countries, where personal, family, and business relationships are closely intertwined. More generally, advisory boards can provide high-level global expertise to a firm while avoiding some of the logistical difficulties of adding outside directors who are based outside the home country. Some international advisory board meetings can be held in conjunction with regular board meetings in order to try to enhance the global awareness of directors.

• Facilitating partnerships and providing useful government or industry intelligence. Some directors are currently recruited primarily for their Rolodex and the valuable set of personal relationships they can bring to the firm. This strategy is particularly common in such sectors as aerospace and health care, where former high-level government officials often make a quick transition to the boardroom. These directors are often criticized for having seats on a dozen or more boards and thus not being able to devote the concentrated time and attention that a fully empowered board requires. In such cases, an advisory board position may be an ideal role, as it leverages the strengths of that individual without causing some of the process problems that arise when a director is absent or not fully prepared for meetings.

• Instant credibility. Advisory boards are often used by high-tech start-ups, who are trying to quickly develop name recognition and gain a better understanding of their marketplace. Participation on these boards can be attractive to high-profile individuals, such as CEOs of larger public companies or experts with a strong reputation in the field, who do not have the time to devote to a full directorship. Although the hours these individuals devote may be limited, their advice can often be invaluable to firms with an inexperienced management team. Because such directors are typically paid primarily (if not solely) in stock options, the cost to the firm of establishing such a board is low.

• Deep technical expertise. Firms large and small can often benefit from establishing an ongoing relationship with leading experts on technologies that are core to the firm's business. Some of these experts, who are generally based at universities or research institutes, may lack the inclination or business expertise to serve as effective full board members, but they can play a vital role in identifying potential future opportunities or threats in the field, serving to guide R&D and strategic investment decisions.

What particular form an advisory board should take will vary from firm to firm. Some may meet in person a couple of times each year; others are virtual, a community of experts on retainer that the board or top managers can call on when needed. The key to getting value from these arrangements is to choose what specific purpose the advisory board is intended to play (separate boards can be established to meet different needs); identify the right mix of individuals to fill this need; and then define the length of time for which the advice is required, reevaluating the usefulness of the advisory board on a regular basis.

Conclusion

In the span of a few decades, the norm for U.S. corporate boards has gone from their being relatively ineffectual "pawns" who could be easily manipulated by management, to becoming strategic resources that can provide advice and exercise independent oversight to ensure that firms stay focused on creating value. Even as the capabilities of many boards have increased, however, what is expected of boards has been growing at an even more rapid rate. Although it is important not to overestimate what boards can achieve—they remain, by necessity, relatively removed from the running of a business—our analysis of high performance boards suggests it is both feasible and beneficial for boards to reexamine their roles and to continue to build their capabilities.

As our discussion in this chapter indicates, however, no one approach to boards is best for all situations. Established large global and national firms need different board structures and policies than do smaller start-ups, joint venture firms, and other forms of organizations. One size clearly does not fit all organizations, but one principle does: all organizations must recognize the value that multiple key stakeholders create in the corporation, and they must give each of these stakeholders a voice in the boardroom.

CONCLUSION

Because boards are becoming more active, they must deal with a basic conflict between the two main roles boards are being asked to play: Can a board be a strategic partner with top management in formulating the strategy and building the capabilities of the organization and still exercise independent oversight of management?

The tension between the different board roles can be clearly illustrated using the hypothetical case of a rapidly growing high-tech firm. The firm was seeking to expand internationally and enter new product markets, and it recognized that upgrading the quality of its board could be a vital asset in such a strategy. The board was delighted to identify a high-profile, fifty-two-year-old chief executive in its industry who had recently sold his firm and was looking for new challenges without the commitment of a full-time post. He agreed to join the board and immediately formed a strong working relationship with the CEO, who frequently called on him outside of board meetings for advice with questions about global branding, his particular area of expertise. When the firm decided to dramatically expand its European sales office to include a center of excellence for research and product development, the CEO asked the director to spend a month in Europe assisting the new president there to launch the new operations. The director was able to leverage his contacts there to help the firm establish several new strategic partnerships and to help the firm avoid several potential European regulatory pitfalls. In recognition of this invaluable service and the significant extra time it required of the director outside of his formal board activities, the company awarded this director a special one-time $50,000 bonus and a grant of one thousand additional shares.

The board was stunned at its next shareholder meeting when it was criticized by some prominent pension funds for having awarded a consulting contract to a director and having therefore increased the percentage of "insiders" on its board.

Although this case is hypothetical, it represents a composite of decisions real boards are facing each day. It illustrates both the increasing potential for conflict among the different roles boards play and the fine line between paid consultant and strategic adviser.

The best way for boards to succeed simultaneously in their multiple, sometimes conflicting missions appears to be to start by putting the structure and set of practices in place that provide the basis for a strong and independent board. Then, with the elements firmly established to ensure careful and ongoing oversight, individual directors and the board as a whole can work closely with top management to enhance strategy and to leverage new resources for the firm. The following are the essential ingredients to the first step of building an independent board:

- Ensuring that independent directors (with no formal business or family ties to the firm prior to joining the board) constitute a clear majority (at least two-thirds) of all board members.
- Assessing the knowledge and abilities of these directors regularly against the firm's changing market and technological demands to ensure that they have the skills necessary to effectively oversee the firm's actions.
- Having independent directors chair and control all key committees: compensation, audit, nominating, and corporate governance. The compensation committee should consist solely of outside directors.
- Providing mechanisms for the outside directors to form a cohesive group and establish clear leadership of the board itself—by separating the chairman and CEO roles, appointing a lead director, having regular executive sessions where no inside directors are present, or some combination of these.
- Creating regular channels of information to the board that are independent of management—for example, direct communication links with employees, customers, suppliers, and investors.
- Providing the board with staff, resources, or both so that it can conduct its own analysis of issues where it feels the need (for example, in benchmarking executive compensation); if individual directors are performing significant duties that go well beyond the requirements of a typical board member, then this role should be recognized and rewarded by the board as a whole, not by company management.

- Conducting an annual, formal evaluation of the CEO, in which performance targets are specified in advance relative to key competitors and the board provides the CEO with clear written and oral feedback.
- Introducing a regular succession planning process that reaches down several levels in the organization.

Although these practices together can help increase the likelihood that boards have the knowledge, information, power, and time needed to provide effective oversight, they leave open the question of to whom the board itself must answer. Corporate boards are in the relatively unusual position of assessing their own performance and setting their own rewards. The de facto solution in many companies—namely, relying heavily on the firm's top managers to hold the board accountable—is fraught with problems, as it compromises the very independence that the board needs to establish. Rather, our analysis suggests that boards should consider the following steps to provide the firm's stakeholders with some assurance that the board is being responsive to their interests:

- Linking a significant percentage of rewards to long-term firm performance through the use of stock grants and options.
- Conducting a regular evaluation of the board and its individual members that includes input from directors themselves, key stakeholder groups, and the firms' managers.
- Using the results of the evaluation and benchmarking of other firms to review corporate governance procedures on a regular basis.
- Requiring directors to offer their resignations when they change their primary job or take on additional board memberships. This can help ensure that the membership mix on the board remains appropriate and independent.

Once these fundamentals for an independent and accountable board are in place, directors can feel free to concentrate their efforts on helping identify potential threats and opportunities to the organization, shaping the firm's strategy to fit this changing environment, and building effective external relationships that can help the board and management leverage the organization's capabilities most effectively. Indeed, with the right safeguards in place, a board that is more actively involved in the strategy process and in formulating strategic alliances can also provide more effective oversight of the organization. Without this involvement and the additional knowledge and information such involvement provides to directors, boards are in effect confined to a reactive mode, forced to assess top managers' decisions well after the fact. In today's rapidly changing global economy, such delays, even when there is the most independent and well-intended stewardship of the firm, may have dire consequences. By becoming more immersed in the strategy formulation and monitoring process, directors are able to raise more penetrating questions to challenge top managers, to suggest potential new avenues to explore, and to identify possible early warning signs of difficulties with the existing approach.

The strategic and network-building roles of the board can be enhanced by a set of practices identified throughout our analysis:

- Ensuring that the board has a diverse, complementary set of expertise, with some directors who have in-depth expertise in the firm's sector(s) and key technologies and others who bring independent perspectives from outside the industry
- Providing regular developmental experiences to increase directors' understanding of the firm's business
- Linking directors directly into the firm's information systems, perhaps with a customized portal to provide the key metrics they want to track
- Minimizing the amount of time spent in meetings on discussion of operating and financial information that can be reviewed in advance, and instead focusing discussions on strategic issues
- Conducting a special annual retreat devoted to longer-term strategy and review of the managers who will be responsible for executing this strategy

In addition to these specific practices, boards may increasingly find it beneficial to experiment with new and different mechanisms for corporate governance that can enable boards to handle the varied challenges they will continue to face in the future.

APPENDIX: RESEARCH BACKGROUND

The research presented in this volume is based primarily on interviews conducted by the authors and on analysis of the Korn/Ferry International Board of Directors Annual Survey. In this Appendix, we briefly describe these sources of data and our methodology. In addition to these two main sources, we drew upon research conducted by others in the fields of board governance, teams, leadership, rewards, and organizational behavior. References are made to these sources throughout the text.

Korn/Ferry Survey: Background and Methods

Throughout the book, we cite data based on our analysis of the Korn/Ferry International Annual Board of Directors Study. This detailed mail survey has been sent to all of the directors of the publicly traded *Fortune* 1000 U.S. firms each year since 1973. The survey consists of ten pages of questions (yes-no and 1–5 Likert scales) asking directors to report on the current governance practices and effectiveness of the board of the largest publicly traded company on which they serve.

In the 1999 version of the study, which is the basis for most of the data we report, surveys were sent to more than seven thousand directors of 902 publicly traded *Fortune* 1000 firms. More than one thousand directors (215 CEOs, 187 inside directors, and 614 outside directors) responded, a 13 percent response rate.

In Chapters One and Two, we also describe links between the Korn/Ferry data and company performance. Starting in 1996, we formed a partnership with Korn/Ferry to aid in the redesign and analysis of the survey to make it more appropriate for research purposes and to try to answer the question, Are effective governance practices related to company performance? The analyses presented in this book are based on the 1996 survey, to which more than 1,150 chief executives and inside and outside directors responded.

In order to investigate the relationship between board practices and company performance, directors were asked for the first time in 1996 to give the name of the company on which their survey answers were based. This question was optional, and directors from 354 companies responded. In cases where there were multiple respondents from the same company, one was chosen at random to represent that particular board.

Firm performance and market data for the 354 company responses were drawn from Standard & Poor's Compustat database and the Center for Research in Security Prices (CRSP) databases for 1996 and 1997. The Compustat data files are compiled by Standard & Poor's Compustat Services, Inc., from balance sheets, income statements, form 10(K)s, and other corporate financial reports. The CRSP, which is a department of the Graduate School of Business at the University of Chicago, developed the other financial data files.

Return ratios were calculated as follows:

$$\text{Return on investment (ROI)} =$$
$$\text{earnings before taxes and interest} / (\text{assets} - \text{current liabilities})$$
$$\text{Market return} =$$
$$\exp\left[\Sigma\ \text{Ln (Monthly Stock Return}_{1-12} + 1)\right] - 1$$

The survey comprised two types of questions designed to measure board practices or perceived effectiveness. The first type was a simple yes-or-no question about whether a particular practice was currently used—for example, "If your chairman is also the CEO, do you have a lead director among the outside directors?"

The second type of question asked directors to rate their boards on a scale from 1 ("strongly disagree") to 5 ("strongly agree")—for example, "Does your board have control over the meeting agenda?" To determine whether a board scored high or low on a particular question, we compared its rating with the mean and standard deviation for all the companies in the sample. Companies were then categorized as "high" if the response was one or more standard deviations above the mean, and "low" if the response was one or more standard deviations below the mean.

Factor analysis was conducted on nine questionnaire items regarding effectiveness in various board roles. The nine items separate cleanly into two factors, which we categorize as "strategy formulation" effectiveness and "external networking" effectiveness. The strategy formulation scale contains six items, with reliability of .81, and the external networking scale contains three items.

Interview Data: Background

In addition to the survey data from Korn/Ferry, we conducted extensive interviews with 110 CEOs, board directors, governance experts, and senior managers to learn in greater depth about governance issues and practices. Participants, whose organizations ranged from start-ups to well-established firms, represented a broad sample of mature to high-growth industries, ranging from natural resources to pharmaceuticals to high technology to finance to consumer goods.

The following interview questions are a sample of the types of questions we asked board directors and CEO participants in our study. In addition to these general questions, we also explored boardroom dynamics and history that were specific to each company.

The Board's Ability to Understand Corporate Performance and CEO Performance

- What performance measures does the board employ to make its assessments of both corporate and CEO performance? Do you have preferred measures? What types of outside data does the board employ? Do you use human resources data, employee attitude surveys, and customer satisfaction data in your assessments?
- How does the board receive information on the progress of strategic initiatives, organizational change programs, employee morale or sentiments, and ethical issues? Do you have vehicles such as a hotline where problems down in the organization can be brought to the attention of the board?
- In what areas do you feel the board needs more or less information in order to assess performance?

Board Membership

- As a CEO, what do you look for in board members? Specific examples of these characteristics with actual board members? Are there specific background experiences or personal characteristics that are helpful? How do you source your directors?
- As a director, what do you look for in board members? Specific examples of these characteristics with actual board members? Are there specific background

experiences or personal characteristics that are helpful? How do you source new directors?

- What is the composition of your board—insiders versus outsiders?
- What do you consider an ideal board size?
- How have board members been chosen to build a director skill set on your board? Can you give examples using specific directors? Is there an ideal mix of backgrounds that you are seeking?
- Do you employ a formal process to determine the ideal mix of directors—for example, a matrix of some sort?
- What selection criteria do you use?
- What role does a board committee play in selection? What role does the CEO play in director selection? What role does an executive search firm play in your director selection?
- What is the mandatory retirement age?
- Have you ever asked a board member not to stand for reelection? Why?

Board Roles and Stakeholders

- As a CEO, what do you feel the principal roles of your board should be? Do you see new roles emerging given the pace of change, technology, the arrival of e-commerce?
- As a CEO, for what do you look to the board in terms of help, support, direction, information? At what roles do you feel directors are less effective? Are there any means to improve in these areas?
- To whom do your directors feel most accountable? Which stakeholders? Why these? Is there one dominant group?
- As a board director, what do you feel are your principal roles? In which of these roles do you feel the board is most effective, as opposed to less effective? Are there inherent tensions between these roles? If yes, which ones? What have you found to enhance your effectiveness in each of these roles? To what group of stakeholders do you feel most accountable?
- Have you been asked to adopt any governance practices by investors such as CalPERS? Have you reviewed any governance guidelines? How have they influenced your board?

Board Leadership

- Who plays the primary leadership roles on your board? Are there any shortcomings with this role? How effective do you find committee leadership? Are there any specific shortcomings?
- Do you have a nonexecutive chair? If yes, how has the experience been with

this role in terms of providing leadership? What roles does this person typically play? If you do not have a non-executive chair, why not?

- Do you have a lead director? If yes, what roles does this person typically play? How has the experience been? If not generally effective, why not? What is the selection process?
- Do you have a board committee that assumes a primary role for the board? If yes, which committee, and why does this committee assume this role? How effective has its leadership been? If it has not been effective, why not?
- Can committees meet without the CEO present? Can outside directors meet without the CEO present? If yes, how successful has this approach been? Is it effective in providing a healthy counterbalance to the CEO's power?

Board Evaluations

- Does your board conduct a performance evaluation of your CEO? Is this a formal or informal process? What are the specific steps involved, and what is the typical timetable? What criteria does the board evaluate to make its judgment? How is this evaluation tied to compensation? How is feedback to the CEO handled? What have you learned from the process? Would you make any changes to improve its effectiveness? If there is no evaluation, why not?
- Does your board conduct a performance evaluation of the entire board itself? If yes, is this a formal or informal process? What criteria do you employ? Why these? What is the typical timetable for the process? How is feedback to the board handled? What have you learned from the process? Would you make any changes to improve its effectiveness? Are there any shortcomings in the overall process? If you do not have an evaluation, why not?
- Do you have an evaluation for individual directors? If yes, what criteria do you use? Why these? How does the process work, and what is the typical timetable? How is feedback handled? If you do not have an individual director evaluation, why not?

Compensation Practices

- What are your current compensation practices for the CEO and directors? Why these? How do they align the board and CEO to stakeholder/shareholder interests?
- What have you learned about their effectiveness in shaping behavior and performance over time?
- Who determines compensation or changes in compensation?
- Do you believe in stock-based compensation and rewards? To what extent and why? Do you use options or stock grants?

- What has been their impact, as best you can assess?
- Is your board planning a shift in its compensation practices? If so, why?
- Do you provide a retirement plan for your directors?

Committees

- Describe the committee structure of your board. Why do you have these particular committees? What are the individual roles? How effective have you found this arrangement to be? What lessons have you learned over the years about board committees?

Crisis Management

- Has your board prepared an action plan for itself if a major crisis were to arise? Have they outlined specific crisis scenarios and corresponding responses? Is a particular committee commissioned to take charge given specific types of crises?
- If a crisis occurs with the company's senior leadership, how will the board provide leadership?
- Does a single individual director have accountability as the leader?

Succession

- How does your board prepare for succession issues? Is there a succession plan already in existence? How do your directors assess potential replacements for the CEO? What role does your CEO play in his or her own succession? Is it a practice to have the CEO's replacement come on to the board sometime before he or she assumes the CEO title? For what time period must the successor be a member of the board before assuming the CEO role? If yes, how effective have you found this practice to be?
- Does your CEO stay on as a board member or as board chair after stepping down from his or her executive role? If yes, what is the impact you see?
- What is the board's involvement in development of the company's senior management pool?

Board Preparation

- What materials do you send out before meetings to prepare your directors for board meetings? What have you found to help in keeping board members well informed both before and during board meetings? Do you hold sessions on special topics, such as strategy? How effective have you found these to be and why? Are there problem areas?
- How do you prepare new directors for their role on your board? Do you have a formal "on-boarding" process? If yes, what is it, and how effective have you found it to be?

Meetings

- Describe a typical board meeting. How frequently does the board meet? What subject areas are covered, and what proportion of time is devoted to these? What is the typical board process with regard to decision making? What makes for a more effective board meeting? How much time is allocated for typical meetings?
- Who sets the agenda for board meetings? Is there a mechanism for board members to surface issues not on the agenda?
- Describe a typical committee meeting. How frequently do these occur?

Emerging Issues

- How will e-commerce affect your board in the future?
- How will liability suits affect your board in the future?
- Are there any hot issues about boards or board members that are currently on your mind?
- Do you see the membership or the role of your board changing in the future?

NOTES

Introduction

1. Hirschman, A. O. (1970). *Exit, Voice and Loyalty.* Cambridge, MA: Harvard University Press.
2. Felton, R., Hudnut, A., and Heeckeren, J. V. (1996)."Putting a Value on Board Governance," *The McKinsey Quarterly, 4,* 170–175.
3. *The Economist,* Oct. 8, 1994, p. 82.
4. Bryne, J. A. (2000). "The Best and Worst Boards." *Business Week,* Jan. 24, p. 146.
5. Bryne, J. A. (1997). "The Best and Worst Boards." *Business Week,* Dec. 8, p. 90.
6. Freeman, S. (1999). "Campbell Soup Says Profits Will Fall Below Estimate." *Wall Street Journal,* June 26, p. B4.
7. Barrett, A. (1999). "Campbell's Wet Noodles." *Business Week,* Jan. 25, p. 48.
8. Ibid.
9. Blair, M. (1995). *Ownership and Control: Rethinking Corporate Governance for the Twenty-First Century.* Washington, DC: Brookings Institution; Kennedy, A. A. (2000). *The End of Shareholder Value.* Cambridge, MA: Perseus.
10. Drucker, P. (1999). *Management Challenges for the Twenty-First Century.* New York: Harper Business, p. 149.
11. Lawler, E. E., III. (1999). *Rewarding Excellence: Pay Strategies for the New Economy.* San Francisco: Jossey-Bass.
12. Quoted in Barber, F. (1999). "Business @ The Speed of Thought." *Business Strategy Review, 2,* 11.
13. Ibid.
14. Blair, M. (1995). Op. cit.

Chapter One

1. National Association of Corporate Directors and the Center for Board Leadership. (2000). *1999–2000 Public Company Governance Survey.* Washington, DC: National Association of Corporate Directors.
2. Jensen, M. C., and Meckling, W. (1976). "Theory of the Firm: Managerial Behavior, Agency Costs and Ownership Structure." *Journal of Financial Economics, 3,* 305–360; Fama, E., and Jensen, M. C. (1983). "Separation of Ownership and Control." *Journal of Law and Economics, 26*(2), 301–326.
3. Pfeffer, J., and Salancik, G. (1978). *The External Control of Organizations: A Resource Dependence Perspective.* New York: HarperCollins.
4. Bainbridge, S. M. (1993). "Independent Directors and the SLI Corporate Governance Project." *George Washington Law Review, 61,* 1034–1083.
5. Lorsch, J. W., and MacIver, E. A. (1989). *Pawns or Potentates: The Reality of America's Corporate Boards.* Boston: Harvard Business School Press.
6. National Association of Corporate Directors and the Center for Board Leadership. (2000). Op. cit.
7. Knepper, W. E., and Bailey, D. A. (1998). *Liability of Corporate Officers and Directors* (6th ed.). Charlottesville, VA: Lexis Publishing.
8. Ibid.
9. Ibid., pp. 77–78.
10. Ibid., p. 122.

Chapter Two

1. Lawler, E. E., III. (1986). *High-Involvement Management: Participative Strategies for Improving Organizational Performance.* San Francisco: Jossey-Bass.
2. Katzenbach, J. R., and Smith, D. K. (1993). *The Wisdom of Teams: Creating High-Performance Organizations.* Boston: Harvard Business School Press.
3. Benson, G., and Finegold, D. L. (2000). "Inside the Black Box: Corporate Board Practices, Effective Governance, and Financial Performance." Paper presented at Western Academy of Management Annual Meeting, Waikoloa, Hawaii.

Chapter Three

1. Finkelstein, S., and Hambrick, D. C. (1996). *Strategic Leadership: Top Executives and Their Effects on Organizations.* Minneapolis/St. Paul: West.
2. Ward, A., Bishop, K., and Sonnenfeld, J. (1999). "Pyrrhic Victories: The Cost to the Board of Ousting the CEO." *Journal of Organizational Behavior, 20*(5), 767–781.
3. National Association of Corporate Directors and the Center for Board Leadership. (2000).Op. cit.
4. Ibid.
5. Finkelstein, S., and Hambrick, D. C. (1996). Op. cit.
6. Ocasio, W. (1994). "Political Dynamics and the Circulation of Power: CEO Succession in U.S. Industrial Corporations, 1960–1990." *Administrative Science Quarterly, 39,* 285–312.

7. Barrett, A. (1999). "Rite Aid Hasn't Treated Its Real Ills Yet." *Business Week,* Nov. 1, p. 48.

8. National Association of Corporate Directors and the Center for Board Leadership. (2000). Op. cit.

9. Ibid.

10. Westphal, J. D. (1999). "Collaboration in the Boardroom: Behavioral and Performance Consequences of CEO-Board Social Ties." *Journal of the Academy of Management, 42*(1), 7–24.

11. Lawler, E. E., III. (2000). *Rewarding Excellence: Pay Strategies for the New Economy.* San Francisco: Jossey-Bass.

12. National Association of Corporate Directors and the Center for Board Leadership. (2000). Op. cit.

13. Ibid.

14. Hillman, A., Harris, I., Connella, A., and Bolenger, L. (1998). "Diversity on the Board: An Examination of the Relationship Between Director, Diversity and Firm Performance." Unpublished manuscript, University of Western Ontario, London, Ontario.

15. Judge, W., and Zeithan, C. (1992). "Institutional and Strategic Choice Perspectives on Board Involvement in the Strategic Decision Process." *Journal of the Academy of Management, 35*(4), 766–794.

16. National Association of Corporate Directors and the Center for Board Leadership. (2000). Op. cit.

17. Dalton, D. R., Daily, C. M., Johnson, J. L., and Ellstrand, A. E. (1999). "Number of Directors and Financial Performance: A Meta-Analysis." *Journal of the Academy of Management, 42*(6), 674–686.

Chapter Four

1. Lorsch, J. W., and MacIver, E. A. (1989). *Pawns or Potentates: The Reality of America's Corporate Boards.* Boston: Harvard Business School Press.

2. Ibid., p. 82.

3. Daily, C. M., and Dalton, D. R. (1997). "CEO and Board Chair Roles Held Jointly or Separately: Much Ado About Nothing?" *Academy of Management Executive, 11*(3), 11–20.

4. National Association of Corporate Directors and the Center for Board Leadership. (2000). Op. cit.

5. National Association of Corporate Directors. (1996). *Report of the NACD Blue Ribbon Commission on Director Professionalism.* Washington, DC: National Association of Corporate Directors, p. 4.

6. Toronto Stock Exchange Committee on Corporate Governance in Canada. (1994). *Where Were the Directors? Guidelines for Improved Corporate Governance in Canada.* Toronto: Toronto Stock Exchange, p. 41.

7. Daily, C. M., and Dalton, D. R. (1997). Op. cit.

8. Henderson, D. (1995). "Redraw the Line Between the Board and the CEO." *Harvard Business Review, 73*(2), 153–161.

9. Ibid., p. 160.

10. Firstenberg, P., and Malkiel, B. (1994). "The Twenty-First Century Boardroom: Who Will Be in Charge?" *Sloan Management Review, 36*(1), 27–37.

11. Lorsch, J. W., and MacIver, E. A. (1989). Op. cit.

12. Firstenberg, P., and Malkiel, B. (1994). Op. cit.

Chapter Five

1. Kaplan, R. S., and Norton, D. P. (1996). *The Balanced Scorecard.* Boston: Harvard Business School Press.
2. Skandia Insurance Company. (2000). [http://www.skandia.com].
3. Eisenhardt, K. M. (1999). "Strategy as Strategic Decision Making." *Sloan Management Review, 40*(3), 65–72.
4. Brummet, A., Flamholtz, E., and Pyle, W. (1968). "Human Resource Management." *Accounting Review, 43*(1), 217–224.
5. National Association of Corporate Directors and the Center for Board Leadership. (2000). Op. cit.

Chapter Six

1. Lawler, E. E., III. (1999). *Rewarding Excellence: Pay Strategies for the New Economy.* San Francisco: Jossey-Bass.
2. Lepsinger, R., and Lucia, A. D. (1997). *The Art and Science of 360-Degree Feedback.* San Francisco: Jossey-Bass; Tornow, W. W., and London, M. (1998). *Maximizing the Value of 360-Degree Feedback: A Process for Successful Individual and Organizational Development.* San Francisco: Jossey-Bass.
3. Conger, J. A., Finegold, D. G., and Lawler, E. E., III. (1998). "CEO Appraisals: Holding Corporate Leadership Accountable." *Organizational Dynamics, 7*(1), 6–20.
4. Lawler, E. E., III. (1999). Op. cit.; Mohrman, A. M., Jr., Resnick-West, S. M., and Lawler, E. E., III. (1989). *Designing Performance Appraisal Systems: Aligning Appraisals and Organizational Realities.* San Francisco: Jossey-Bass.

Chapter Seven

1. Conger, J. A., Finegold, D. L., and Lawler, E. E., III. (1998). "Appraising Boardroom Performance." *Harvard Business Review, 76*(1), 136–148.
2. Mohrman, S. A., Cohen, S. G., and Mohrman, A. M., Jr. (1995). *Designing Team-Based Organizations: New Forms for Knowledge Work.* San Francisco: Jossey-Bass.
3. Russell Reynolds Associates. (1998). *The Structure and Compensation of Boards of Directors at S&P 1500 Companies: 1997–1998 Board Practices Survey.* New York: Russell Reynolds.
4. Lawler, E. E., III. (1999). *Rewarding Excellence: Pay Strategies for the New Economy.* San Francisco: Jossey-Bass.

Chapter Eight

1. Christensen, C. M. (1997). *The Innovator's Dilemma: When New Technologies Cause Great Firms to Fail.* Boston: Harvard Business School Press.

2. Oppel, R. (2000). "The Higher Stakes of Business to Business Trade." *New York Times*, Mar. 5, p. 3.

3. *New York Times*, Jan. 4, 2000, p. A1.

4. Habeck, M., and others. (2000). *After the Merger*. Harlow, England: Financial Times/Prentice Hall.

5. Scully, A., and Woods, W. (1999). B2B Exchanges, USA: 1S1 Publications.

6. Malone, T., and Laubacher, R. (1998). "The Dawn of the E-Lance Economy." *Harvard Business Review*, Sept.–Oct., pp. 145–152.

7. Ibid.

8. Reingold, J. (1999). "Dot.Com Boards Are Flouting the Rules." *Businessweek*, Dec. 20, pp. 130–135.

9. Kaplan, R. S., and Norton, D. P. (1993). "Putting the Balanced Scorecard to Work." *Harvard Business Review*, Sept.–Oct., pp. 137–147.

10. National Association of Corporate Directors. (1996). *Report of the NACD Blue Ribbon Commission on Director Professionalism*. Washington, DC: National Association of Corporate Directors.

11. Daily, C., Certo, S., and Dalton, D. (1999). "Pay Directors in Stock? No." *Across the Board*, Nov.–Dec., 46–50; Kaback, H. (1996). "The Case for Cash for Directors." *Directors & Boards*, Winter, 14–24.

Chapter Nine

1. Quoted in Vance, S. C. (1983). *Corporate Leadership, Boards, Directors, and Strategy.* New York: McGraw-Hill, p. 5.

2. Lorsch, J. W., and MacIver, E. A. (1989). *Pawns or Potentates: The Reality of America's Corporate Boards*. Boston: Harvard Business School Press, p. 7.

3. Ibid.

4. Berle, A., and Means, G. C. (1967). *The Modern Corporation and Private Property*. Orlando: Harcourt Brace.

5. Ibid.

6. Useem, M. (1993). *Executive Defense: Shareholder Power and Corporate Reorganization*. Cambridge, MA: Harvard University Press.

7. Ibid.

8. Ibid.

9. Jensen, M. C., and Murphy, K. J. (1990). "CEO Incentives—It's Not How Much You Pay, But How." *Harvard Business Review*, *68*(3), 138–153.

10. Useem, M. (1993). Op. cit.

11. Drucker, P. (1991). "Reckoning with the Pension Fund Revolution." *Harvard Business Review*, *69*(2), 106–109.

12. Useem, M. (1993). Op. cit.

13. Icahn, C. (1988). "Icahn on Icahn." *Fortune, 117*(5), 54–58.

14. Useem, M. (1993). Op. cit.

15. Brancato, C., and Gaughan, P. A. (1988). *The Growth of Institutional Investors in U.S. Capital Markets*. New York: Columbia University Institutional Investor Project.

16. "The 1991 Pensions Directory." *Institutional Investor, 25*, 153–192.

17. Useem, M. (1993). Op. cit.

18. Grant, L. (1992). "GM Shuffle May Be Watershed in Reining in CEOs." *Los Angeles Times,* Apr. 13, pp. D1-D2.

19. Ibid., p. D2.

20. Useem, M. (1993). Op. cit.

21. Hanson, D. M. (1990, Dec. 6). "Letter to J. Peter Grace." Sacramento: California Public Employees' Retirement System.

22. Allen, W. T. (1992, Apr. 13). *Our Schizophrenic Conception of the Business Corporation.* Paper presented to the Samuel and Ronnie Heyman Center on Corporate Governance, Cardozo School of Law, Yeshiva University, New York.

23. Ibid., p. 10.

24. Ibid., p. 6.

25. Ibid.

26. Ibid.

27. Ibid., p. 7.

28. Blair, M. (1995). *Ownership and Control: Rethinking Corporate Governance for the Twenty-First Century.* Washington, DC: Brookings Institution.

29. Hamel, G., and Prahalad, C. K. (1994). *Competing for the Future.* Boston: Harvard Business School Press.

30. Allen, W. T. (1992, Apr. 13). Op. cit.

31. Ibid.

32. Ibid.

33. Ibid.

34. Ibid.

35. Blair, N. (1995). Op. cit., p. 239.

36. Rousseau, D., and Shperling, Z. (2000). "Pieces of the Action: Ownership, Power and the Psychological Contract." (Technical Report). Heinz School of Public Policy and Management, Pittsburgh, PA, January.

37. Ibid.

38. Ibid.

39. Lawler, E. E., III, Mohrman, S., and Benson, G. (2001). *Organizing for High Performance.* San Francisco: Jossey-Bass.

40. Ibid.

41. Osterman, P. (1999). *Securing Prosperity.* Princeton, NJ: Princeton University Press.

42. Ibid.

43. Vitols, S. (1995). "Corporate Governance Versus Economic Governance." W2B Discussion Paper FS195-310, Berlin, November.

44. Dore, R. (1986). *Flexible Rigidities.* Palo Alto: Stanford Univeristy Press; Streek, W. (1989). "Skills and the Limits of Neo-Liberalism." *Work, Employment and Society, 3*(1), 89–104.

45. Vitols, S. (1995). Op. cit.

46. Ibid.

47. Osterman, P. (1999). Op. cit.

48. Friedman, T. (1998). *The Lexus and the Olive Tree.* New York: Farrar, Straus & Giroux.

49. Osterman, P. (1999). Op. cit. See p. 174 for summary of proposed pro-labor reforms.

50. Blasi, J., and Kruse, D. (1991). *The New Owners.* Champaign, IL: Harper Business.

51. Lawler, E. E., III, Mohrman, S., and Benson, C. (2001). Op. cit.

52. Blasi, J., and Kruse, D. (1991). Op. cit.

53. Ibid.
54. Ibid.
55. Putterman, L. (1984). "On Some Recent Explanations of Why Capital Hires Labor." *Economic Inquiry, 22,* 171–187.

Chapter Ten

1. Chase, D., and Reznick, M. (2000). "Director Pay at Internet Companies." *Directors and Boards, 24*(2), 44–47.
2. Christensen, C. M. (1997). *The Innovator's Dilemma: When New Technologies Cause Great Firms to Fail.* Boston: Harvard Business School Press.
3. Stewart, T. (2000). "How Teradyne Solved the Innovator's Dilemma." *Fortune, 141*(1), 188.
4. Ibid.
5. Ibid.
6. Kanter, R. M. (1994). "Collaborative Advantage: The Art of Alliances." *Harvard Business Review, 72*(4), 96–108.
7. Barlett, C. (1990). "Corning Incorporated: A Network of Alliances." (Case Study 9-391-102). Boston, MA: Harvard Business School.
8. Kanter, R. M. (1994). Op. cit.
9. Galbraith, J. (1998). "Designing the Network Organization." In S. Mohrman, J. Galbraith, and E. E. Lawler III (eds.) *Tomorrow's Organization.* San Francisco: Jossey-Bass.
10. Levine, D., Adler, P. S., and Goldoftas, B. (1995). "NUMMI: A Case Study." In D. Levine (ed.), *Reinventing the Workplace: How Business and Employees Can Both Win* (pp. 10–35). Washington, DC: Brookings Institution.
11. Kenny, R. (1999). "Rediscovering Advisory Boards." *Directors & Boards,* Fall, 26–30.

ACKNOWLEDGMENTS

We are deeply indebted to the Korn/Ferry organization for support for our research on corporate boards. They provided data from their annual study of corporate boards, as well as financial support for our writing, data gathering, and data analysis. We would particularly like to thank Richard Ferry for his help in guiding our research efforts and for the many introductions he made for us to key executives and board members. Throughout our work with Korn/Ferry, Kay Kennedy and Stephanie Rosenfelt-Berger have provided support, asked key questions, and helped us define our research. Finally, Norman Clement of Korn/Ferry gave us many helpful comments and insights at the beginning of our research.

Several members of the Center for Effective Organizations have helped us greatly in producing this manuscript. Beth Neilson did the majority of data analysis and provided us with outstanding analytical support. Sabrina Moreno gave outstanding support in the production of the manuscript. And, as is true of all projects of the Center, we are deeply indebted to our corporate sponsors, who provide us with financial support; many of them also participated in our study.

Last but not least, we want to thank the many corporate board members and CEOs who contributed to this study. Many of them gave freely of their valuable time to help us understand the operation of corporate boards and how they can be more effective. We are deeply appreciative of their willingness to help corporate America improve the effectiveness of boards and corporate governance.

THE AUTHORS

Jay A. Conger is a professor of organizational behavior at the London Business School and is senior research scientist at the Center for Effective Organizations at the University of Southern California in Los Angeles. Formerly the executive director of the Leadership Institute at the University of Southern California, Conger is one of the world's experts on leadership.

Author of over seventy articles and book chapters and nine books, Conger researches leadership, innovation, boards of directors, organizational change, and the training and development of leaders and managers. His articles have appeared in the *Harvard Business Review, Organizational Dynamics, Business & Strategy, Leadership Quarterly,* the *Academy of Management Review,* and the *Journal of Organizational Behavior.* He is currently the associate editor of *Leadership Quarterly.* One of his books, *Learning to Lead* has been described by *Fortune* magazine as "the source" for understanding leadership development. His book *Charismatic Leadership* (with R. N. Kanungo, Jossey-Bass, 1998) received the Choice Book Award in 1999. Other books include *Building Leaders* (with B. Benjamin, Jossey-Bass, 1999), *The Leader's Change Handbook* (with G. M. Spreitzer and E. E. Lawler III, 1999), *Winning 'Em Over* (1998), and *Spirit at Work* (Jossey-Bass, 1994).

Outside of his work with universities, Conger consults with private corporations and nonprofit organizations throughout the world. His insights have been featured in *Business Week, The Economist, Forbes, Fortune,* the *Los Angeles Times,* the *New York Times, Training,* the *Wall Street Journal,* and *Working Woman.* A popular speaker and outstanding teacher, Conger has been selected by *Business Week* as the best business school professor to teach leadership to executives. In his role as a university professor, he has received numerous teaching awards and the Center for Creative Leadership's H. Smith Richardson Fellowship. He received his B.A. from Dartmouth College, his M.B.A. from the University of Virginia, and his D.B.A. from the Harvard Business School.

Edward E. Lawler III is a professor of management and organization in the Marshall School of Business at the University of Southern California. He is also director of the school's Center for Effective Organizations.

After receiving his Ph.D. from the University of California at Berkeley in 1964, Lawler joined the faculty of Yale University as assistant professor of industrial administration and psychology. Three years later he was promoted to associate professor. Lawler moved to the University of Michigan in 1972, as professor of psychology, and also became a program director in the Survey Research Center at the Institute for Social Research. He held a Fulbright fellowship at the London Graduate School of Business. In 1978, he became a professor in the Marshall School of Business at the University of Southern California and, in 2000, he was named Distinguished Professor of Business. During 1979, he founded and became the director of the university's Center for Effective Organizations. In 1982, he was named professor of research at the University of Southern California.

Lawler is a member of many professional organizations in his field and is on the editorial board of five major journals. He is also the author and coauthor of more than two hundred articles and thirty-two books. His most recent books include *The Ultimate Advantage* (1992), *Organizing for the Future* (with J. R. Galbraith, 1993), *From the Ground Up* (1996), *Tomorrow's Organization* (with S. A. Mohrman and J. R. Galbraith, 1998), *Strategies for High Performance Organizations—The CEO Report* (with S. A. Mohrman and G. E. Ledford, 1998), and *Rewarding Excellence* (2000), all published by Jossey-Bass. His articles have appeared in the leading academic research journals, as well as in *Fortune, USA Today*, the *Harvard Business Review,* and the *Financial Times.*

David L. Finegold is an associate research professor at the Center for Effective Organizations in the Marshall School of Business at the University of Southern California. He graduated *summa cum laude* from Harvard University and was a Rhodes Scholar at Oxford University, where he received his D.Phil. in politics. Prior to joining the Center for Effective Organizations in January 1996, he was a social scientist at RAND in Santa Monica, California.

Finegold has conducted research, published, consulted and provided executive education to public and private sector organizations on the changing employment relationship and successful talent strategies for attracting, developing, and retaining employees. His work has focused on the key role of employee development improving firm performance. His current research projects include work in the following areas: the impact of the Internet on organizational design and human resources, the psychological contracts and career paths of temporary workers, design of effective corporate boards, and managing technical excellence— leading practices in the management of knowledge workers and the leveraging of the knowledge that they create.

Finegold is the author of more than twenty-five journal articles and book chapters and has written or edited four books, most recently *Are Skills the Answer?* (Oxford University Press, 1999) and *The German Skills Machine* (Berghahn Books, 1999). His forthcoming book from Jossey-Bass is *Net-Enabled: Designing Organizations for the Internet Economy.*

Finegold is a member of the Academy of Management and a reviewer for *Sloan Management Review, Industrial Relations, California Management Review, Industrial and Labor Relations Review,* and *British Journal of Industrial Relations.*

INDEX